Ron Graham

All the King's Horses

Politics Among the Ruins

Macfarlane Walter & Ross

Toronto

MACFARLANE WALTER & ROSS
37A Hazelton Avenue
Toronto, Canada M5R 2E3

Canadian Cataloguing in Publication Data

Graham, Ron, 1948-
    All the king's horses : politics among the ruins

Includes index.
ISBN 0-921912-88-9

1. Canada – Politics and government – 1984-1993.*
2. Canada – Politics and government – 1993-   .*
I. Title.

FC635.G73 1995   971.064'7   C95-932170-5
F1034.2.G73 1995

The publisher gratefully acknowledges the support
of the Ontario Arts Council and the Canada Council

Printed and bound in Canada

To Susan, Robert, Margot, Anthony, and Ian
with my love

and to the memory of
Charles Ritchie
(1906-1995)

and Stephen Godfrey
(1953-1993)

Today it is different: cities are still built over decades, but rulers often change every few years or even every few months. The political stage revolves many times faster than the stage of our daily existence. Regimes change, governing parties and their leaders change, but man lives just as he previously had – he still does not have an apartment or a job; the houses are still shabby, and there are potholes in the roads; the arduous task of making ends meet still goes on from dawn to dusk.

Perhaps that is why many people turn away from politics: it is for them an alien world, animated by a rhythm different from the one that punctuates the life of the average human being.

– Ryszard Kapuscinski, *Imperium*

Contents

CHAPTER ONE

The Taming of the Shrew

Party Girl

K IM CAMPBELL came quickstepping into the plain, window-less room down in the bowels of Ottawa's Civic Centre like she had come quickstepping into Canadian politics: blonde head bobbing to a loud western tune, bright eyes searching for a connection to the crowd, buoyant to the point of manic. Though she shouted, her words could not be heard above the frenetic chanting of her name. The focus of everybody's attention, she soon vanished into a throng of supporters and the bleaching glare of the television lights.

No one could have guessed the incredible pressure the minister of national defence had been under that day in April 1993. She had had to answer thorny questions in the Commons about the Canadian troops in Bosnia and Somalia. She had had to defend her departmental estimates before a parliamentary committee. She had had to deal with the multitude of problems that were plaguing her month-old campaign to win the leadership of the Progressive Conservative Party of Canada. "There's steel in there," an organizer said, watching from the sidelines as Campbell grabbed hands, kissed colleagues, hugged friends, waved, grinned, jumped, and clapped to George Fox's overamplified rendition of "Clearly Canadian."

"When I entered the race in Vancouver," she told the crowd of young Tories once the song was over and the cheering had stopped, "I said that 'under this cool, arrogant, intellectual, urbane exterior, there beats the heart of a Texas line dancer.' Well, tonight I'll show you what that means!" For this was a "stomp 'n' chomp" fund-raiser, with a couple of bales of hay to evoke the Wild West, chili steaming in kettle pots on the back of a chuck wagon, and a squad of young women moving in a line dance to the rhythm of a country band, a couple of steps to the left, a couple of steps to the right, backward and forward, with a spin and a hop and a clap.

For an hour or so Campbell, wearing an unflattering pair of jeans and a black shirt with a fringe, exchanged pleasantries, posed for photographs, chatted up potential delegates, and spun in the arms of men who already appeared to be bragging about having once danced with a prime minister. Then, suddenly, without signal or invitation, she took a place in the rank and file of the dancers.

Line dancing looks simple, but doing it gracefully requires the right sway in each soloist and a synchronized smoothness among the entire troupe. The variation Campbell joined, "Slappin' Leather," is especially complex, and she was soon falling over herself trying to tap the heel of her left shoe with each hand after a fancy turn step. Her line dancing turned out to be no better than her Russian. But gosh – to use one of her favourite expletives – was she ever determined to learn! The vertical frown lines, which came from nowhere whenever Campbell got serious, suddenly appeared between her eyebrows. Her back became bent with the concentration she brought to studying the steps. Sometimes she had to move awkwardly to avoid being buffeted by the other women, and the music did not last long enough for her to become either proficient or relaxed.

Kim Campbell no longer looked like the front-runner for the most powerful public office in the land. She looked like the oldest, shortest, and least talented hoofer at a chorus-line audition. Yet there was something endearing about her effort. If she had any design other than to learn – to demonstrate, say, that she was not simply a cello-playing, operetta-singing, Tolstoy-reading elitist – she must have understood that she risked looking like a fool. Instead, she seemed oblivious to the people watching her – except perhaps to the young dancers whose expertise she was trying so hard to absorb.

Though born in 1947, she seemed comfortable among these college students. Her kinetic bounce and blonde shock were those of an all-Canadian cheerleader. Even her humour was laced with a varsity crudeness. After informing the stomp 'n' chompers that her boots were from Kamloops and her fringe was from Regina, she had added, "And my underwear is from Vancouver!" – which, to judge by the stunned response, was one intimate detail the party members preferred not to know.

This was, by many accounts, the real Kim Campbell. The undergraduate who had organized a baby-buggy race in which the contestants wore diapers and ate pablum. The law student whose fantasy had been to "just be a writer of comedies and sit at home with a lampshade on my head." The minister of justice who had joked, "Say, fella, is that a prohibited weapon with a barrel length of less than eighteen inches, possession of which is grandfathered by those who satisfy the requirement of being a genuine gun collector on or before October 1, 1992, in your pocket, or are you just glad to see me?"

She may not have gone into show biz, as her father had expected because of her precocious love for composing songs and performing skits, but politics was proving close enough. A crowd-pleasing speech has been as much a source of entertainment as a matter of state since the days of Pericles, after all, and television has blurred whatever line once existed between vaudeville and public affairs. Professional jokesters knock off a few gags for the politicians to use as warm-up material; drama coaches lead them through performance exercises; looks overwhelm words; delivery supersedes thought. While Canadians have yet to produce their Ronald Reagan, by casting a professional actor to play the part of prime minister, they have often turned a number of media celebrities into politicians – from William Aberhart to René Lévesque, from Lise Payette to Ralph Klein – and transformed their politicians into media celebrities.

Indeed, in a country where non-fiction books outsell novels and made-for-TV movies tend to resemble documentaries, where homegrown stars are lured to the United States and there aren't enough familiar personalities to sustain a local version of *People*, politics has become the national theatre across whose stage heroes and villains stride in nightly episodes fashioned as the news. To most of the people cadging an autograph or snapshot from Kim Campbell that night, she did not represent power so much as fame.

Her talent for stand-up comedy and amateur theatrics had found a fortuitous outlet, and in a happy encounter such as the stomp 'n' chomp she could charm an audience with her sisterly exuberance, the sparkle in her eyes, and her captivating smile – the very attributes that had got her elected as first female student president at Vancouver's

Prince of Wales Secondary School and first female frosh president at the University of British Columbia. She was lucky, too, that television made her attractive qualities even more attractive than they were in real life.

In conflict situations, however, television did not make Kim Campbell seem attractive at all. Her facial muscles tightened, her frown appeared, her humour vanished, her eyes became icy blue, and she attacked with the alarming frenzy of a rabid fox. The hotter the argument, the faster she talked, the more her mouth fluctuated between ironic smiles and ugly sneers. Her face became such a chaos of rapidly changing expressions that viewers often found it hard to make a good guess about her true character.

Father Knows Best

If her personality was fully integrated, as she claimed, it was nevertheless multifaceted. One longtime friend knew of four Kim Campbells: the warm and down-to-earth glad-hander, the serious and hard-working cabinet minister, the shy and lonely-hearted divorcée, and the irreverent madcap cutting loose with her older sister Alix and a few close chums. Campbell herself more than once exposed a dichotomy in her soul: the brainy lawyer with the goofiness of a comedienne, the policy wonk with the soul of a wood nymph, the powerful politician with the heart of a line dancer.

"I might run for the leadership," she teased before Prime Minister Brian Mulroney's resignation, "or I might run away with a gigolo to Brazil." Which must have caused any psychotherapist who heard it to sit bolt upright, for Campbell's mother had in fact run away from her husband and two children when Kim was twelve – not with a gigolo to Brazil, to be precise, but with a boyfriend to the Caribbean. A part of Campbell's complexity, she had inadvertently implied, was the tug between the personalities of her warring parents.

On one side was Lissa Cook, bright-minded, strong of will and free in spirit, a Shavian frontierswoman who had worked as a wireless operator during the war and filled her daughters' heads with notions of personal fulfilment and the equality of women. "I was raised to be a feminist," Kim once remarked. "I was raised on Charlotte Whitton's wonderful comment that a woman has to be twice as good as a man in order to be considered half as good."

On the other side was George Campbell, old-fashioned, quick of wit and distinguished in manner, a Crown attorney who had served overseas with the Seaforth Highlanders and raised his girls to respect financial prudence and traditional values. "I'm a Conservative," he declared, "in that I believe in free enterprise and in people taking some measure of responsibility for their own development. Governments can't pay for everything. And I've always been a royalist. Sometimes I bleed for my country because a lot of those values seem to be lost."

But his was an easygoing Conservatism. His own parents, though Tories in Scotland, had become Liberals after they emigrated to Montreal, and George himself had occasionally voted Liberal in British Columbia. Once he even voted for the socialists to help an army buddy. "If Kim had any conditioning at all in the home," he thought, "it probably would have been more socialist, not in any philosophical sense but because of her mother's acquaintances who were socialists. I never had time to be concerned about politics."

Shortly after her parents' separation, young Avril Phaedra dropped the exotic names her mother had chosen, converted to the Anglican church, and began defining herself as a Conservative. Even during the political and social turbulence of the 1960s, she stood out as a neatly dressed goody-goody amid the dishevelled radicals on the UBC student council. "I had studied too much about socialist countries to be captivated," she explained to the journalist Peter C. Newman. "I thought socialism was well motivated but highly unrealistic as to how to get from *A* to *B*, and it seemed to me that the Conservatives had a much more realistic view of human nature."

Beneath George's traditionalism, however, she retained a fair share of Lissa's independence, which no doubt contributed to Kim's being progressive on many social issues and unhappy in affairs of the heart. Indeed, after an estrangement caused by her father's second marriage to a woman not much older than his daughter, she seemed to repeat her mother's desertion by running off with a man not much younger than her father. A math professor, chess wizard, *bon vivant*, and Winnipeg Jew who had become an outrageously loud devotee of Ayn Rand, Nathan Divinsky offered his young wife the kind of cerebral and sensual relationship her mother had apparently craved.

Together Nathan and Kim gambolled among the groves of Academe, where she thought she might like to pass the rest of her life arguing about Plato and Hobbes. In 1970, before completing her M.A., she accompanied her husband to London and began studying for a doctorate in Soviet government at the London School of Economics. But she dropped that too in order to return to Vancouver and take care of his three daughters from a previous marriage. Eventually, condemned by her lack of a graduate degree to the lowest levels of postsecondary teaching, she chose instead to train as a lawyer.

She was, by the energy of her mind and the aggressiveness of her manner, more a lawyer than a scholar. Though she relished the give-and-take of ideas, she lacked intellectual depth. Her virtues – like her jokes – were those of a first-rate undergraduate: always asking the insightful questions, always challenging the traditional answers, always anxious to sit at the front of the class. She also suffered the undergraduate's vices: presuming she knew better than her teachers, showing off her knowledge with long-winded expositions, unwilling to sacrifice a clever retort for the sake of someone's feelings.

In 1980, while still in law school, she carried both her virtues and her vices into her true calling, politics, by replacing Divinsky as an elected member of the Vancouver School Board. "Most people have an image of politicians as people who want to be loved, it's like being an entertainer," she told the *Vancouver Sun* in 1983. "But I have discovered I don't need to be loved by the public, that I will only say what I think."

Politics in British Columbia has always been a primordial struggle between the unionized workers in the resource industries and the entrepreneurial pioneers in ranching and commerce for control of the Lotusland in which both dreamed of building their heaven on earth. Their clash became especially polarized following the provincial election of 1933, when the Great Depression triggered the collapse of the governing Conservatives and the sudden success of a new socialist party – the Co-operative Commonwealth Federation (CCF) – as the official Opposition. At first the anti-socialists had no choice but to rally around the victorious Liberal party. In 1952, however, they were presented with a more genuinely right-wing alternative, Social Credit, a rural and small-business party led by a folksy hardware-store owner named W. A. C. Bennett.

Bennett held power for the next twenty years by convincing the province's Liberals and Conservatives that he was their best champion against the Red menace. Then, in 1972, the victory of the CCF's successor, the New Democratic Party, further intensified the conflict between left and right, translating almost every public issue into a matter of class struggle. When Social Credit was returned to power in 1975 and 1979 under "Wacky" Bennett's dull son Bill, it saw its mandate as the restoration of rugged individualism and the protection of free enterprise.

This ideological war was fought at the school board level in battles between the Committee of Progressive Electors, who were NDP supporters for the most part, and the Non-Partisan Association, a right-wing alliance to which Nathan Divinsky and Kim Campbell belonged. And battles royal there were. Campbell's four years on the board, including a stint as chairperson, coincided with a severe recession in British Columbia and the consequent effort by Bill Bennett's government to slash its spending. Campbell applauded the Socreds' restraint policy even when it affected school budgets, and that led her to rail against "the unacceptable face of trade unionism" during a confrontation with teachers.

The leftist trustees amused themselves by calling her an arrogant blowhard and bombastic snob until she got redder and redder and finally shrieked at them to fuck off. "She always had this superior air and big mouth that she decided was wasted on nineteen-year-olds," said one. "She'd preach for hours to us little people who wouldn't understand about the Big Picture she had learned at the London School of Economics. She used fancy words to sound smart and she loved hanging around highbrow types in order to be seen as a highbrow herself, but she was just a middle-class girl out to make an impression on the world and get a pat on the head from Daddy."

Her father did approve of her fiscal responsibility. "Kim understood the value of a buck from an early age," he said. "When she was little and I was a law student, she used to watch me leave for the midnight shift in the plywood mills on Friday night and again at six o'clock on Sunday morning. She was brought up on the ethic that you only got out of life what you were prepared to work for." But not all her causes were reactionary ones. She fought for a French-immersion program against hostile parents in Vancouver, for example, and she refused to pick up her husband's torch for the back-to-basics "genuine education movement," mostly because it was not popular with the mainstream. Nathan Divinsky had been unable to brainwash her, in other words, except perhaps with the lyrics of Gilbert and Sullivan. "It's not true that he was my Svengali," she later protested. "I had as powerful an influence on him as he had on me."

"I didn't see him changing her political orientation," George Campbell confirmed. "But her time on the school board was a big learning experience, because of its ideological fights. Kim would have loved to get consensus, for the sake of the kids, but she was pushed to declare herself on the right or the left. If fiscal responsibility meant being a conservative, then that's what she was."

When her eleven-year marriage ended in 1983, Kim Campbell became more than ever her father's daughter. She graduated in law from UBC, like he had, and she described herself in those days as "very much in the middle of the political spectrum . . . either left-wing Socred or right-wing NDP." When she decided to enter provincial politics as a Social Credit candidate – losing in 1983, winning in 1986 – she treated the party as a practical rather than an ideological vehicle. And, having worked as a policy adviser in Bill Bennett's office for a few months, she was a lot closer to his technocratic, top-down view of government than to his father's populism.

Within the Socred coalition, certainly, Campbell was not perceived as either an ideologue or a populist. Her quixotic run for the party's leadership in 1986 was a conscious gesture toward attracting a more urban, feminine, educated, and youthful constituency, and her widely reported dictum that "charisma without substance is a dangerous thing" was as much an attack on Bill Vander Zalm's "simplistic vision of a past that can never be recaptured" as on his slick salesmanship. She subsequently scuppered any chance she had of getting into Vander Zalm's cabinet by condemning his religious opposition to the public funding of abortions.

But if she had not picked up Divinsky's extremism, she had absorbed some of his legendary abrasiveness and conceit, based upon the presumed superiority of the intelligentsia. Though her friends intuited a deep, dark chamber of vulnerability – from which flowed her obsessive competitiveness, her hypersensitivity to criticism, and her relentless necessity to crow – her enemies thought her insufferably condescending. Her intelligence became a bludgeon; her wisecracking became a weapon; and once she developed a conviction, she was reluctant to change it, for change would have been an admission that she could be wrong. She often came across like some overstimulated "Jeopardy!" contestant, eagerly determined to push every button first. When she did give the right answer, she could hardly resist adding a snide put-down or supercilious crack to make sure her opponents knew that they had been bettered. Thus, of Premier

Vander Zalm, she once remarked, "I only wish I knew him before his lobotomy."

As a result, she often sounded more doctrinaire and authoritarian than she was because she was usually defending her convictions from a position of power. As school board chairperson, when asked what she would do if the Vancouver parents voted against French immersion, she joked, "We'll shove it down their throats!" While she came to see herself as an outsider – her "quite poor" childhood (which her father denied), her factory jobs as a student (which were more from choice than necessity), her alienation as a woman and a westerner (which did not slow her climb up the greasy pole) – Campbell had spent almost all her life in middle-class comfort and none of her time in political opposition. Any reformist tendencies, therefore, had been tempered by the benefits she enjoyed from the status quo and her duty to defend the actions of those in power.

"What are you people so afraid of?" she screamed sarcastically at some opponents of the Free Trade Agreement during the 1988 federal election. They may simply have been afraid, with reason, of losing their jobs.

Naked Launch

Though Kim Campbell had shown little interest in federal politics before the battle for free trade, and though she was reluctant to leave the West Coast (perhaps foreseeing that her second marriage, to lawyer Howard Eddy, would not survive her career in Ottawa), she fled the eccentricity of the Vander Zalm Socreds for the pragmatism of the Mulroney Tories. In 1988 she scored a narrow victory in Vancouver Centre. Elevated almost immediately into the cabinet, she widened her British Columbia focus into a pan-Canadian perspective and worked at subduing her British Columbia belligerence under the tutelage of the Grand Schmoozemeister himself.

In the months before Brian Mulroney announced his resignation on February 24, 1993, no one had expected to see a Kim Campbell coronation. She had only been a Progressive Conservative since 1988, after all, and though she had been recognized as a bright and effective comer soon after arriving in Parliament, she did not know the Tory party and – more to the point – the Tory party did not know her. Even her cabinet colleagues tended to see her as a loner, intimate with few and aligned to no ideological clique.

Nor did the Ottawa media know her any better, except perhaps for the four hundred women journalists she had impressed at a conference with her heartfelt remarks about the "unspeakable loneliness" of public life. At first the press gallery merely transmitted the Barbara Woodley photograph of the bonny justice minister standing as though naked (another bit of sexual innuendo) behind her legal robes. Then they passed on a potted, and not always accurate, biography. The graduate student who had not completed her M.A. became, by error or inference, a Soviet scholar and university professor. Her time as a trustee and MLA became a thorough political apprenticeship at the municipal and provincial levels of government. Her legislative score as a Tory minister became, as she was among the first to suggest, a remarkable record of accomplishment. And more impressive than her CV, apparently, was her personality.

"Indeed," the Montreal *Gazette* said of Campbell three days after Mulroney resigned, "she is an attractive politician: bright, articulate, witty, self-confident, sophisticated – surely the only cabinet minister in Canada's history to speak Russian, and one of the few to hold a Ph.D. She also speaks French, and has been working to get to know Quebec. She is not afraid to be different (witness the famous bare-shoulders picture) and she is not a member of the party's far-right wing. No wonder she stands out from the suits."

After a generation of politicians who had been packaged like dog food to be sold on TV, after a decade of Brian Mulroney's unctuous slickness and apparent duplicity, Canadians were understandably suspicious of old-style smoothies. Kim Campbell, in contrast, spoke like a baby boomer. She behaved like a British Columbian. She was funny, feisty, frank, and fresh. She was a woman. "I'm much less shy about showing my imperfections," was how she summed up the difference between herself and Mulroney, "going to the door with my hair messy kind of thing, just letting it all hang out. I think people want to feel there's that spontaneity, that something *real*."

The feeling was apparently enough for a plurality of citizens and a plethora of columnists to forgive the Conservatives for the Free Trade Agreement, two constitutional fiascos, a made-in-Canada recession, the 7-per-cent Goods and Services Tax (GST), 11-per-cent unemployment, record deficits and debt, shameless patronage, and a host of scandals.

With Campbell as leader, the pollsters declared, the Tories would win once more. The party and the press rushed to embrace the phenomenon. The phenomenon spiralled into a mania. "Defence minister marches toward a victory of unprecedented ease," the *Ottawa Citizen* trumpeted. At that point she had not even declared her candidacy.

Contrary to later conspiracy theories, that was not at all what Brian Mulroney had plotted. He had certainly positioned Campbell to be a contender, by training her in Justice and Defence and tolerating a bit of premature organization by her backers, but his game had been to position half a dozen ministers for a slugfest from which the best person would lead a revitalized party to another election victory. When Michael Wilson, Don Mazankowski, Perrin Beatty, Bernard Valcourt, Benoît Bouchard, and Barbara McDougall all retreated before the onslaught of Campbellmania, Mulroney urged Jean Charest into the ring. His grand design would not unfold if Kim Campbell were allowed to grab the party and carry his legacy in whatever direction she pleased.

The contest was barely under way before Mulroney started feeding the *Globe and Mail* editorialists their line that Campbell was the puppet of "such haggard devotees of politics-as-usual" as Dalton Camp and his brother-in-law Senator Norman Atkins. Veterans of the Big Blue Machine, Ontario's legendary network of organizers and strategists, both had fallen out with Mulroney since the 1988 election, not least because they were considered wet on economic and social issues. He therefore had cause to try to scare Campbell away from the "Atkins-Camp bid for re-eminence," as his friends at the *Globe* called it, but he was either badly informed or downright mischievous about their influence.

True, one of Campbell's closest friends and advisers was David Camp, a Vancouver lawyer who also happened to be Dalton's son and Atkins's nephew. His father had only met the candidate once at a public reception, however, and his uncle had cast one of the fateful votes that killed Justice Minister Campbell's abortion bill in the Senate in 1991. Neither played any role in her campaign. Dalton Camp was seriously ill and awaiting a heart-transplant operation, in fact, and Kim Campbell seemed to flee the room (as though to avoid guilt by association) whenever Norman Atkins appeared.

Initially, at least, she did not require much propping from the prime minister, the party pros, or even the press. She simply caught the fancy of the Canadian people. "My campaign unfolded in a way that I neither wanted nor predicted," she later remarked. "It was a bandwagon that ran the risk of getting mired in the mud." If fate had not been so kind, she might well have thrown her hat into the ring, as she had for the leadership of the Social Credit party in B.C., and emerged in last place. But fate had given her a dangerous temptation as well as a golden opportunity. Since she had come so far so fast seemingly by being herself, beholden to no particular faction, why shouldn't she quick march the rest of the way to the beat of her own drum?

Kim Campbell was vulnerable to that temptation because she was already in the habit of beating her own drum. She had never lacked for confidence about her God-given abilities nor hidden her self-developed talents from the world. As first female minister of justice and first female minister of national defence, her approach remained constant: "To be who I am, to articulate my vision and run it up the flagpole and see if anybody salutes." Now she was trusting that her singularity would make people salute her as the first female prime minister of Canada.

"The great thing about line dancing," Kim Campbell said as she walked from the stomp 'n' chomp toward her limousine, "is that you don't need a partner."

At the time it seemed a brave, even poignant, acceptance of her aloneness. The long day finally over, with her staff and supporters heading home to unwind with their families, she was going to be left by herself at midnight – with only her terrifying responsibilities – in the all-white apartment in a fashionable brownstone on Metcalfe Street, as cold as it was elegant, as austere as it was orderly, a large Gordon Smith and some Inuit prints on the walls and a small stack of books and magazines beside a sofa: Paul Kennedy on the twenty-first century, *Maria Chapdelaine*, a few issues of *Shape* and *Vanity Fair*, and the paperback autobiography of Ava Gardner.

Later, however, Campbell's offhand comment took on another meaning. She had missed the essence of line dancing, which is the integration of individual movement into the harmony of everyone else's. In the same way, it seemed, she had entered the leadership contest as something she could do by herself – in her own style, with her own words, for her own purposes. It was not that simple in the doing. Stumbling and bumping, she would have to move left and right, backward and forward, to pick up the dance of the political class.

The Political Class

An old Ottawa hand, now retired and on his way to a round of golf, sat in the lobby of the Chateau Laurier Hotel during the Tory leadership campaign and talked about Kim Campbell. He admired her brightness and sincerity, respected her practical attitude and hard work, and liked her as a person. Not the least of her qualities, from his point of view, had been her willingness to learn from seasoned bureaucrats such as himself. She used to called him Sir Humphrey, after the manipulative bureaucrat in the British satirical series "Yes, Minister," and he had liked that.

The sketch he drew was of a clever young minister, freshly arrived from the West Coast with a satchel of parochial concerns and opinions, who had been sent to him for instruction in the ways of the world. Blessed with a quick and orderly mind, bursting with enthusiasm and good questions, anxious to succeed, she had absorbed the basics of national government and blossomed into an effective politician. But when he considered Campbell's weak grasp of economics and her limited experience in office, he had reservations about her becoming prime minister just now. "It is an amazing indication of the state of our public life that she is so far ahead," he concluded. "She may be up to scratch in three or four years, but when I compare what she doesn't know to the hard issues we face, I think, Holy shit!"

His assessment may have been patronizing, but it was not uncommon. All around the capital that spring, at dinner parties and watering holes, among party organizers and parliamentary reporters, there was the same uncertainty. At lunch a powerful operative in the Prime Minister's Office, surveying the dim sum cart, mused, "She may improve – look at Mulroney between the convention of 1983 and the election of 1984 – but it's no sure thing." A Conservative senator, over a cup of coffee in his East Block office, moaned about "the bunch of teenyboppers" Campbell had put in charge of her campaign. "She might be able to squeak through a leadership race with them," he said, "but she'll have trouble winning an election." And, west along Wellington Street in the National Press Building, a *Globe and Mail* reporter opined that a half-hour grilling by a first-rate mind would easily expose Kim Campbell as an intellectual fraud.

Each was the voice of Canada's political class, the informal network of men and women who regularly occupy themselves with national politics at the highest level. Not as hereditary as a caste, it is nevertheless a distinct group to whom Canadians normally delegate the management of their public affairs. Not as exclusive as a guild, it is nevertheless a fraternal clique adept in the black arts of power. Its MPs go after each other's jugulars in front of the cameras in the House of Commons, then slip "behind the curtains" to share a smoke and a joke. Its reporters build careers by exposing the foibles and falsehoods of ministers, then gush the most saccharine tributes the moment one of them retires.

"Whatever the party or jurisdiction of politicians," Prime Minister Jean Chrétien once observed, "you all are elected officials, and that gives you a community of interest. When you aren't talking business, you tend to talk about your problems as politicians, your successes and your failures, and the partisan element vanishes. The warmth of friendship can do much to thaw the chill of political tensions or the coldness of technical negotiations."

Within the loop, competing and conniving for influence or office, are the elected politicians and appointed senators, the senior mandarins and media correspondents, the ministerial assistants and parliamentary workers, the party activists and hired pollsters, the special-interest lobbyists and think-tank consultants, with cameo appearances by corporate presidents, union leaders, church dignitaries, aboriginal chiefs, royal commissioners, best-selling authors, prominent intellectuals, and various other "talking heads" on "Prime Time News" and "Canada A.M." Though individuals may come and go with death or defeat, the political class itself remains remarkably consistent. The party elders hand down their esoteric knowledge and insider lore. The veteran bureaucrats dole out their expert advice and technical jargon. The eminent pundits pass along their pickled wisdom and cynical pose.

In the United States, the political class is said to include all those who work "inside the Beltway," referring to the highway that encircles Washington, D.C. In Ottawa, it tends to be everyone whose life revolves around what is happening "on the Hill" (as chronicled in the *Hill Times*). It's an apt metaphor. From the Olympian height of their personal accomplishments, the movers and shakers cannot help but look across to each other and down on everyone else: the *average* citizen, the *common* people, the *ordinary* Canadian. However hard they may try to dislodge each other in order to rule the roost, they are usually careful not to rock the roost itself. They all hear, from beyond or below, the dreadful howling of a mob.

They are, to switch to the most common metaphor, the players – on different teams wearing different colours, to be sure, but in the same league nevertheless. "You need a game plan, you need a play book" was how Ray Castelli explained his job as operations director of Kim Campbell's leadership campaign. "Execution is important, and you can't score points unless you have the ball." One side scores with a devious tactic, another suffers a brutal blow, but both are joined together by rules, experience, necessity, and an absolute devotion to the game. "It's like hockey," Jean Chrétien explained. "You can fight on the ice and still have a beer together afterwards."

"The players," observed the journalist Stevie Cameron about the small and isolated burg in which they play, "no matter how much they hate each other, will meet in the aisles of the IGA or around the table of a small dinner party or at an Arts Centre concert and be unfailingly polite." That goes deeper than the code of conduct that a civilized social life requires, the mutual respect that adversaries often develop in war and sports, or the utter fascination that insiders share about this morning's headline. It is rooted in the fact that all of them – politicians and bureaucrats, journalists and lobbyists, friends and foes – are caught in a web of symbiotic relationships. Everyone is of potential use to everyone else.

If the members of the political class are the ones on the field, the voters are the spectators booing or cheering in the stands. That's why, despite the ruthless clash of parties and ideas, both wealthy tycoons and welfare recipients rail against "the system" that offers them no real choices. And that's why, though the voters are as divided by conflicting interests as the players, the political class tends to lump the people together just like professional athletes lump together their fans. How easy things look from a seat in the stadium! How obvious things seem on Monday morning! How disruptive things become when hooligans storm on to the field!

"The worst kind of slavery is the slavery to public opinion," Pierre Trudeau declared. To which Brian Mulroney added, "You can be a popular prime minister or you can be an effective one, but you can't be both." Kim Campbell, according to her habit, was even blunter. "A lot of people that you're out there working for," she once said, "are people who may sit in their undershirt and watch the game on Saturday, beer in hand."

The Confidence Game

The tension between the political class and the people is as old as democracy, and it is based primarily on fear. The masters of the game fear the fantasies and prejudices of the multitude of amateurs who have the ultimate authority to oust them. The public, on the other hand, feeling powerless despite that authority, fear the greed and ambition of those who are supposed to be their servants.

"All communities divide themselves into the few and the many. The first are the rich and wellborn, the other the mass of the people," Alexander Hamilton argued during the American constitutional debates of 1787. "The people are turbulent and changing; they seldom judge or determine right. Give therefore to the first class a distinct, permanent share in the government. They will check the unsteadiness of the second."

In the past, because French Canada and English Canada were both founded upon the rejection of two great popular revolutions, Canadians exhibited a Hamiltonian deference to authority. They trusted government – certainly more than the Americans ever did – and seemed content to leave its tedium and tribulations to a few elected representatives, a cabal of bureaucrats, and the press gallery. However much politics itself was considered "a rather unworthy pursuit," as Lester Pearson put it, "like running a confidence game or managing a prizefighter in New York," public service remained a noble calling, somewhere between civic duty and religious self-abnegation, and public institutions remained objects of respect. Democracy may never have been pure in Canada, but it was worth life itself in two great wars.

"Elite accommodation" even became an accepted definition of the Canadian system. The people were sectioned, as it were, into regions, communities, or "client groups" whose barons brokered among themselves for compromise solutions and political favours. The provincial premiers got fiscal transfers; the business lobbies got tariffs; the farmers and fishermen got subsidies; the workers got minimum wages; the underdeveloped regions got grants; the ill got medicare; the unemployed got insurance; the old got a pension; the young got an allowance. Indeed, it was assumed, in a country as geographically vast and ethnically diverse as Canada, politics could not operate in any other way. The federal system was itself a deliberate repudiation of majority rule in a unitary state.

The men at the top – for men they almost always were – were judged primarily by their ability to extract benefits from the national wealth for their particular factions. If successful, they were seldom begrudged their power or perks. Canadians wanted honest and efficient government, which basically meant a fair division of an ever-increasing pie. After that, they wanted to be left alone.

Usually they were – until election time, when various agents of the political class suddenly began pounding on their doors in the middle of supper, jamming their mailboxes with promises and exaggerations, interrupting their radio and TV shows with paid appeals and incomprehensible debates, filling their newspapers with thundering denunciations and patriotic gabble, clutching at their hands and babies, arousing the whole country to a pitch of false hope and partisan excitement in a shameless quest for votes. Somebody won, somebody lost. The names in the news changed, but little else.

The government itself seldom changed, in fact. For most of the twentieth century, from Wilfrid Laurier to Pierre Trudeau, the Liberal party won so regularly that it became known as Canada's Natural Governing Party. The Liberals understood, better than either the Conservatives or the New Democrats, how to accommodate the elites and straddle the ideological centre. Their religious tolerance guaranteed the loyalty of most French Canadians. Their immigration policies attracted the support of most new Canadians. They allowed entrepreneurs and financiers plenty of freedom – and plenty of assistance – to make plenty of money. In exchange, they required them to contribute their fair share toward the construction of a generous welfare system, which further assisted business by creating social stability, health and education benefits, and consumers for its products. Despite cyclical downturns, despite regional and linguistic disparities, despite a chronic underclass of native peoples and the impoverished, the Liberals oversaw the transformation of a pioneer colony into a middle-class, middle-power, middle-brow hallucination.

However haphazard and inequitable, the system functioned reasonably well as long as Canada remained a cornucopia of fertile fields and limitless resources, with historic links to the richest markets of the world and ready access to foreign capital. Following the Second World War, especially, with much of Europe and Asia in ruins, Canada enjoyed an unprecedented boom in exports and investments.

By the 1960s, indeed, prosperity and progress were taken for granted, and the political class was able to preoccupy itself with the redistribution of the nation's wealth through universal social *entitlements*.

But the very foundations of that wealth were soon weakened. Aggressive competitors arose from the debris of war and the cheap labour markets of the Third World. More supply and less demand forced resource prices down. In 1971 Canada's largest customer, the United States, levied a 10-per-cent surcharge on all imports. In 1973 the OPEC cartel conspired to quadruple the world price of oil, which doubled again as a result of the Iranian revolution, causing double-digit inflation and regional inequities. Productivity growth, job levels, and disposable incomes began to descend. Welfare payments, real interest rates, and budget deficits started to climb. Then, in the early 1980s, and again a decade later, the worst recessions since the Great Depression wrecked economic and social devastation across the land.

More subtly, yet of greater consequence, all the Western economies were undergoing a revolutionary shift from raw materials and manu-facturing to information and services. Industry and finance began using computers and satellite telecommunications to construct global orga-nizations beyond the control of nation-states. World trade barriers were gradually lowered by the General Agreement on Tariffs and Trade (GATT) and other international treaties. Traditional jobs rapidly disappeared, while the new high-tech jobs required unprecedented levels of education and training. As governments grew in size and cost, they created uncompetitive distortions in the marketplace and a psy-chological dependence in every sector of society. And the old macro-economic tools, whether inspired by John Maynard Keynes or Milton Friedman, could no longer fine-tune national economies that were subject to the vagaries of bond markets and planetary events. Economists are still arguing about all the causes, but no one can deny the effects.

"Taking stock of the past four decades," a government report con-cluded in 1994, "the most striking feature has been the long-term deterioration of overall economic performance since the mid-1970s. This was a watershed in the economic history of the postwar era and marks the beginning of two decades of relatively disappointing performance for the Western economies as a group – a performance characterized mainly by low productivity growth, stagnating real incomes, and rising unemployment rates. In Canada, the productivity slowdown was not sufficiently offset by reduced public and private consumption, resulting in an extraordinary buildup of debt, both foreign and domestic."

Canada's economic downturn, in other words, was more than a cyclical adjustment or management problem. It signalled not just the end of an extraordinary boom, but also the end of the industrial era that had dawned in the early nineteenth century. And since that era had coincided with the development of Canada, nothing was secure any more: not the political institutions, not the social structures, not the assumption of prosperity, not the guarantee of standards, not even the faith in progress. As the demands and expectations of the public exceeded the ability of the political class to fulfil them, the compliance and satisfaction gave way year by year to disappointment and cynicism.

Kick Ass, Kiss Ass

"When incomes stagnate, fear starts to take over," Pierre Trudeau reflected in one of his rare interventions in public life since his retirement in 1984 to Montreal, where heads of state, corporate chiefs, and people on the street still seek out his advice on world affairs and Quebec politics. "As faith in government declined, the pursuit of personal gain became the driving force not only in the economy but in society as a whole. The Love Generation of the sixties was moving towards the Me Generation of the eighties."

Trudeau certainly knew of what he spoke. Because the postwar climb in Canada's productivity and wealth peaked and began its decline when he was in office, he had to bear the first, ferocious rage against the political class. The left accused him of being a mere agent of the business elite. The right dismissed him as a socialist in a tailored suit. To an increasing number of mainstream Canadians, he appeared deceitful and smug. Worse, he appeared incompetent. He mocked the idea of wage and price controls during the 1974 election, then imposed them in 1975. He dabbled in Crown corporations and industrial strategies, then tossed huge subsidies and tax breaks to the private sector. He ran up a string of deficits, then slashed public spending. In truth as well as in appearance, Trudeau and his Liberal government were floundering in the economic malaise and global upheavals of the times. As he himself confessed at the end of 1975, "We haven't been able to make it work – the free-market system."

For much of the 1970s, moreover, Canada's epic economic troubles were overshadowed – and exacerbated – by an epic political crisis that threatened the federation itself. Quebec nationalism had arisen in the previous decade, first as a cry for provincial autonomy, then as a movement for outright independence, primarily because French-speaking Canadians had been denied a just proportion of the national wealth and effective power in Ottawa. Not only had Trudeau entered federal politics to correct that injustice, but events such as the FLQ terrorist crisis in 1970, the Victoria constitutional talks in 1971, the Quebec language law in 1974, and the election of the separatist Parti Québécois in 1976 kept him fixated on Quebec.

As a result, and against his better judgement, he was forced to waste an inordinate amount of time and effort on constitutional reform. It proved an expensive diversion, too, because Quebec's demands for more money and power inspired every other provincial government to produce its own inexhaustible list. By the end of the decade, Canada had become the most decentralized federation in the world (with the possible exception of Switzerland), and Ottawa became "increasingly powerless," as the Economic Council of Canada warned in 1979, "to the peril of the country as a whole" at the very time when strategic management was most needed. Yet all the constitutional negotiations resulted in little more than the defeat of the Liberals in 1979.

Fed up with the cantankerous and unproductive conflicts of the political class, many Canadians had come to blame both the tone and the matter on Pierre Trudeau. Joe Clark did not have much better luck, however, during his few months of Conservative rule. Elite accommodation was predicated, after all, upon prosperity and payoffs. As revenues grew scarcer and responsibilities clashed, the ritualistic quarrels between Ottawa and the provinces became fights to the finish. As capital grew tighter and taxes increased, the mutual alliances between government and business degenerated into open hostility. The consequence, more often than not, was conflict and impasse.

When Pierre Trudeau was re-elected in 1980, he returned to power with a new resolve based on a simple – yet profoundly important – question: Who shall speak for Canada? "We had tried federal-provincial cooperation," he recalled with exasperation. "We had tried to cooperate with business and labour. We had tried to cooperate with the energy-producing provinces. But for all our cooperation we were finding it hard to get anything done. I decided that enough was enough."

So he set about to override the particular interests of the elites and re-establish Ottawa as the champion of the national interest. His government got ready to act unilaterally to patriate the British North America Act from London and append to it a new charter of rights. It instituted the National Energy Program over the virulent objections of the energy-producing provinces, the business lobbies, and the American multinationals. It tackled such intractable problems as the Atlantic fisheries and the western freight rate. It browbeat labour into accepting an anti-inflation agreement and threatened to reduce the fiscal transfers to any province that contravened the standards of the Canada Health Act. The whole thrust of Pierre Trudeau's final mandate was an activist, centralist, and expensive exercise in nation-building. "It was my feeling," Trudeau said, "that the major decentralization being demanded by the provinces would endanger Canada's survival as a country, and I was determined to resist it."

Coincidentally, for reasons that had more to do with American monetary policy and the collapse of world oil prices than with any domestic policies, Canada suffered the severest recession in thirty-five years. Inflation climbed above 10 per cent; interest rates soared above 20 per cent; unemployment mounted above 11 per cent; and the federal debt jumped by $30 billion a year to reach $200 billion in 1984. The popularity of the Liberals, indeed of their entire interventionist approach, plummeted. If their programs had succeeded in returning Canada to the glory days before 1973, Canadians might well have forgiven them the extravagance and waste, the corruption and patronage, the arrogance and remoteness. With failure, however, the people went looking for change.

After almost twenty solid years of Liberal rule, they were ready to give the Progressive Conservative party another try. By 1984, too, they were susceptible, as perhaps never before in Canadian history, to the appeal of the decentralist, free-market, private-enterprise conservatism that Ronald Reagan and Margaret Thatcher had been promulgating in the United States and Great Britain. But only up to a point. "Between 1980 and 1984," Allan Gregg, the Tories' very bright and articulate pollster, noted at the time, "satisfaction with the government dropped from 50 per cent to 20 per cent. Yet there wasn't one scintilla of change in the belief that governments can wholly or partly solve the problems that concern people. They may have to do things differently, but the system can still work if changed."

Brian Mulroney knew that better than most of his fellow Tories. Though he had taken the Tory leadership from Joe Clark in 1983 as a right-wing businessman, determined to increase domestic productivity and reduce government spending, he was a longtime bit-player in the political class who understood how the Liberal party had maintained power for so long. Essentially, he sought to steal the Liberal formula, first by opening his party to French Canadians and immigrant voters, and second by restoring the quid-pro-quo entente between the public and private sectors. And because the Liberals had moved further to the left than usual, the Conservatives were given an opportunity to occupy the centre and expand their core vote – which Mulroney astutely seized.

"In political history," he declared, in a revealing summation of his philosophy, "you can be nice and decent and kind and all those things, but if you don't win, you don't go anywhere."

His victory represented nostalgia for the past as much as hope for the future. It evoked a once-upon-a-time Canada when government was small and budgets were balanced, when federalism was cooperative and jobs were plentiful, where business was smug and social programs were sacred. It implied the return of old-style elite accommodation under a former labour negotiator who bragged about having "sown harmony and understanding" wherever he had gone. Despite Mulroney's working-class background as the son of an electrician in the Quebec mill town of Baie Comeau, he had built a successful career in Montreal by stroking the rich and powerful in the Mount Royal Club and the Ritz. That had given him a profound conviction that the world only went round by getting "the boys" together, over a friendly drink preferably but to hammer heads if necessary, in order to reach a deal.

There were, in this modus operandi, only two sides to human nature: vanity and greed. There were no principles that could not be bent. There were no ideals that could not be purchased. At his best, he flattered all and sundry with personal kindnesses, phone calls, handwritten notes, floral bouquets, official honours, a private joke, a sympathetic look, or a slap on the back. At his worst, he tempted them with appointments, contracts, grants, tax breaks, sinecures, clout – or threatened, as a Tory senator once expressed it, "to cut off their balls."

Mulroney often boasted, with ample justification, of his achievement in holding together the notoriously fractious Tory caucus through good times and bad. It was, after all, an unlikely alliance of Quebec nationalists, Ontario and Maritime Loyalists, and western individualists, who shared little more than an aversion to Liberals and a desire for power. The pleasures and privileges of high office were the key to party unity, of course, to which Mulroney added his theatrical ability to make his MPs laugh or cry, his real concern about their marriage troubles or alcohol problems, and the speed with which he condemned anyone who resisted his wishes to some desolate political Siberia. "His caucus knew when he was bullshitting and having them on," Allan Gregg remarked with the foul-mouthed frankness that, along with his ponytail and rock-musician appearance, had made him such an exotic oddity in the back rooms of the Tory party, "but his leadership style of 'kick ass, kiss ass' made people afraid to cross him and want to please him at the same time."

Mulroney's base appeals triumphed, at least in the short term. His carrots and sticks kept the donkeys obedient; his solemn vows and weak opponents brought him two terms in power. But in time, as though in a morality tale, the whole edifice so artfully constructed from cunning and deception came tumbling down on the Tories' heads. Brian Mulroney himself only escaped the wrath of the people by fleeing behind the thick walls of a mansion in Montreal.

No Way

For much of his first term Mulroney slithered and slid, trying to please everyone, desperate to be loved. He gave grants to big businesses and tax exemptions to small investors. He provided jobs for thousands of Tories and slush funds for regional development. He defended the indexing of old-age pensions to inflation and the principle of universality in social programs. "His grand agenda, if there was one, seemed to shift in response to the day's headlines," Michel Gratton observed at close range as press secretary in the Prime Minister's Office, "so that we had major policies which had never been presaged in the election campaign – such as the free-trade initiative – and sudden switches that seemed to come from nothing more than a reading of the previous day's headlines."

But a series of ministerial scandals and broken promises undid whatever harmony and reconciliation Brian Mulroney had tried to establish. Worse, his government was continuing to run deficits that averaged above $30 billion a year. As Trudeau had discovered, Ottawa no longer had the money to buy consensus. In fact, it was going to have to borrow just to pay the interest on what it had already borrowed. When the Conservatives hit that truth, they did the opposite to what the Liberals had done. They downsized, they privatized, they deregulated, they withdrew. Instead of confronting the elites, Mulroney basically surrendered to them.

That was seen most clearly in his two boldest manoeuvres, the Meech Lake Accord and the Free Trade Agreement. The first was a deal in which Mulroney and the ten premiers agreed to recognize Quebec as a "distinct society" with certain entrenched rights in exchange for its signature on Trudeau's 1982 constitutional reforms; the second was a treaty with the United States in which Canada dismantled most of its tariff and non-tariff barriers to American goods and American investment in exchange for guaranteed access to the U.S. market. Both were deals cooked up by "the boys" behind closed doors. Both represented major concessions by the Canadian government to the leaders of special-interest lobbies. Both were announced as *faits accomplis,* not only impossible to alter now but virtually impossible to undo ever. Both were unpopular. The last thing Mulroney wanted, in fact, was to put either to the Canadian people. In the public imagination, according to Allan Gregg's polls, he went from being "Willy Loman – the guy who was prepared to kiss any ass to win favour, to get the population with him – to being Idi Amin – a guy who's got his own view, who just doesn't listen."

In the heyday of elite accommodation, the factional chiefs had struck a bargain, then sold its benefits to their followers. If there was something unpalatable in the compromise, there was bound to be some compensating goody. If there was something dubious about the issue, the political class was usually given the benefit of the doubt. Brian Mulroney certainly proved a master at pulling unlikely deals from his magician's hat. One on one, he appealed with remarkable acumen to the crudest desires and noblest sentiments of human beings. He had an uncanny instinct for when to alternate the charm with the heat. Experience had taught him how to back someone into a corner and use the pressure of a deadline. It helped, too, that getting a deal seemed more important to him than getting anything for the national government. But neither Mulroney nor the elites had much success in selling the pacts he had so skilfully brokered – except, on a couple of important occasions, in Quebec.

"Though the role of the elites has evolved over time," Jean Charest suggested, "there is still a small group of people who are capable of determining the orientation of a much larger group in Quebec society, and there has never been the same degree of cynicism about the political process. Even those middle-class Quebeckers who are in revolt against high taxes and too much government recognize that the state has a key role to play in the survival of their language and culture. And they always recognized, in Brian Mulroney and the Conservative government, an openness toward Quebec."

That did not do the federal Tories or their strange bedfellows in the provincial Liberal party much good, however, when it came to the Charlottetown Accord and the next election. In Quebec, as in the rest of the country, education, the mass media, and the inability of the political class to halt Canada's economic decline had shaken the public's deep-rooted faith in its leaders. Brian Mulroney's patent partisanship, calculated bonhomie, and extravagant life-style (culminating in his $600,000 farewell visit to the important capitals of the world) only aggravated the growing contempt for old-style political posturing. Indeed, his cynical view of human nature seemed to have permeated the cabinet, the caucus, the civil service, the media, and eventually the nation itself.

Private gain was exalted over public service – as Mulroney admitted in 1984, while still leader of the Opposition, "I would have been the first with my nose in the trough, just like all the rest of them." The private sector was esteemed over the public good. Downgraded, too, were the very values of community responsibility, social justice, national unity, and popular sovereignty that had held Canada together for more than 125 years. Mulroney described the Constitution itself as not worth the piece of paper it was written on. Even when he tried to appeal to a sense of fiscal restraint or civic duty, his fancy shoes and blatant self-glorification made his platitudes unconvincing.

"A prime minister is a moral anchor of a government," explained Arthur Kroeger, a tall, courtly, and highly regarded deputy minister, who retired to become chairman of the Public Policy Forum and a lecturer at the University of Toronto, "and if the anchor is not firmly wedged, you get drift. My sense of those years was that ministers of great integrity could be put in a very uncomfortable position because they weren't sure they would have the backing of the prime minister in defence of the public interest."

Underlying that, moreover, was the question of whether the public interest any longer corresponded to the interests of Canada's elites. Was the Meech Lake Accord, for example, really for the sake of national unity, or was it in fact a tacit power grab for the political advantage of Brian Mulroney and Robert Bourassa? And was the Free Trade Agreement really for the benefit of the national economy, or was it in fact an elaborate corporate plot to help shift jobs and investments to the United States?

That kind of skepticism was even found among Progressive Conservatives. Below the Hill, beyond the range of Mulroney's sweet whispers and sudden tantrums, many of them felt betrayed. Hadn't they voted against the Liberals' constant "appeasement" of Quebec and their persistent deficits? Hadn't they voted against patronage, corruption, presidential pretensions, and all the back-room sleaze of the political class? Hadn't they voted for an effective national government and jobs, jobs, jobs?

Instead, they got two constitutional follies to placate Quebec nationalists, a federal debt that was more than twice what the Tories had inherited, and a string of colossal deficits brought on by high interest rates and a devastating recession. One and a half million citizens were unemployed, two million were on social assistance, and a record number of Canadian children were living in poverty. There had been thirty-eight tax increases, including the hated GST that had sent many law-abiding consumers into the underground economy, and real family income had been stagnant for a decade. Tens of thousands of small businesses were either crippled or destroyed. Schools and hospitals were in obvious decline. The nation's capital had become a refuge for money-grubbing scoundrels who had been sent to do good for the country and ended up doing very, very well for themselves.

By providing government that was no better than Trudeau's – if not, in many instances, worse – Mulroney turned a question of confidence in the nation's leadership into a crisis of confidence. More insidiously still, by providing bad government, the Tories bolstered their case that government itself is bad. According to a 1993 Environics poll, 39 per cent of Canadians had come to believe that Ottawa actually *harmed* the public interest. "People have lowered their expectations of the political processes that managed the country for generations," concluded Michael Adams, whose firm had conducted the poll. "Canadians now look at governments not in terms of what they will give but in terms of what they are likely to take away."

Justly perhaps, the more the Tories alienated Canadians from their national government, the more the people became alienated from them. But the entire political class suffered as well. Mulroney's favourite defence against accusations of corruption or deception, after all, was that the Tories were only doing what the Liberals had done before. So why should the people trust any politician if they are all duplicitous and self-serving? Why should anyone even vote if no party will keep its promises or heed the electorate? "Why," as Kim Campbell herself asked, "should Canadians respect a system that does not show respect for them and their needs?"

The effect of this mutual disrespect became dramatically apparent with the 1992 referendum on the Charlottetown constitutional agreement, yet another deal concocted by Mulroney and the premiers to satisfy Quebec by honouring it as a distinct society, giving all the provinces a host of new powers as well as equal representation in the Senate, and entrenching native self-government to boot. Despite its many impractical details, the accord garnered the support of the three major parties in the House of Commons and all ten premiers, as well as a majority of business groups, union leaders, aboriginal chiefs, and newspaper editorialists. In a show of unity seldom seen outside war and natural disasters, the political class worked together in a coalition committee and campaigned hard to sell the deal as the best – and probably last – hope for the survival of the nation. Opposing it was not just lunacy, it was tantamount to treason. Prime Minister Mulroney referred to its opponents as "enemies of Canada," no less.

Yet defeated it was, by nearly 55 per cent of the population, representing majorities in six provinces and the Yukon, both official languages, and most native communities. Canadians had come as close as they probably ever will to lining up their governing elites and chopping off their heads in what one TV commentator called "a revolution for the status quo." As Allan Gregg learned from his focus groups, "Any notion that the country was going to fall apart was rebutted by people saying, 'These are the same fuckers who told us that free trade was going to make us prosperous and the GST was going to reduce the deficit. We're not going to be fooled again!' They were so uninformed and so cynical that there was a veneer through which logic couldn't penetrate."

Whatever the particular reasons, whether logical or emotional, progressive or reactionary, thoughtful or glib, voting "No" signalled a massive rejection of the judgement and agenda of Canada's political class, not just of Brian Mulroney and the Conservatives. It turned into a vote against brokerage politics, elite accommodation, party fixers, sectoral trade-offs, and abstract issues that had no apparent connection to the realities of ordinary lives. It was also, no doubt, a plea for a vision in which the good of the whole transcended the benefits to the parts.

"If you're going to engage in this kind of collective decision making and make it valid," said Arthur Kroeger, who had been seconded from the Department of Employment and Immigration to work on securing the accord, "all the major interests have to be represented. In my view, there was one interest that was not at the table – the national interest. The federal government just wanted a deal, and as long as it could give away this or that in order to placate a group, it was ready to do so. There was nothing in the package that could make Canadians feel good about being Canadians."

With Mulroney's resignation, too, the Canadian people sent an unexpected message to the political class by rocketing Kim Campbell to the top of the polls, ahead of all the better-known and more experienced Tory contenders, ahead of the Liberals' Jean Chrétien and the NDP's Audrey McLaughlin. At first impression, however loyal a member of the government she might have been, Campbell looked and sounded like a human being, not some brainwashed emissary from another plane. And she reinforced the impression with an easygoing, plain-speaking launch to her leadership campaign on March 25, 1993, in Vancouver.

"Government isn't something that a small group of people do *to* everybody else," she said. "It's not even something that they do *for* everybody else. It should be something that they do *with* everybody else. There is such a yearning in Canada today to be part of the process. If we can't capture it and find ways of making it a reality, we will have failed not only our party but our country."

Though Campbell herself may not have understood what that meant in practice, she had struck the right note. And though the Conservative party owed Brian Mulroney for its two terms of power and plunder, it was also indebted to him for the precept that winning was all that mattered. If Canadians wanted Kim Campbell, the pros would toss aside whatever loyalties and principles stood in her way. Representatives from every region and faction of the party rushed to embrace her as their saviour.

Running on Empty

Kim Campbell was the right person in the right place at the right time more because of her image – bilingual female baby boomer from the urban West Coast – than her ideas. As a member of Mulroney's inner cabinet she had been orthodox about free trade, deficit reduction, constitutional reform, and the GST. As minister of justice she had been active regarding abortion, gun control, homosexual rights, and sexual assault. Significantly, however, when she stood at the top of the polls, no one seemed to know – and few seemed to care – where she stood on the political spectrum.

She was a fiscal conservative who wanted to spend over $1 billion on the KAON physics project for her province and billions more on the EH-101 helicopters for her department. She was committed to the Free Trade Agreement but in favour of cultural protectionism, tough on crime but against capital punishment, ardent about the rule of law but willing to admit its "systemic" racism and sexism. The left called her a reactionary ideologue; the right called her an unprincipled opportunist; she called herself a pragmatic democrat.

"One of the reasons why the prime minister has had confidence in me is that he saw me handle difficult issues without breaking up the caucus," Campbell remarked, with her typical blend of forthrightness and boastfulness, while still a member of Brian Mulroney's cabinet. "He knew he could count on me not to be divisive, to be patient, to be very careful, and to pull back when I got into a situation that was too fractious." (On the contrary, revealed Mulroney's unofficial spokesman, the *Globe*'s editor-in-chief Bill Thorsell, he had not been impressed with "her ability to manage difficult policies through the Tory caucus" and "remained unsure of her political instincts.")

Getting things done was always a higher priority than ideological consistency, which was why she belonged to none of the gangs in Mulroney's cabinet. Her allies were as diverse in style and thought as a brain like Lowell Murray and a boob like Tom Siddon, a *nationaliste* like Marcel Masse and a Loyalist like Perrin Beatty. "She is particularly comfortable in the realm of ideas," said Beatty, one of her earliest friends in Ottawa and an influential adviser, "and she is open to persuasion if you can make a good argument. I've never found her defensive or brittle. She genuinely listens, and then she makes a decision."

Campbell's pleasure, indeed, was to use the prestige and resources available to a federal minister to hear a cacophony of opinions and examine a plethora of options, as though she were leading a crowded undergraduate seminar on every given matter. "I believe," she once explained, "that when people sit around a table, even with people that they've been taught to think of as their enemies, they have to take account of their humanity – it's no longer an abstract idea, it's no longer a title, it's a real flesh-and-blood human being that they have to face – they can then begin to talk meaningfully and in a productive way about their goals and aspirations and what they need from government."

"I've seen her grow tremendously in terms of learning to deal with people who disagree with her," said Mary Collins, another Tory minister from British Columbia. "She's learned that, to do politics effectively, you have to build consensus." On the abortion issue, for example, Campbell put aside her pro-choice belief, consulted a broad range of interest groups and legal experts, laboured over the details with her bureaucrats, negotiated with her caucus colleagues, and reached a middle ground in which abortions became both available and criminal.

In this, she was a fair reflection of most federal Tories. Government and Mulroney's persuasive techniques had united the loose coalition of outsiders and malcontents into a sophisticated network of brokers. Age and the Reform party had removed most of the Ontario imperialists and western cowboys who used to scare off francophones, women, immigrants, young people, and moderate voters. Unlike in 1983, therefore, there were few ideological battles raging within the party's ranks and looking for champions. Instead, the Progressive Conservative party, while still oriented toward business and the white upper-middle class, was more interested in keeping office than keeping faith.

But, again like most Tories, Kim Campbell had had to learn consensus-building on the job in Ottawa, and it rubbed against some bad habits. She did not abandon her tone of conviction so much as postpone it. Once the most rational solution became fixed in her mind as though in cement, her brusque and often moral certitude would reappear, ready to trample over any argument she encountered and gloat over every enemy she defeated. The week after she won federal funding for the KAON project after a heated cabinet debate with William Winegard, for example, she humiliated him in front of their colleagues with a triumphant dig. "Bill was liked and respected by everyone," one witness recalled, "and he understood he had lost fair and square. But she just had to rub his nose in it."

Psychologically torn between the personalities of her mother and father, deeply conflicted between her need to be hugged and her wish to be independent, she herself seemed confused about whether she was a consensus politician or a conviction politician. "I'm still aggressive and combative and very tough about things I need to be tough about," Campbell said during the leadership campaign. With the next breath, however, she claimed to have become "a mellower person" who did not rise to the bait so easily.

Compounding the confusion, she had not entered the race with a set of detailed policies. She felt inhibited about making catchy statements from which she might have to backtrack as prime minister. She could not storm ahead with her own ideas without jeopardizing her public commitment to attracting "talented people to participate in fleshing out the programs." Mostly, she did not have a grasp on the issues, even though she and her staff had been plotting a leadership run for more than a year. From the very first, it seemed, the emphasis was going to be on style, image, and process, what one private memo called "almost a non-partisan, non-policy approach."

Whatever the reason, as the self-described "master of the thirty-*minute* sound bite," she had yet to discover her own way of compressing complicated issues into thirty-second answers for radio and television. Nor was she ready to read lines written by the old pros of the political class. "Even my own people didn't really understand what kind of a candidate I was," Campbell lamented later. "They didn't give me what I needed, which was time to think and reflect and get comfortable. I'm uncomfortable talking about something if I haven't had a chance to figure it out. I don't like to respond if I don't know the background or take ownership of a position that may not be my position. I couldn't go out and do instant policy."

Continental Drift

Policy, instant or otherwise, seemed especially hard to formulate in the last decade of the twentieth century. The economic and social transformations were so overwhelming, the global and technological forces so powerful, the political and fiscal assumptions so precarious, that only the foolhardy rushed in with five-year plans and concrete promises. With both the state and the marketplace in public disgrace, the familiar solutions of the left and the right had lost their ability to convince, and there had not yet emerged many new ideas or any obvious alternatives.

Democratic politicians, not just in Canada but around the world, faced the unenviable task of presiding over disintegration, disappointment, decline, and despair. Their governments were essentially broke. That was, as Kim Campbell said, "not a question of ideology, it's a question of reality." As proof, she had only to point to the example of Bob Rae, the NDP premier of Ontario.

Coincident with his election in 1990, Canada's largest and wealthiest province was walloped by the worst recession since the 1930s, the short-term turmoil of free trade, the negative effects of a high dollar, the reduction of federal fiscal transfers, and the major shifts in the North American economy. Rae's amateur government watched helplessly as its revenues plunged, its welfare payments almost trebled to $6 billion, and the provincial deficit skyrocketed to over $10 billion a year. Interest payments on the debt, more and more of which was held overseas, threatened to surpass government spending on health or education – "which," as the premier succinctly put it, "is nuts." The NDP's initial strategy to pump more cash into the economy had to quickly U-turn toward cutbacks, rollbacks, buyouts, and layoffs.

"If we had been in government longer or with a greater degree of experience, we might have taken things a little bit differently at the beginning – except that the numbers surprised the public service as well," Rae mused one afternoon in April 1993, in the premier's corner suite on the second floor at Queen's Park, looking south to the towers of Toronto's financial district. "The dimensions of the deficit didn't really emerge until into 1991. At that point, we said we'll run it up, but then we will start to bring it down."

Every premier, mayor, school board, and hospital administration across Canada stared into the same dark reality. The result, not just in Ontario but everywhere, was higher taxes and fewer services, and since the political and economic limits to increased taxation were soon reached, the fiercest battles were fought over the size of government and the cost of social programs. To New Democrats such as Bob Rae, who was trying to save $2 billion by negotiating a new "social contract" with his 900,000 public-sector employees in the spring of 1993, that created an agonizing conflict with the party's basic beliefs and core supporters. To Conservatives such as Brian Mulroney and Kim Campbell, however, the lack of money conveniently reinforced the right wing's bias toward less government as a good in itself.

Tory economic policy was really anti-policy, un-policy. The most vigorous action was the washing of hands. Instead of regulation, deregulation. Instead of public enterprise, privatization. Instead of federal-provincial partnerships and national standards, offloading and devolution. The best thing Ottawa could do for prosperity and growth, went the Conservatives' refrain, was to get the deficit down, get inflation under control, and get out of the way. And, sure, that meant that 10 per cent of the population was unemployed, but as the Tories' finance minister, Don Mazankowski, liked to remind the cabinet, it also meant that 90 per cent of Canadians were working!

The Free Trade Agreement emerged from that *laissez-faire* approach and led back into it. Originating as the enthusiasm of a few businessmen and bureaucrats, then gathering support among corporate lobbyists and party thinkers, it seized Brian Mulroney's imagination while his first government muddled through scandal and controversy. Continental free trade offered him a grand initiative of historic significance that would, at the same time, permanently weaken the authority of the federal government, suit his desire to make Canada the lapdog of American foreign policy, and earn him the eternal gratitude of his rich friends in Montreal and New York.

What appeared like courageous, even visionary leadership was in essence an abdication of national power to international pressures, market forces, and regional interests. Mulroney's first line of defence, in fact, was that Canada had no choice. Continentalism was as inevitable as gravity. After a century of tariffs and subsidies, Canadian industry had outgrown the small domestic market. The biggest conglomerates dominated the economy, which raised concern about the concentration of wealth and the lack of competitiveness, and even small businesses were realizing that they would have to export their products if they wanted to remain productive and solvent. Despite the Liberals' efforts to develop other markets around the globe, 75 per cent of Canada's exports went to the United States by 1984, and most of that trade was already without tariffs.

"I eventually came to the conclusion," Trudeau reflected, "that Canadian businesspeople have it so easy with the United States –

where they already know the customers, the techniques, the language, and the geography – that they are a little lazier and less inclined towards initiatives in Asia or Africa or other parts of the world, even Europe."

As the forces of American protectionism gathered strength during the recession of the early 1980s, Canadian companies began to panic about the effect on their remaining sales and profits. In 1983 Gerald Regan, the minister of international trade in Trudeau's last government, opened discussions on sectoral free trade, similar to the lucrative automotive pact the Liberals had negotiated twenty years earlier. In 1984 the Royal Commission on the Economic Union and Development Prospects for Canada, under the chairmanship of Donald Macdonald, Trudeau's former minister of finance, urged a "leap of faith" into a comprehensive bilateral agreement in order to assure access to the American market, secure jobs, and force a long-neglected modernization of Canadian industry.

Within a remarkably short time much of the political class became persuaded by the idea. The American multinationals, the Business Council for National Issues (BCNI), provincial premiers in Quebec and the West, and senior bureaucrats in Finance and Trade were early advocates. Soon they were joined by traditional protectionists such as the Canadian Manufacturers' Association and the Canadian Federation of Independent Business, by fresh converts in the Privy Council Office (PCO) and External Affairs, and by a growing bandwagon of economists, editorialists, and opinion makers. What had been politically unspeakable in 1984 became the cant of 1988: a common-market deal with the United States was the only route to continued prosperity.

Even among the opposition, the quarrel was not with free trade in general, but with specific concessions in the Tories' deal or the dangers of getting entangled with the United States in a bilateral trading bloc. What looked like a titanic clash of elites – Conservatives versus Liberals and New Democrats, Ontario versus Quebec and the West, business versus labour and the nationalists – disguised the developing consensus within the political class. Despite John Turner's vigorous defence of Canadian sovereignty, he articulated no credible alternative to the Free Trade Agreement, except perhaps to suggest that the same goals might be achieved through the multilateral GATT negotiations. The Liberal premier of Ontario at the time, David Peterson, demonstrated his own ambivalence by absenting himself from much of the national debate.

But there was no such consensus among the people. Canadians had been sharply divided about the benefits of free trade with the Americans even before Canada formally existed. John A. Macdonald had won one election by opposing it in 1891. Wilfrid Laurier had lost another by proposing it in 1911. Mackenzie King had consequently backed away from it in 1947. Brian Mulroney himself had warned against it in 1983. "It affects Canadian sovereignty," he declared during his bid to replace Joe Clark, "and we'll have none of it, not during leadership campaigns, nor at any other times." Haunted by his own rhetoric, Mulroney had hoped to tie up the deal before the election. When he couldn't, he had no choice but to put its fate – and his – in the hands of the voters.

In the normal course of events, the desire of most Canadians to preserve a national community based upon an east-west economy and a distinctive culture would have been enough to defeat the Free Trade Agreement in 1988 – and it was defeated in the sense that the Liberals and New Democrats together won a majority of votes. The Tories won the majority of seats, however, by garnering almost all of Quebec and the West and by splitting the opposition two ways. They benefited, too, from the $5 million the Canadian Alliance for Trade and Job Opportunities spent to promote the FTA and from the plain fact that almost no one – most Liberals included – really wanted to see John Turner as prime minister.

The moment the FTA was in place, it was too late to unravel it. The business community began an immediate restructuring of its Canadian operations, including shutdowns and layoffs. The political parties began a thorough overhaul of their economic policies. Even the most passionate nationalists seemed to have been crushed into hopeless resignation by their defeat. "A lot of jobs have disappeared in Canada because of the Free Trade Agreement," said Turner's successor, Jean Chrétien, while leader of the Opposition. "Scrapping it will not necessarily bring them back. You cannot go back to square one five years later. You can never gain back your virginity."

Among the people, however, as factories closed and investments moved south, as unemployment rose and adjustment programs failed to materialize, opposition to the FTA only grew broader and deeper. It joined the common litany of complaint that parliamentary democracy no longer worked in Canada. Not only had the agreement passed without the approval of a popular majority, it effectively prevented all future governments from reversing it. And given the hundreds of thousands of jobs that it soon rationalized out of existence, it again raised the disturbing question: In whose interest is the political class governing?

"Its own," many Canadians answered. Or, an even more common response: "Big business."

And Deeper in Debt

There was little new in the political influence of business. Canada was essentially a private-enterprise polity with a free-market economy, after all. Even its interventionist tradition, from the Lachine Canal to the St. Lawrence Seaway, from the National Policy to the National Energy Program, from the Canadian Pacific Railway to Petro-Canada, had often taken the form of public assistance to the private sector. What was new, however, was business's increasing inability to guarantee well-paying jobs for life and its growing reluctance to contribute to the assistance of the poor, the young, the old, the sick, and the unemployed.

Business CEOs did not state it quite that way, of course. Their general target was public spending. Though the Tories had managed to reduce Ottawa's operating expenses below its revenues, the federal debt climbed above $500 billion in 1993, equal to 60 per cent of Canada's Gross Domestic Product (GDP), and the compound interest alone was producing huge annual deficits. The result was higher interest rates, higher taxes, higher amounts of foreign borrowing, and fewer jobs. According to the BCNI and other corporate lobbyists, Ottawa had no option but to slash dramatically into pensions, welfare payments, unemployment insurance, health care, and all the other entitlements – including business subsidies – that accounted directly or indirectly for more than half of the federal program expenses.

Yet those programs had become identified with Canada itself – its political fairness, its social peace, its moral superiority over the United States. Not only were they considered politically untouchable by the middle class, but they represented the difference between well-being and hardship for poorer Canadians. Business leaders, it seemed, were no longer content with their high incomes and their disproportionate share of the national wealth. Now, while demanding fewer taxes and regulations for themselves, they wanted the lower- and middle-income earners to forfeit even more − or else, they threatened, they would move their jobs and capital to Tennessee, Mexico, or South Korea.

That wasn't an idle threat. In the age of global corporations, international finance, and technological communication, money could speed around the world in search of the cheapest labour force or the highest investment yield. As all governments got deeper in debt to their domestic and overseas bondholders, they had less liberty to set their own political and social agendas. In the United States and Europe, in Latin America and Asia, amid the ruins of the Soviet Union and the chaos of Africa, power was shifting from the state apparatus to the private sector as a result. And Canada was hardly exempt. The Free Trade Agreement was but one manifestation of that shift in *realpolitik*.

Since Brian Mulroney was obviously a kindred spirit − if not a hired hand − of the business interests, their true clout could be better seen in the pressures at work on Bob Rae in Ontario. He rapidly discovered how little control his provincial government had over most of the major decisions affecting the lives of its citizens. Business ultimately determined where the new plants would be located and how many employees would be laid off. Investment dealers controlled most of Ontario's accelerating debt and assessed the credit level at which the province could borrow more. So when the business lobbies wanted Sunday shopping or gambling casinos, tax holidays or development grants, Rae was in a weak position to refuse.

"Fundamentally," he admitted, "it's the private sector that's going to create 80 or 85 per cent of the jobs in our economy. That's what living in this kind of society is all about, and I don't know anybody who wants to live in any other kind of society. Since that's true, the argument that we need governments to spend a whole lot more money to stimulate the economy − well, maybe there're some limits to that."

But, for all the free market's logic and power, most Canadians remained highly suspicious. Companies that had built on tax dollars and government protection did not hesitate to transfer work and research to the southern United States. The celebrity tycoons and yuppie stockbrokers who flaunted their sudden wealth demonstrated little understanding of the old social and moral responsibilities of money. Corporate taxes came down, trade barriers came down, regulatory hurdles came down — but executive salaries and mass layoffs went up. Indeed, by denigrating community values and altruistic ideals in the pursuit of individual gain and personal gratification, many CEOs undermined all their appeals to collective austerity and selfless sacrifice, just as Brian Mulroney had with his expensive tastes and greedy friends.

"Although it is customary in democracies to blame all our problems on governments, I do not believe that business should be let off too lightly," confessed Hal Jackman, a member of the Toronto elite and a prominent Tory whom Mulroney appointed lieutenant-governor of Ontario. "Free-market or classical economic theory was misinterpreted in order to justify the pursuit of selfish and shortsighted aims at the expense of long-term growth and industrial stability. Although we may rightfully criticize the growth in public-sector debt, private corporate debt grew equally apace. The tragedy, of course, is that too little of this increased debt resulted in any net increase in productive investment. Where are the new factories? The new jobs or the new industries in this country? The vision that motivated business leaders in the 1950s seems to have been lost. Instead, needed resources were used for takeovers, leveraged and management buyouts, the building of corporate empires at the expense of the tax system — empires which seem to have no social or economic purpose."

The political class, convinced by business or merely at its mercy, was deeply implicated. With no comprehensive alternatives, it had to carry the corporate agenda to a skeptical public. It was not a happy or even hopeful agenda. Ahead loomed more cutbacks and more layoffs. Old-age pensions and free access to health care could no longer be taken for granted. RRSPs and unemployment insurance were under scrutiny. The next generation of Canadians could not be assured the standard of living of their parents or grandparents. Even the business establishment was not sure whether globalization and technology would create enough jobs in Canada to return the unemployment rate to the old norms. Nor was it certain whether the Canadian economy would fully recover from the quadruple whammy of free trade, the world recession, the GST, and the Bank of Canada's Draconian fight against inflation by means of high interest rates and a high dollar.

Kim Campbell admitted as much at the start of her leadership campaign. Whenever she pressed the Finance Department for demographic trends or structural changes that might bring some relief to the debt and deficit, the only conclusion she drew was that "the light at the end of the tunnel is always an oncoming train."

The government to which she belonged, meanwhile, hardly had enough energy to even try to get out of its way. After creating a kind of media hysteria about the debt, the Tories produced a budget with a 1992-93 deficit of $35.5 billion ($8 billion above the previous budget's forecast) and a projected deficit for 1993-94 of $32.6 billion (which turned out to be a record $42 billion). Its marginal cuts had more to do with creative bookkeeping than reduced spending; there were no new taxes; there still seemed to be plenty of loose cash with which to play politics or accommodate the boys; and the entire responsibility for social-program reforms was left to Mulroney's successor. Not wanting to jeopardize their chances for re-election, they merely placed their trust in the private sector and hoped for a return to economic growth of more than 4 per cent a year.

Campbell herself could not offer anything more substantial or innovative. Her understanding of macroeconomics was slight, she had never held an economic portfolio, and her much-vaunted experience in small business had consisted of being a minor shareholder in a Vancouver restaurant. Confused and unimpressed by all the contradictory advice emanating from the mob who claimed her attention, trusting in her quick mind and motor mouth, she flew woefully unprepared into the first all-candidates' policy forums in Toronto and Montreal. The result was a bunch of sophomoric answers and a case of bad nerves. She was, as the *Globe and Mail* stated, "the heir apparent without apparent views."

Stung by such criticism, she commissioned a series of policy proposals on everything from a national debt management plan to environmental technologies. Even those, however, proved short on detail and imagination. Essentially Campbell thought that the Mulroney government had been on the right course – if only the people could be educated to see that! – and except perhaps for a little dabbling in research and development or the better administration of the GST, she wasn't going to win many Conservative delegates by quarrelling with her prime minister. "I have no desire to distance myself from policies or priorities that I have had a role in creating," she declared, "whether they are unpopular or not."

Inwardly, too, she did not believe that the role of a party leader is to be "a policy encyclopedia" on every issue. Once, when pressed to produce a grocery list of how she would cut the deficit, she replied, "I'm not running for minister of finance, I'm running to be the leader." That meant articulating a vision of Canada and inspiring

Canadians to achieve it, which in turn meant changing the process of government so that people would understand the reality, lower their expectations, and accept the big changes ahead.

"The process *was* the substance," explained Senator Lowell Murray, her friend and adviser, a shy and rather formal man with whom she shared a wicked sense of humour, a love of British institutions, a taste for Canadian culture, and a strange blend of pleasantness and arrogance. "The journalists kept looking for something more, but there was nothing more. There was nothing radical about what she was proposing. It was, in fact, quite conservative. She wanted to get the system to work as it was intended to work." In short, to redeem the political class all by herself.

Inside Out

Kim Campbell looked at the Progressive Conservative party left by Brian Mulroney and asked, "Why were we so low in the polls? What had gone wrong in a party where we felt that we had been taking courageous decisions and facing evident realities? As someone who had gotten results in very difficult areas, I felt that bravado wasn't enough. We had to understand people, and how to bring them together, and how to listen, and how to create the constituency to make change."

Time and again she cited "changing the way we do politics" as the very reason she wanted to be prime minister. For, unless she could undo Mulroney's legacy of public alienation and cynicism, nothing else could be achieved. Even the deficit was more a political problem than an economic one, because the *what* of politics had become totally dependent upon the *how*. Campbell called it the "politics of inclusion." In essence that meant broadening the range of consultation far beyond the caucus, the bureaucrats, and the special-interest groups. The political class had to reach out to uncommitted citizens and bring them into the decision-making process, not least through the communications channels and policy conferences of the party system. Against a politics of "insiders, privilege, and influence," Campbell imagined a politics of accountability, fair access to power, and responsive institutions. Against a politics of "confrontation, threat, entrenched self-interest," she evoked a politics of reason, mutual understanding, and sincere attempts to pursue the common good.

"The politics of inclusion is more than a slogan," a poster in her campaign offices declared. "It's a way of life."

At a noon rally in Ottawa on April 19, Campbell issued the most extensive policy paper of her leadership campaign to try to explain what that meant. Among its twenty-five proposals were an annual party policy conference, ongoing party policy commissions, a permanent party think tank, more free votes and private members' bills in the House of Commons, prebudget hearings, an ombudsman, citizens' initiatives, and new regulations about lobbying. And, deferring to the spirit of the whole enterprise, she stressed that these were only her views and suggestions.

"I want to know what YOU think," she told party members and the Canadian people. "The quickest and easiest way to convey your views to me, *personally*, is by calling my hotline at 1-900-5615-KIM." (Fifty cents for the first minute, thirty-five cents for each additional minute.)

Precisely twenty-five years earlier, another fresh face had stormed on to the public stage with much the same message. Pierre Trudeau called his version "participatory democracy," and it was as important an issue for him as national unity and social justice. He had dedicated his formidable intellect and prolonged education to the study of democratic principles, after all, and the liberal precepts of his book learning had been reinforced by the very real struggles in Quebec during the 1950s against the corrupt and autocratic regime of Premier Maurice Duplessis. "'Democracy first!'" Trudeau declared in 1958, "should be the rallying cry of all reforming forces in the province."

Ten years later, during his first election campaign as prime minister, his principal message to Canadians was that "if they are to be governed well, they will have to participate in the governing; that there are no magic solutions; that there is no charismatic leader with a magic wand which will produce great solutions."

To that purpose he gave members of Parliament, including those in the opposition, the money and staff to improve their research and better connect with their constituents. He rationalized the procedures of the House of Commons, televised Question Period, and strengthened the parliamentary committees. He changed the electoral laws to decrease the influence of corporate donations and facilitate the involvement of more citizens. He allowed members of the Liberal party regular input into the formation of policy and significant power over the selection of their riding candidates. He funded "public-interest groups" in order to bolster their claims before the government and the courts. He revamped the cabinet decision-making process to shift authority from the bureaucratic cabals to the elected ministers. Above all, he entrenched the Charter of Rights and Freedoms in the Constitution in order to protect individuals and minorities from tyranny.

The charter was the most concrete expression of Trudeau's philosophy, because, in his words, "it sought to strengthen the country's unity by basing the sovereignty of the Canadian people on a set of values common to all, and in particular on the notion of equality among all Canadians." It made supreme the direct bond that exists between individual citizens and their national government – above any other allegiance to region, province, ethnic group, or association – and, by happenstance as much as by design, it gave Canadians a personal sense of ownership of their Constitution. When the premiers resisted elements of the charter, Trudeau prevailed by threatening to take his "people's package" to a general election or national referendum. Later, when the political class tried to tamper with it unilaterally, through the Meech Lake and Charlottetown accords, the people reclaimed it as *theirs*.

"If our cause was right," Trudeau reminded Liberals, "all we had to do to win was to talk over the heads of the premiers, over the heads of the multinationals, over the heads of the superpowers to the people of this land."

That was a repudiation, of course, of the cozy arrangement by which Canada's elites had traditionally divvied power and lucre among themselves. Despite his inherited wealth and superior mind, Trudeau had spent most of his life combatting the self-serving interests of provincial leaders, business executives, officious bureaucrats, church leaders, and media commentators. And despite his years as prime minister, he still considered himself a solitary interloper among the political class because of his iconoclastic ways and democratic ideals. There were certainly a lot of old-fashioned Liberals who felt uncomfortable with his unusual suggestion that the elites be bypassed rather than accommodated.

Trudeau's very activism was grounded in a democratic supposition: Governments have to govern. They cannot carelessly abnegate their responsibilities, either by decentralizing to the point where the system can no longer function or by capitulating to the demands of every loud bully. And because Canadian nationalism was not based on the supremacy of a single cultural or religious group, the Foreign Investment Review Agency and the National Energy Program did not contradict his deep abhorrence of ethnic nationalism, specifically Quebec nationalism. Instead, in Trudeau's view, they were merely useful tools for advancing the interests of the Canadian people against the competing interests of entrenched elites and other societies.

Similarly, his interventionism did not contradict his lifelong desire for personal freedom. Laws and regulations were necessary to ensure that as many individuals as possible could feel free and fulfilled in a just society. Whether they were fair laws and good regulations depended on the wisdom of the people's elected representatives and the participation of a well-informed citizenry. "We can't all be good cobblers," was how he explained it, using A. D. Lindsay's analogy, "but we can all tell if the shoe fits." And if centralization became necessary, Trudeau believed, it had to be structured so that as many players and ideas as possible could be brought to the table. He and his chief bureaucrat, Michael Pitfield, deliberately constructed a complex and coordinated process to make cabinet decision making collegial and diffuse.

In practice, decentralized decision making proved costly and time-consuming for both the party and the government, and it was often confused with either direct democracy or getting one's own way. When the cabinet overruled the arguments in the caucus for a guaranteed annual income, for example, or when the MPs ignored the opinions of their constituents on capital punishment, or when a Liberal convention defeated a riding's resolution to legalize marijuana, it was easy for the losers to become cynical and retreat into apathy or interest groups. Sometimes, of course, there was genuine cause for cynicism. The tendency of the political class – then as always – was to withhold influence from whatever grassroots mechanisms it did not ultimately control. People could air their views and pass judgement on the results, but they were not supposed to run away with the agenda of the party brass.

"Party members did not want or expect to be only a vehicle for electing the leader or members of Parliament who would then act without reference to their ideas or objectives," observed Liberal Senator Lorna Marsden, a warm and energetic sociology professor from the University of Toronto who served on the party's executive from 1973 to 1984. "They were frustrated and disappointed to find that influence did not run through the party, but through the principal secretary, senior officials, and ministers."

Perhaps, but most Canadians – including most members of the Liberal party – preferred leadership and goodies from the political class to Socratic dialogues and policy conventions. In a way, Trudeau's own charisma undermined both the need and the desire for the sort of democratic involvement he had always preached. "The voters wanted a leader to guide them, and I was giving them a professor," he later said of the 1972 election, which he came close to losing. "The members of my party wanted to jump into combat, and I was giving them a lecture. The electorate was eager for its regular dose of eloquence, attack, riposte, cheers, and rallies, and there I was giving them calm, lucid propositions in pedagogical terms. That is not how you win elections."

So he immediately invited such experienced professionals as Keith Davey and Jim Coutts back in from the cold. The prime minister and his PMO soon became almost presidential in style and command. Anonymous bureaucrats in the Privy Council Office were accused of manipulating policies and programs for their own goals. MPs were seen as ineffectual "nobodies" at the beck and call of grey eminences at Liberal headquarters. The broadcasting of Question Period had exposed the House of Commons as a rowdy and irrelevant circus of buffoons and hysterics. Even the charter seemed to have moved too much decision making into the hands of a few federally appointed judges and unelected interest groups. Meanwhile, the role of the Liberal faithful as bearers of the local news and disseminators of the party line was increasingly usurped by the prime minister's pollsters and advertisers. As a result, according to Senator Marsden, "the party gatherings were used more as an opportunity to deliver the message from the leader and the caucus and less as a method of sampling party opinion."

Invariably, as Trudeau himself had often warned, whatever the intention, whatever the safeguards, power corrupts. It bullies. It seeks to expand. It becomes smug and self-righteous. Most insidious of all, it isolates those who have it from those who do not. After almost sixteen consecutive years in office, Trudeau had little notion of the daily struggles of ordinary folks. They, in turn, seemed incapable of behaving in a natural manner whenever he walked into a room. The people and their leader circled each other at a safe distance, with a respect that carried a trace of hostility.

By the time of Trudeau's retirement in 1984, other forces had conspired to make Canadians feel even less powerful than they had in 1968. As wealth and authority continued to move upward, from small businesses to mammoth conglomerates, from local communities to international superpowers, fewer and fewer people were masters of their fate. Even their elected governments buckled under the impact of economic globalization. While the provinces and the business groups were condemning the centralist powermongering of Trudeau's policies in the early 1980s, those very policies were being undone by the tightening of the American money supply, the collapse of world oil prices, the rise of bank rates, the lowering of trade barriers, and the onset of recession. Ironically, a growing proportion of the cost of asserting Canada's national sovereignty was funded by borrowed money, which eventually did more to undermine that sovereignty than any machinations by Washington or Exxon.

"No elites! No rainmakers!" John Turner promised Liberals during his bid to succeed Trudeau, and everyone understood he was referring to Keith Davey. Less than three months later, having won the convention and called the election, Turner was begging Davey to help save the Liberals' disastrous campaign. And Brian Mulroney, after overcoming the Tory elites who had supported Joe Clark, also returned to the old cadre of strategists, pollsters, bureaucrats, advertisers, and organizers to help him win the 1984 and 1988 elections.

Mulroney's two terms were characterized by the further concentration of whatever power remained in Ottawa. Almost all the checks and balances that Trudeau had put in place to democratize the system were removed or rendered useless. Power moved up from MPs and parliamentary committees to political chiefs of staff and cabinet committee meetings; then up to "supercrats" in Finance and the PCO and a handful of ministers; then up to the PMO and the prime minister himself. "There emerged a term never before heard in Ottawa – 'the Centre,'" Arthur Kroeger had observed from his perch as a deputy minister. "Mulroney disliked structures, procedures, meetings, documents. He loved to operate out of his own office, making a hundred phone calls a day to stroke or cajole or threaten people. And the absence of system removed constraints. It left the prime minister and his agents free to move in on any subject they wanted."

In effect, the PMO and PCO placed most of the key ministries under a kind of receivership. The clerk of the Privy Council, following orders from the prime minister, would intervene in the details of industrial development grants or immigration levels. Finance got Stanley Hartt, an old friend of Mulroney's from Montreal, as its senior bureaucrat, and later the department was taken over by the deputy prime minister, Don Mazankowski, who also functioned as the "chief executive officer" for the operations that Mulroney chose to ignore. Almost everything to do with Quebec, from government contracts to patronage jobs, had to be approved by the Centre. Cabinet ministers, trying to check the abusive demands of bullyboy lobbyists, were themselves checked by someone's private deal with Mulroney or a hectoring call from the prime minister. Deputy ministers were over-ruled, as one former mandarin observed, by "inexperienced campaign workers, political buddies, cronies and friends appointed to influential positions where they were indeed able to push aside experienced pub-lic servants."

"The public's cynicism wasn't rooted in the belief that politicians are inherently corrupt or that the system simply cannot respond to the needs and largeness of the problems," Allan Gregg argued. "Instead, the public had come to believe that the key decision makers were so far removed from the real world that they had insufficient input to provide the proper output. They were so self-absorbed that they only made decisions by and for themselves, only talked to people like themselves, and only did things for people who were for them. And the fact that Mulroney pursued the elite agenda of free trade, deficit reduction, and constitutional reform just added credence to that."

Only when the Meech Lake Accord came a cropper, not least because the Canadian people had been excluded from the process, did Mulroney resign himself to extensive public hearings on constitu-tional reform. Even so, he ignored most of their findings and ham-mered out the final draft of the Charlottetown Accord with the ten premiers alone. Its defeat in the 1992 referendum, coupled with the growing impact of the Reform party's populist protest among western Tories, alerted the entire political class to the wide gulf that now stretched between the governors and the governed.

"The growing alienation of Canadians from their government has reached crisis proportions," declared a 1993 report of the Public Pol-icy Forum, a non-partisan association of prominent executives, bureaucrats, and academics dedicated to improving relations between the public and private sectors. "It threatens the health of our democ-racy and our future prosperity. How can we manage our nation's affairs or bring people together to face up to tough issues, when Cana-dians have so little confidence in national decision makers?"

Over Her Head

Like Pierre Trudeau's participatory democracy, Kim Campbell's politics of inclusion did not really mean power to the people. It meant fine-tuning the existing institutions to better reflect the wishes of the people. "In our political system," she said, "the party must be preeminently the forum where particular interests are reconciled and the national interest is defined."

She wasn't even happy about the use of a referendum to ratify the Charlottetown Accord, wondering whether it wasn't best left in the hands of the "civicly competent" and "responsible." She had reservations, too, about the idea of citizens being able to force a referendum. There were, she said, "legitimate concerns to be addressed about the predominance of majoritarian principles in a country where regional equity, the fair treatment of language and other minorities, the reconciliation of special interests into a national consensus, and the regulation of the political power of money are integral to our national philosophy." And, as an admirer of Edmund Burke's precept that an elected representative owes his first duty to "his unbiased opinion, his mature judgement, his enlightened conscience," she did not favour giving constituents the power to recall MPs who strayed too far from the opinions of the majority.

Despite her basic idealism and honesty, a cynic – and there were plenty of those around – might have suspected that Campbell's populist rhetoric was nothing more than the traditional stuff of leadership campaigns. Bashing the insiders is the most convenient way by which candidates can create a sense of newness, without actually disowning either the previous leader or the party's policies, and it plays to the fact that almost everyone has some sort of grievance against the Old Guard. In Campbell's case, certainly, she valued the support of most of the insiders, she paid close attention to the advice of her bureaucrats, she worked in constant consultation with special-interest groups, she depended heavily upon the expertise of lobbyists, and she had only marginal links to the lives of most Canadians.

Brian Mulroney had been teaching her the tricks of elite accommodation, after all. Though never as dazzled by wealth and luxury as her mentor, she made an effort to charm the Eatons and Bassetts in

Toronto. She picked up a softness for Quebec nationalism from her friend Marcel Masse, perhaps the most nationalistic of the Tories' Quebec ministers, who instructed her to blast "the arrogant, domineering, centralizing federalism of the Trudeau-Chrétien years" in a Montreal all-candidates' debate. She took pride in how fast she had learned to stroke the caucus and mobilize the vested interests for her legislative goals. Nor had her unexpected rapport with the Canadian people been the result of years of effort and a history of mutual regard. On the contrary, it had arisen mostly because she had all the virtues of a clean, white, blank piece of paper.

Often, in fact, Campbell left the impression that inclusion was less a matter of giving a more powerful microphone to the people than of giving a more effective megaphone to the politicians. Sheer ignorance, she suggested, had prevented the Canadian public from supporting the purchase of the military helicopters, as though there was not any substance to the opposition and nothing pigheaded or corrupt about the government's decision. If she could just give her Politics 101 lectures directly to the masses, without her opponents' partisan negativism or the media's deliberate mischief, then enlightenment would reign from sea to shining sea and discontent would melt like snow in the sun.

"We haven't communicated our priorities in terms that have been meaningful to the people affected by them" was usually the worst she had to say about the Mulroney record. "That's part of doing politics differently: from being what government *does* to people to an agenda where people understand the reason *why*."

But if Pierre Trudeau had not been able to bring reason to bear over passion, with all the power of his charisma and his rigorously developed code of democratic principles hardened in the fire of the anti-Duplessis movement, what hope had Kim Campbell with her apprenticeship at the feet of a technocrat like Bill Bennett? And if Brian Mulroney had not been able to usher in an era of national reconciliation, despite the magnetism of his sunny ways and his readiness to give away the store, what hope had Kim Campbell without any of his Tammany Hall talents? The conflicts between Ottawa and the provinces, between federalists and separatists, between the business lobbies and the social agencies, between the political class and the people, reflected deep divisions that were getting harder to bridge with limited trade-offs and little money.

Jeffrey Simpson, the *Globe*'s political columnist, expressed her dilemma well. "The politics of inclusion, to mean anything, requires compromise, listening, painstaking negotiations and consensus," he noted. "The politics of honesty requires decisiveness, farsightedness, boldness, courage and an exceptionally thick skin. The synthesis of the two is a fragile one."

In truth, Kim Campbell had to learn even more about politics than she did about policy. Call it shyness, call it arrogance, she retained a distance from most people that neither her smiles nor her embraces could close completely. Call it idealism, call it naivety, she was disturbed by crass partisanship or irresponsible demagoguery in public debate. She preferred to armwrestle people to her point of view with the force of her arguments rather than do deals with them, in Mulroney fashion, with pressure tactics and patronage appointments. She really believed in a government without secrets or hidden agendas, and she adamantly refused to push the "hot buttons" of language rights or government bashing to win delegate support. When her failed marriages and childlessness became character issues, her image makers had to pry her teeth apart with a crowbar for a single mention of Nathan Divinsky's three daughters, because Campbell did not want to demean her loving relationship with her stepchildren.

Unlike Flora MacDonald or Barbara McDougall, she was seldom at ease amid the backslapping haw-haw-haw of what remained a man's game. She hated gabbing on the phone, even with her best friends. She often leapt from insensitive curtness to tedious lecturing, blissfully unaware that people had taken her lack of graciousness or her instruction as an insult. When Joyce Milgaard confronted her as justice minister to reopen the case of her son David, who was eventually found innocent of a crime for which he had spent twenty-two years in jail, Campbell's instinct – unlike Mulroney's – was to opt for a legal technicality over a half-minute of human sympathy.

As her campaign faltered, these quirks of character were magnified into major concerns about her political judgement. She was held accountable for the amateur organizers who had been letting delegates slip away while most of the old-timers in her entourage jabbered on their duffs or fought each other for a place at her side. And since little distinguished Kim Campbell from Jean Charest in terms of policy, except with regard to Quebec nationalism, the media began probing for nuances that would expose her as either a right-wing ideologue or a nasty bit of goods.

Suddenly, on May 18, in the eighth week of her campaign, just when she was beginning to feel more confident about the process and the issues, Campbell woke up in a Halifax hotel room and turned on the radio news. What she heard made her blood run cold. Great Scott, she thought, what's going on here? And with the thought came a sinking feeling and a terrible sense of powerlessness.

Wild Turkey Shoot

If the mania around Kim Campbell conjured up the memory of Pierre Trudeau arriving as if by magic to rescue his tired old party from defeat, Canadians in general and Tories in particular were bound to be disappointed. "Couldn't we call it Campbellrationality," she herself had asked in March, "or Campbelldiscernment?" The first time she did anything less than perfect, she knew, everybody was going to jump on it.

Which was exactly what happened, on April 15, 1993, the night of the first all-candidates' forum at Bassett Hall in Toronto. Without the hype, she might have come as a pleasant surprise, a splash of bright fuchsia amid the four dark suits, earnest, sincere, reasonable, and more than able to hold her own in both official languages. The next day, however, the big news was that she had lost in energy, charm, wit, comfort, and substance to Jean Charest.

"Crazy over Jean," screamed a headline in the *Toronto Sun*, above a photograph of a merry Charest bestowing a kind of papal blessing with his two raised palms and another of a witchy Campbell looking as if she were about to strangle someone with her two sharp claws. "Very chilly. Haughty eyebrow raises. Real Margaret Thatcher qualities" was how the *Sun*'s reporter described Campbell.

"I never ever treated the campaign like it was won, until the numbers came in on the second ballot," she said afterwards. "But the media were treating me with the kind of scrutiny as if I was already prime minister. I couldn't understand what was happening. All of a sudden I was dealing with a press gallery that didn't know what I had done, with a presumption of bad faith, and it was really hard for me to deal with."

The entire press corps had an instinctive interest in bringing her down a few notches. The tighter the race, the more dramatic the contest, the better the story, the higher the ratings, the bigger the newsstand sales. There may also have been an element of guilt among the reporters and editorialists who had built her up so uncritically in the first place. And on the practical level, given that Campbell seemed the sure winner, everyone's time and money could be spent digging into her past and hunting for her ideology. Certainly no other candidate had to withstand the same amount of investigation.

"But what does she stand for?" the editors of the *Globe and Mail* cried in the wind. The next day, by way of contrast, they sang the praises of her "hard-working, thoughtful, transparently honest" opponent, Etobicoke MP Patrick Boyer, "a man with ideas on policy, who wants to be Prime Minister to put them into effect, rather than a man who first decides he wants to be Prime Minister, then collects some ideas he thinks will help get him there." High on his list of ideas, moreover, were parliamentary and electoral reforms designed to increase the public's influence over the political class. The *Globe* even suggested that the Conservative grassroots might surprise all the "smirking pragmatists" wise in the ways of the political world and "embrace the candidate who means to give power back to the people." (In the end, of course, Boyer came last with only fifty-three votes, and the *Globe* didn't support him either.)

"For people who rise each day as do editorial boards," Dalton Camp observed with a barely concealed smirk, "charged with the duty of advising entire nations and all their tribes on what is best for them, the very idea of Kim Campbell has been a humiliation to say the least; more sinister, there is the uncontrolled nature of present public opinion which has not, according to the polls, been seized of the need to know more about policy, either hers or that of anyone's morning paper."

In fact, after an initial flurry of demands for more substance and solutions from her, the press joined the party pros in dismissing the policy forums as dull and the policy papers as old hat. There was little print space or air time for issues and analysis. There was hardly the space or time to report the highlights, let alone the details, what with all the personality profiles and family gossip about Campbell herself. The *Toronto Star* scored an exclusive interview in which the candidate's mother vented forty years' worth of grievances against the candidate's father. ("I spent eight years working to put George through university," Lissa declared, "and he ended up a lawyer and I ended up with no skills to earn a decent living that would have enabled me to look after the girls.") *Maclean's* followed with the scoop that Kim Campbell and Nathan Divinsky had been living under the same roof at least three years before their marriage in 1972. The Montreal *Gazette* reported, apropros of Campbell's second marriage, that she was a self-confessed "sucker for highly intelligent men." And Peter C. Newman informed the readers of *Vancouver* magazine – and subsequently the nation – that the future prime minister had been conceived on top of a timber lookout near Port Alberni.

By June, the *Globe and Mail* itself was into the fun. In a dramatic front-page revelation, its regular sports columnist told a pathetic tale: little Kim, not yet two, gasping for breath, was rushed to the hospital and operated upon for septic laryngitis, then quarantined for two weeks. "When her parents came to collect her," the *Globe* solemnly stated, "she treated them as betrayers. Her mother smiled and reached to lift her from the bed. Avril flinched and turned away. Some in the Campbell family say it was never quite the same after that. They say Avril, who would change her name to Kim as an adolescent, never again felt as strong an affection for her parents."

The value in this kind of revelation went beyond the crassly commercial or the merely prurient – or so the media claimed. Since issues change and crises arise, people want a *personal* take on their leaders more than a batch of speeches and position papers. "When delegates or voters weigh the record of a candidate for office," Norman Webster argued in his Montreal *Gazette* column, "they consider a host of factors – schooling, travel, job experience, haircut, friends, enemies, eloquence, successes, failures, whether he or she has damp palms, and sometimes even policy. Mainly, what people are looking for in their politicians is character, judgement and an ability to understand their concerns, and a man's or woman's family life cannot be kept out of the equation."

"And, in this particular case," added John Honderich, the *Star*'s editor at the time, "because she basically adopted the government's policies as her own, the greater unknown was Kim Campbell herself. Who is she? Can we trust her? Is she a leader?"

That Kim Campbell had once tried marijuana or twice tried marriage might have revealed something, positive or negative, about her character. So might the social background of her parents and the political orientation of her husbands. But what public service was performed by hounding her mother and father into trading insults and recriminations about their marital troubles of thirty years before? None, of course, for that was more about the selling of advertisements, not the eludication of character. It was about politics as soap opera, not as intelligent discourse. And so, having already spooked many people of good mind and serious purpose who weren't prepared to make the follies of their youth the topic of national discussion, the media proceeded to scare away from public life the many more who didn't wish to subject their nearest and dearest to a ceaseless pounding on the door by every news outlet from Victoria to St. John's. (That did not prevent the same media, of course, from wringing its collective hands over the apparent decline in the quality of candidates running for office in the election a few months later.)

"Kim was saddened at the thought that her family had been dragged into something that related to her own career," George Campbell said. "Reporters would call me up and say that they *had* to ask me certain questions. But why did they *have* to ask me anything? My guiding principle was, if it's likely to cause Kim some personal upset, then I won't comment. But that came across like some sort of sin."

Even in the realm of policy, the media were ever ready to skip matters of substance for a slip of the tongue. The sport, as routinely played in the Commons and press scrums, consisted of hurling question after question – probing questions, hypothetical questions, insinuating questions, rude questions, contradictory questions – whose intent was less to elicit information than prompt a gaffe. The mere garnering of facts and arguments was considered a disappointment, akin to failure, and reporters who had been giving Campbell the third degree for having done something would switch without an ounce of shame to grilling her in the same indignant tone about why she *hadn't* done it.

"Earnestness is tolerated among the parliamentary press gallery," Robert Mason Lee observed in the Vancouver *Sun*, "but beliefs in any form are viewed with downright suspicion. Most desirable is a tired and detached wit, demonstrating that one is a knowing partner in an unsavoury game." As a result, he added, political journalism is "neither objective nor conspiratorial. It's a wild turkey shoot."

"It's a good game," Pierre Trudeau remarked from the other side. "They try to corner me, and I try to get out of the corner." Nor was he the only politician to delight in being evasive, whether through obfuscation, ambiguity, misrepresentation, state secrecy, or bald-faced fibbing. Mackenzie King's "Conscription if necessary, but not necessarily conscription" remains after fifty years a perfect model of its kind. But, from time to time, stupidity, inadvertence, fatigue, anger, confusion, or plain bad luck will cause the verbal equivalent – Gotcha! – of stepping on a land mine. Though there is no boom or flash, everyone feels the wave of destructive energy and receives a premonition of the devastating consequences. The television reporters have that night's clip. The newspaper reporters have tomorrow's headline. The opposition has this week's outrage.

Journalism has always been something of a turkey shoot, but never perhaps wilder than now. The rebelliousness of the 1960s, conditioned to a significant extent by the lunacy of the Vietnam War, called political authority into contempt as well as question. The Watergate scandals of the 1970s made investigative reporters appear morally superior to elected politicians and considerably more glamorous. The financial shenanigans of the 1980s reinforced the media's presumption that the only thing standing between every public figure and jail is a cover-up waiting to be uncovered. Nothing became more derided, consequently, than a soft question or the benefit of a doubt.

"I can remember, for example, going to Press Gallery dinners as a much younger man," Brian Mulroney told two *Maclean's* interviewers in a goodbye kick at the media. "We would have a good night, sing songs, chat with everybody, talk it up. Everybody gossiped a blue streak; it was a fun evening. Now, these same people will go across the street rather than shake hands with you because you're a politician and they don't want to compromise their journalistic integrity. And so they will operate out of sheer ignorance rather than know something about what's going on." The other side of the coin, of course, was that if the media had known what was *really* going on in the back rooms of the Prime Minister's Office, Mulroney would probably have been run out of Ottawa long before 1993. Certainly the Canadian people would have saved themselves a lot of headaches and heartburn if they had paid attention to his off-the-record gotcha, made during the 1984 election campaign, that "there's no whore like an old whore."

Television, too, has had a deleterious impact on public debate. Trading as it does in images and emotions, it is a notoriously poor vehicle for ideas and issues, and its commercials merely reinforce the fantasy that all problems have a quick and happy solution readily available to everyone who wants it. Its strength is in the direct exposure of personalities and the simple telling of stories, which is why its news reporters are on the constant hunt for confrontations and dramas. A vale of tears or a flash of anger, a tale of heroism or an account of villainy, it doesn't really matter so long as the entire thing can be illustrated visually and explained in a minute. And then it is gone, before anyone has time to get bored and zap the channel, lost in the onrush of newer pictures and dramas, leaving behind (if anything) the vaguest memory of a face or a disconnected piece of trivia.

Not only does the public – and the politically uncommitted, in particular – now get most of its information from television, but the written press has either sought to imitate its snappy, unnuanced style in order to attract the TV audience or has surrendered to it much of journalism's fact-gathering responsibility in order to provide analysis and opinion to the elites. As Keith Davey noted, "It is print which determines, as well as rank orders, society's agenda; but today it is principally television which determines how we will respond to the items on that agenda." More often than not, that means with brevity, sensation, and conflict.

"If politics is like show business," Neil Postman remarked in *Amusing Ourselves to Death*, his convincing critique of the effect of television on contemporary life, "then the idea is not to pursue excellence, clarity or honesty but to *appear* as if you are, which is another matter altogether." And if the political class has always known that perception is much more important than reality, it now understands that perception can be conveyed in thirty seconds while reality takes a little longer.

Pulp Fiction

Kim Campbell bragged about seldom watching TV, and she often exhibited a perverse pleasure in goading the media even when they had been particularly kind. When she launched her campaign in the fever of Campbellmania, for example, she unnecessarily berated the press for their ignorance about her service to the party and their criticisms of her performance as minister. Their current infatuation with her, she said dismissively, "was likely to be a short-lived relationship and I expected to be left at the altar."

Her campaign headquarters almost immediately picked up her hypersensitivity to criticism and "I don't need anyone" conceit. A couple of *Maclean's* reporters, preparing a major cover story about Campbell, were left dangling for weeks in their request for an interview, then offered a half-hour of her time if they flew to Vancouver for it. When the article appeared, Campbell publicly called attention to some minor errors, which had only slipped past the magazine's fact-checking process because her staff had not bothered to respond to a score of phone messages. To add insult to injury, on the night of Campbell's victory, when the same reporters asked a senior Tory strategist if they could get an exclusive with the new prime minister, his reply was, "What the fuck have you ever done for us?"

Every reporter, it seemed, nursed a personal grudge about the incompetence and rudeness of someone on Campbell's team – often Campbell herself. Being human, a good many reporters were on the alert for a chance to extract petty vengeance. It finally came their way on May 13, the night of the fourth policy forum in Vancouver. For two hours the Tory candidates talked in laborious detail about free trade and small business, immigration and forestry, parliamentary reform and social welfare. By now their positions had become so pat that the journalists could recite the more familiar lines in unison. And then, in the final minutes, Kim Campbell described the opponents of Tory economics as "the enemies of Canadians." Not only was it similar to the phrase by which Brian Mulroney had branded everyone who opposed the Charlottetown Accord, it was the evidence the media had been seeking to expose Campbell as Mulroney in a wig and skirt. Though she instantly realized her error and tried to undo it, she knew she was too late. "The snapping of tendons could be heard from the old press room," she later remarked, "as they said, 'Aha! Okay, boys, now we have this.'"

Innocent *faux pas* or Freudian slip, it pushed everything else aside. Even the *Globe*, for all its editorial lamentations about the politics of style over substance, devoted a lengthy analysis to those four words alone. "In the space of a few moments," it concluded, "the Conservative front-runner may have jeopardized her efforts to portray herself as a different leader." (It could have concluded just as accurately that, in the space of a few paragraphs, the *Globe and Mail* may have jeopardized its efforts to portray itself as a different newspaper.)

While the national media were in Vancouver busily deconstructing "the enemies of Canadians," they missed the biggest story of the campaign – even though it had been hand-delivered to their hotel rooms by Campbell's own organizers – in the guise of a long and complimentary profile of "Citizen Kim" by Peter C. Newman in *Vancouver* magazine. They had a good excuse to miss it, however: it was not a story yet, not for another five days, not until it had been twisted and distorted and spun into one by Jean Charest's spin doctor and a compliant reporter.

"Campbell slams critics for 'apathy,'" the *Toronto Star* declared as its headline story on May 18. "Kim Campbell says ordinary Canadians who don't belong to political parties have little right to criticize politicians." Furthermore, the *Star* reported, "She is infuriated by people who sit back and criticize while politicians like her are working hard for the country. 'Who do they think is working to keep this country intact so they can have the luxury of sitting back and being such condescending SOBs?' she tells interviewer Peter C. Newman. 'To hell with them.'"

According to the full text in *Vancouver* magazine, however, she had not slammed "critics" for apathy, nor had she referred to "ordinary Canadians who don't belong to political parties" or "people who sit back and criticize" as condescending SOBs. "The thing that infuriates me is apathy" was what Newman had reported her saying. "People who boast about how they've never been involved in a political party." Confusing the matter further, Newman himself had quoted her differently in a private newsletter the previous March. In that version she had railed quite specifically against "people who are arrogant or who talk almost with pride about how they've never involved themselves in a political party."

Then, even more irresponsibly, the *Star* had Campbell stating bluntly that "she became an Anglican 'as a way of warding off the evil demons of the papacy.'" It seemed like the nutty babble of an anti-Catholic bigot. In context, during the rambling three-hour Sunday brunch she and Newman had had at Victoria's Empress Hotel, it was a wry aside, dripping with irony, about why she had converted to the Anglican church during her year at a Roman Catholic convent school.

The story no doubt was a triumph for its reporter, Patrick Doyle, who was known to amuse himself during press conferences by focusing a politician between his thumb and forefinger and chanting under his breath, "I crush, crush, crush your head!" His editors, in their wisdom, put it on the front page. From there it was picked up, in even more truncated form, by the wire services and electronic media across Canada. It stirred the wrath of non-partisan activists and the Canadian Conference of Catholic Bishops. It provided the grist for radio talk shows, coffee shop arguments, and office humour. It made Kim Campbell start the day in her Halifax hotel room with a groan of horror and, by disrupting her methodical march to the Tory leadership, nearly altered the course of Canadian history.

Unfortunately, it was no triumph for Doyle's profession, still less for Canada's public life. To the degree that gotcha journalism is a corruption of democratic accountability, this story was a corruption of gotcha journalism. For want of being able to catch a mistake, it manufactured one. And Kim Campbell, whose public image had been largely contrived by a single photograph, saw it almost destroyed by the contrivance of a single paragraph.

"Reporting is all about doing précis, often of long, complicated material," said John Honderich in his newspaper's defence, "and our responsibility is to do that to the best of our ability, as fairly as possible. Her comment about the papacy, I would say on reflection, was the only one that was out of context, though the Canadian Conference of Catholic Bishops still had problems with it when we ran the full context on the op-ed page. But all the other comments were reflective of a certain tone she was expressing that gave Canadians a sense of unease about her, that she was disdainful of them and patronizing. Her theme was inclusiveness, yet a lot of her talk was exclusive."

At first Campbell tried to laugh the controversy away. Then she tried to defuse it with an apology, in which she maladroitly suggested that people were thick if they felt offended. Even when it was commonly understood that she had been the victim of a rather shoddy piece of work, the trouble did not go away. "Defiant Campbell won't alter her style," the *Star* declared in yet another major headline a week later. "I am not a loose cannon," the "unrepentant" candidate was quoted as saying. But the newspaper showed itself equally defiant and unrepentant, for it again twisted her original remark into an attack upon "Canadians who don't join political parties as apathetic 'SOBs.'"

For the rest of the campaign, in item after item, on television and in the press, "condescending SOBs" and "evil demons of the papacy" were repeated as examples of Campbell's snobbery or evidence of her naivety. Her "foot-in-the-mouth disease" became more of an issue than what she had to say about universal social programs or the North American Free Trade Agreement. "Ms. Campbell's outspokenness has increasingly been called reckless and her tone judged callous and elitist," the *Globe* reported, with an air of stern rebuke, in what must be a classic example of the pot calling the kettle black. As a result, many Canadians – including many Tory delegates – began to wonder whether, if she were another Trudeau, she wasn't more West Coast flake like Margaret than worldly iconoclast like Pierre.

Not only did this commotion distract from more important matters, it undermined the very sort of candour and irony the media and the people claimed to be seeking from their politicians. It also illustrated how deeply conservative the media are – as powerful players in the political class – for all their blustering about change. They often sounded as shocked as an old-fashioned Methodist minister about some of the details of Campbell's personal life – She's lived in sin! She's been divorced! She's tried pot! – when, in truth, she was a paragon of virtue compared to many journalists. As Susan Riley observed in the *Ottawa Citizen*, "The political culture – and it includes the media – doesn't like spontaneity. Its genius is taking someone as bright as Kim Campbell, as sincere as Audrey McLaughlin, as earthy as John Crosbie, as ordinary as Jean Charest and making them sound the same: false and predictable."

Despite her ordeal, Campbell kept insisting throughout the campaign that Canadians want "honest talk" from their politicians. "You're either going to blandify yourself so nothing you say will ever be taken out of context, or you insist that people be mature enough to take you as you really are." The political class knew, however, what she had yet to grasp: Even if you do not trip yourself, even if you hedge every statement and weigh every word, there will always be someone at the back of the room vowing to crush, crush, crush your head. If you want to win, you have to play the game. And, in the rule book of politics, the front-runner should always play safe.

"Are you going to play the 'getcha, gotcha' game," Campbell again demanded of the media in exasperation, "or are you going to allow a politician to be a person?" The media answered by citing her very question as further evidence of her belligerent nature.

Gotcha!

Conventional Wisdom

To those who were resisting the notion of a woman as prime minister, Kim Campbell's candour proved she was unstable. To those who believed that she was a neo-conservative elitist, it proved she was mean-spirited. To those who feared for the future of the party or their influence, it proved she was a loose cannon. Unstable, mean-spirited, a loose cannon – each became a code for those in the political class to whom Kim Campbell was a threat.

Though the Conservative establishment had been pressed by the public-opinion polls to support her at the start of the race, it grew increasingly uneasy about her unpredictability and independence. Party insiders did not know the host of women, British Columbians, and young people who showed up to work in her campaign headquarters. Senior consultants did not know who was making the final decisions in her name or putting the last word in her ear. Mulroney's good old boys did not know if they would get a place on her staff or in her cabinet. More alarming, she still seemed to think she did not need them. "For me," she insisted on May 23, three weeks before the leadership convention, "it's only worth doing if you can do it on your own terms."

What if she really did represent a shift of power away from Central Canada or toward a new generation? What if she actually did go after the special-interest groups and the friends-of-Brian lobbyists? Good God! What if she truly believed that the party, the media, and the public all had to adjust to her unconventional ways of doing politics, because they were based on her very identity as a woman?

Week by week the coronation of Kim Campbell became less and less certain, as delegates and reporters alike began to look at the alternatives. They found only one other candidate who had a real chance of beating her: Jean Charest, the minister of environment from Sherbrooke, Quebec. When he entered the leadership race, at Mulroney's urging, everyone assumed he was really running to position himself as Kim Campbell's Quebec lieutenant and probable successor. It simply was not the moment for another prime minister from Quebec or a mop-headed, thirty-four-year-old male.

Charest turned out to be a more pleasant discovery than Kim Campbell. He wooed delegates with his prodigious charm; he flattered reporters on a first-name basis; he gave the crowds tub-thumping speeches with remarkable ease and eloquence in both official languages. He radiated decency, sincerity, optimism, energy, competence, and an effervescent delight in old-style politics. He epitomized the traditional politician of the best sort, in fact, as though he were Brian Mulroney without the sleaze. Most people could not help but like him, and the polls soon reflected his popularity. By June there were even indications that Charest, not Campbell, was the Tories' best hope for winning the election.

For much of the political class, too, he represented a more familiar, more manageable continuity. As a son of Quebec, he would appeal to its tribal loyalties, yet he championed the national dream of a bilingual and united country. As a veteran of the Conservative party, he would remain loyal to its record, yet he personified a more honest and approachable style of leadership. His platform, while hardly revolutionary, was clear: "More jobs, less debt, better results."

His campaign, chaired by a soft-spoken but very hardened professional named Jodi White, whose decent, down-to-earth personality had survived more than a decade in the inner circles of the Conservative party, was a model of political organization. "Kim was never able to express what 'doing politics differently' meant, other than blunt talk," White said, "and the fact that some of her blunt talk was somewhat offensive to people created a dissonance with her message. Jean, on the other hand, had a magic that made people feel good about him and about themselves. He was young and thin on substance, but he created excitement. Hope was the key word, and he could have provided it."

Just before the convention, former prime minister Joe Clark, Fisheries Minister John Crosbie, a number of high-powered insiders such as Harry Near and Hugh Segal, and a host of influential newspapers – including the *Globe and Mail*, the *Toronto Star*, the Montreal *Gazette*, the *Ottawa Citizen*, and Quebec City's *Le Soleil* – declared themselves for Charest. Agriculture Minister Bill McKnight publicly compared Campbell's supporters to the suicidal followers of cult leader Jim Jones. Brian Mulroney himself was heard muttering privately that Charest would now make the better choice.

Behind the scenes, however, Kim Campbell had been taking steps to prevent the political class from abandoning her altogether. While outwardly trying to establish some distance between herself and the Mulroney regime – by symbols if not by substance – she had come to realize that she could not ignore the old ways of doing politics without risking defeat. The revelation occurred on April 29, the eve of the all-candidates' forum in Calgary, her last opportunity to prove herself in a public debate before the closing of the delegate-selection meetings. All at once the full implications of her decision to run for the leadership sank in, as did her personal obligation to those working day and night for her victory.

"At the beginning," she said, "it was almost unreal and so much seemed to be generated externally. I even heard that it would be 'an abdication of responsibility' if I didn't run. But in Calgary I felt I could do the job, and I wanted to do it, and I allowed a set of inhibitions to fall away."

Casting aside her doubts and delusions, she resolved to do whatever was necessary not to fail. She demanded to be briefed as thoroughly as a prime minister would be. She vowed to remain resilient and good-humoured, however much her opponents tried to needle her into a hot counterblast. She steeled herself never to burst into tears. And, turning her back on the overcrowded bandwagon of amateurs and office seekers, she took her policy advice from a committee of three experienced ministers – Lowell Murray, Perrin Beatty, and Gilles Loiselle – and her political advice from veteran lobbyists such as Bill Neville, Nancy Jamieson, and Paul Curley, or back-room operators such as Patrick Kinsella, Ray Castelli, and Michael Ferrabee. She also began taking instruction from an image consultant, Barry McLoughlin, who rehearsed her in the arts of concise, unpedantic speech and premeditated spontaneity.

"I controlled the briefing process," McLoughlin told the *Globe*. "We simulated the debate and absorbed the feedback, telling her what sounded good, training her to a forty-five-second rhythm pace."

"She got rid of her handlers!" many of her grassroots supporters said of her crisper answers and peppier spirit in Calgary. "She's finally being herself!" In reality, she had been more herself in Toronto and Montreal: overconfident, overblown, and over her head. If she looked and sounded better, it was largely because she had let herself be programmed into becoming a better politician by the Old Guard and a better performer by Barry McLoughlin.

"I always get stronger through a campaign," Campbell protested later. "As I think things through and have experience speaking about them, I get tighter and tighter in my arguments. Barry helped me to get more and more focused and to think strategically of the best way to make my points. What am I trying to communicate? What is the telling argument? What metaphors, what imagery? I never changed anything about myself – the way I dress or the way I do my hair – but he helped me build on my strengths and minimize my weaknesses."

Perhaps, but one of McLoughlin's first suggestions was to throw out her politics of inclusion, which sounded fuzzy and empty. Her campaign certainly did not fulfil Campbell's hope that it would "show not just what I'd like to do, but how I'd like to do it." Far from inspiring masses of Canadians to participate in a new form of politics, it became mired almost immediately in the familiar customs of the political class. Some 2,800 delegates were selected by party members at meetings invariably manipulated by a few riding organizers. Another 800 or so got an automatic vote at the convention by virtue of their position in the party. More than two-thirds of them were men; almost all were white; a substantial majority had English as a first language and a university degree. As a group they averaged about $70,000 a year in income and between fifteen and twenty years in party politics.

"A leadership race is a back-room powerbrokers' game," Charest said afterwards. "The reason I was able to go as far as I did was because of all the potential candidates from Ontario who refused to run. That opened up a whole group of delegates who were less vulnerable to manipulation and could be persuaded, and we won most of them. We were also able to cause some surprises by breaking the stranglehold on Quebec. But, for those who wanted a coronation, to show up and fight in the ridings was literally bad manners! They were *offended* that we would question the fact that Campbell should win."

Elected or *ex officio*, most had made up their mind about which candidate to support before the policy forums were even over, and most only cared about the candidate's winnability. And despite Campbell's weaknesses and Charest's strengths during the course of the campaign, most were holding to their initial belief that the party would do better with a woman from B.C. than another Québécois, especially against the Reform party. As Dalton Camp argued on the eve of the convention: "There has been much talk about the need for national renewal and change. That is what the Tory leadership convention is supposed to be about – setting the country on a new course, changing the dynamics of power, and – to use a word emphasized by Kim Campbell – expanding on the politics of inclusiveness. One could go a fair piece towards those objectives by choosing the first woman prime minister in Canadian history and by making headroom for people from Canada elsewhere [than Quebec] in the vast business of power sharing and power wielding in government and governance."

With the possible exception of refusing to accept $75,000 for a breakfast meeting with a stockbroker because the offer smelled of influence-peddling, however, Campbell clung to the politics of business-as-usual as to a raft in a turbulent ocean. "We're going to wrap her in plastic until this thing's over," one strategist said during the final stretch of the campaign. Even Kim Campbell's smile started to look like a well-rehearsed device to make her seem friendlier. The person who promised more public access to caucus discussions and cabinet decision making refused to let the press into her meetings with delegates. The person who claimed to be "the least-scripted candidate you'll ever have seen" stuck to a trite convention speech that had been patched together by a committee from the polling results of what the majority of delegates wanted to hear.

Ultimately, on the sweltering Sunday evening of June 13, she squeaked to victory on the second ballot – with 1,817 votes to Charest's 1,630. She would not have won if the party establishment had not rallied behind her the moment Mulroney resigned and tied up almost half the delegates before Campbell's campaign suffered the bad press and bad polls. She would not have won if the bagmen had not helped her raise over $3 million for her campaign, more than twice what had been budgeted. She would not have won if Paul Curley's organizational wizardry, in which computers and trackers kept constant tabs on every delegate, had not prevented many defections during convention week. And she would not have won if her campaign manager, Ross Reid, had not struck a secret deal with John Laschinger, the very epitome of a back-room boy who struck the same sort of deal with Charest's people, to have Jim Edwards come over to Campbell's camp after the first ballot.

"People will try to tell you that you became prime minister because of them," Brian Mulroney told Campbell as a bit of farewell advice. "You became prime minister because of you. Follow your heart." But Mulroney, as a master political tactician, had better cause to believe that vanity than she did. Within days, Mulroney himself had to rescue Campbell when she almost lost Charest from her cabinet in the "civil war" (as one staffer called it) that erupted over her failure to soothe his wounded feelings with anything more empathetic than "Jean, you're a hell of a tortoise!"

With barely a moment for reflection or repose, the new leader was caught up in a vortex of pressures and demands by political and bureaucratic heavies who suspected her mind was up for grabs and were anxious to clutch it for themselves. "The guys with guns have moved in, the transition is under way," said one minister, riding in his limo through the deserted streets of Ottawa in the wee hours after the convention. "Tomorrow morning the entire apparatus of the state will start to mobilize behind her."

Queen for a Day

Having won the leadership, Kim Campbell again became determined to keep her own mind. "As prime minister," she said a few days after being sworn in, "I can start to do things in my own way, and I can do a lot. Without the problems of running a line ministry, I can stand back a bit. I'm looking at ways of reaching beyond the structure of government to bring other sources of expertise and advice into the policy-making process."

When designing what she called "the most significant downsizing and restructuring of government ever undertaken in Canada," she even secluded herself in her apartment for two days, and was amused to imagine how nervous the bureaucrats must have been by her mysterious fiddling with the number and names of their ministries. Apparently the only people not included in the politics of inclusion, some of the Old Guard were heard grumbling, were those with any experience.

Campbell was still under pressure, of course, to demonstrate that she was different from Brian Mulroney. She also wanted to give Canadians a real choice in the upcoming election. There were hopes of drawing up a list of fifteen "markers" that would define the Tory agenda. There were plans to deliver a series of substantial speeches. There was even talk of recalling Parliament during the summer in order to present a package of reforms that would become the Tories' call to arms. As it turned out, she was not able to go much farther than cutting the size of the cabinet from thirty-four to twenty-five and ordering her ministers to show up at the swearing-in ceremony in taxis rather than limousines.

On Canada Day she flew from the Atlantic coast at dawn to Parliament Hill at noon to the shores of the Pacific at sunset for an extended photo-op. Then she met with all but one of the provincial premiers to discuss the economy. Then she dashed off to Tokyo for a Group of Seven summit meeting, with a thick briefing book under her arm and a phalanx of senior bureaucrats at her back. Almost as soon as she returned, she was hijacked by the Mulroney advisers she had chosen to retain – including campaign co-chairs John Tory and Pierre Blais, Ontario chair Paul Curley, Quebec chair Pierre-Claude Nolin, party director Tom Trbovich, and party pollster Allan Gregg – who sent her back on the road to be "test-marketed" with Canadians.

"She felt frustrated and had to be talked into it," said Jodi White, the efficient Charest operative whom Campbell had lured into the PMO as her chief of staff. "She wanted time to develop policy, and she needed time to get hold of the fact that she was the leader, but there was no time."

The lack of time only exacerbated her government's greater problem, the lack of money. The enormity of the federal debt and deficits prevented the Tories from proposing all kinds of obvious ideas, from a national child-care system to the elimination of the GST, while intellectual consistency – and threatening phone calls from Brian Mulroney to John Tory – forbade them from disowning their own legacy. Not only had Campbell and the other leadership candidates tried to outdo each other in their vows to reduce the deficit, but pressure from the Reform party and the financial community ruled out any significant backsliding. Winning a Conservative convention was not the same as winning a national election, however, and wooing the right risked abandoning the centre. Talk of slashing the deficit scared half the nation to death and bored the other half to tears. If it meant eliminating waste and trimming someone else's program, well and good, but only 15 per cent of Canadians rated it their top priority.

"First and foremost," Gregg advised senior Tories in June, "there is a desire for government to address the question of diminished opportunity, that is, what new industry and jobs will be available for those who find themselves displaced or crowded out of economic prosperity? Secondly, the public wants more empathy from its leaders, both substantively in terms of a focus on social policy and stylistically in terms of empathy with real people and their problems."

But Kim Campbell's empathy had not emerged from the convention unscathed. Unlike Jean Charest, who had managed to seem folksy and accessible even when defending the Conservatives' policies, she had not been able to put a compassionate face on the grim economic statistics. From her years on the Vancouver School Board to her time in Mulroney's cabinet, she had habitually compromised to the right, and it had been no different during the leadership campaign. She raised the possibility of a user fee for health care. She trumpeted the support of former finance minister Michael Wilson, the godfather of the GST. She larded her keynote speech with hard-line rhetoric to attract the support of Jim Edwards and Garth Turner. Rather than treating the race as the first leg of a long-distance run, as some of her advisers had urged, she had not seemed concerned about what lay ahead so long as she was leading at the halfway mark.

Nor was her government able to exude much freshness and change. Though thirteen ministers – including Joe Clark, Don Mazankowski, Barbara McDougall, Michael Wilson, and John Crosbie – had opted to leave with Mulroney, Campbell felt obliged to weigh her cabinet toward the veterans and the loyalists, and so it suffered the double curse of looking second-string and yet all too familiar. It met only three times all summer, while the prime minister hopped from barbecue to baseball game and the ministers tried to get a grip on their rejigged departments. A draft Speech from the Throne, which Mulroney later exaggerated into a complete election platform that he had handed to Kim Campbell as a parting gift, turned out to be a cautious, empty-headed rehash.

"We had a lot of trouble getting stuff out of the system," Jodi White said. "Allan Gregg was telling the ministers that we had to have new policies, and I called in their staffs and said we needed ideas, announcements, concrete measures to show that there was a new government. But it was a weaker cabinet, and maybe these guys assumed that they didn't have a role in preparing a platform. We were pretty disappointed with what we were getting back."

Gregg was more than disappointed. He was stunned. "I arrived in Ottawa during the summer to find the policy cupboard absolutely, utterly bare," he recalled. "The cabinet and policy machinery were completely *unable* to come forward with any new ideas, and when new initiatives were put before them, they were completely *unwilling* to endorse them. There was virtual decision-making gridlock."

The problem, he realized, went deeper than an inability to square the political class's panic about the deficit with the public's demand for jobs, social programs, and good news. "The Tories had become the stewards of the status quo, the architects of a do-nothing strategy," he explained, "by virtue of believing that the only real problem was that the population hadn't come to appreciate what a wonderful job they had done. So there was never any impetus for any new policy initiatives, let alone any *mea culpa*. I had fights with people who said that we had to make a virtue out of *doing nothing!* Someone even suggested that our policy should be '*Not One Dollar More!*'"

How, then, given the continuity in personnel and policy, could the Conservatives position themselves for an election in just a few weeks?

One answer was to link the necessity of spending cuts to the desire for job creation: lower deficits produce lower interest rates, higher business confidence, greater investment, and therefore more work. But Gregg insisted that the linkage was too complicated for most voters to understand. Instead, he suggested in a secret memo, the Tories should try "to offer more left-of-centre or liberal reasons" for their right-wing policies and have the new leader "demonstrate a change in style as much as substance."

"There was a certain complacency," Lowell Murray admitted afterwards. "We didn't really wrestle with the possible contradictions in our approach or the possible problems that would arise in sustaining it over a period of time. We should have given a lot more thought than we did to coming up with an approach that was failsafe."

In the absence of such thought, dancing with ordinary Canadians became the literal as well as the figurative strategy. Just as Campbell had line danced at the stomp 'n' chomp in April, now she did the twist at the Art Gallery of Ontario and the fling at a Highland festival to establish herself as an empathetic kind of Tory. All through July and August, at considerable public expense, she tripped the light fantastic from coast to coast, on what one of her assistants called "a cream-puff royal tour," with much of the Ottawa press gallery in tow. (Between June 13 and August 16, according to the National Media Archive, she received 75 per cent of the total mentions of Canadian party leaders on the CBC's main newscasts and only 5 per cent less on CTV's.) Whenever she paused to deliver a serious speech, both she and the reporters seemed less concerned about the growing size of the debt than about the growing size of her bottom. And, lo and behold, when the music stopped at the end of the summer, her popularity had soared to 51 per cent, the highest recorded for any prime minister since Lester Pearson in 1963.

"This pattern would suggest foremostly that our campaign must be about leadership, the comparison of the two main leaders, and the appropriateness of the Campbell style of leadership for the 1990s," Allan Gregg wrote in a campaign memo on August 31. ("Indeed, while we must never be seen to be saying this outright, the campaign which seems to be to our greatest advantage right now is one which would emphasize style over substance.") Two months later, when the Campbell cabinet met for the last time, the words "style over substance" would be remembered with bitter guffaws.

"In the full context of the memo, that isn't as egregious as it sounds," Gregg explained in his own defence. "We knew that people *hated* the government record, yet we were winning! So you didn't have to be a genius to figure that they weren't making their evaluation, at that time, on substance or policy. That this was interpreted by some as a licence to be completely insubstantive over the course of the campaign is ridiculous. The new style of leadership was simply one of four points in the plan I presented to the cabinet."

Nevertheless, the party pros seemed to have convinced Kim Campbell to defer once again to the tricks of their trade. They even persuaded this lady who was "not for turning" to sacrifice her credibility for the sake of the latest polls by turning against her own oft-repeated position that Canada could not possibly do with less than fifty brand-new EH-101 military helicopters. On September 2, under pressure from her election team, she took what she called the "toughest decision" of her politicial life and announced that only forty-three would now be purchased. She had been readied – or so it appeared – to be sent into battle on behalf of the Progressive Conservative party and the political class of Canada.

"In my experience there are two kinds of campaigns," Lowell Murray said to Jodi White as they strolled on Parliament Hill one summer day shortly before the election. "There is the campaign in which everything goes right, regardless of what mistakes you make. And there is the campaign in which, no matter what you do, everything goes wrong. I wonder which kind this one will be."

CHAPTER TWO

Beauty and the Beast

Swing City

"I'VE NEVER been through an election quite like this one," said Dr. Bob Horner, the Conservative MP for Mississauga West, during a lunch at the end of week two of the campaign. Though he had already lost twenty-one pounds, he was squeezed tightly into a booth at Lime Rickey's, just a few steps from his campaign headquarters in an office-tower mall beneath the spanking-new core of Mississauga, Canada's ninth largest and fastest-growing city, immediately to the west of Toronto's Pearson Airport. "We used to get the undecideds down to 10 or 12 per cent. Now they may be as high as 40 per cent. And I get the feeling that they really are undecided. Some of them may go into the polling booth without knowing who they're going to vote for."

Horner seemed, at first sight, like Jackie Gleason's Poor Soul, pear shaped and slow moving, a kind-hearted softie with a rueful voice and wonderful smile. But the more he talked, the more he revealed the toughness of the RCMP officer he had once been and the shrewdness of the veterinarian who had parlayed his practice and real estate into a couple of million bucks. "People always think that you're in politics for the money," he cracked, "but if you tell them that what you earn in Ottawa doesn't pay your income tax, then they get mad at you!"

Even though he was the sixth Horner to have served in a Tory caucus – including his infamous cousin Jack, who had defected to the

Liberals – his two terms as an MP had only given him a junior and temporary membership in Canada's political class. Dr. Horner, indeed, had never given a speech before he was fifty. Then, in 1983, a friend suggested that he put his name forward for the Conservative nomination, on the basis of his being known and liked around town, and to his own great surprise he won it. A year later, after canvassing the whole riding and going off to candidate school, he received his first real lesson in party politics.

It came, out of the blue, with a summons from David Crombie, the Tory boss in Toronto at the time. Crombie came bearing a message: Brian Mulroney wanted Horner to step aside so that one of the new leader's pals could run instead. "Say you're ill," Crombie suggested. "Say anything." Upset and perplexed, Horner took a day to consider the idea before rejecting it as a betrayal of his supporters. But the next week he got another invitation to lunch, this time with a college buddy of Mulroney's and two other back-room guys. They had an offer. If Horner dropped out, the Tories would appoint him to the National Parole Board.

"I said I wasn't running for the National Parole Board," he recalled. "So things got hot and heavy, and they got a little ugly, and I told them to tell Mulroney that I'll be around after he's gone. I learned that I shouldn't have said that."

Despite a series of organizational blunders caused by his total inexperience, Horner was carried by the Tories' 1984 sweep into the House of Commons. ("They could have run a spotted dog and won," he admitted.) Shortly after his arrival in Ottawa, the new members were taken to meet the prime minister. When Horner went in, Mulroney said, "Every time I look at you, I think of your goddamn cousin Jack!" They did not speak to one another for two years. "I could have given a shit less," Horner said. "I mean, I could buy him and sell him and keep him for a pet."

Green though he was, Horner understood that crossing Brian Mulroney was not a wise career move. But he had few personal ambitions and very little patience with the "silly games" of politics. "I will never be a great orator," he confessed, "and I will never get used to getting up in the Commons before three people – two asleep and one reading a newspaper – and pretending in front of the TV cameras that I am making a great speech that means something to anybody. It doesn't mean snap. The only way you get things done is by fighting like hell for them in caucus and committee."

In 1989, after barely surviving the ups and downs of the free-trade election, Horner had to fight like hell with his party's Whip and the Prime Minister's Office to get the one thing he did want, chairmanship of the Justice committee. Though not a lawyer, he was deeply concerned about crime issues, both as an ex-Mountie and Justice committee veteran, and he was being pushed by his riding association to raise his public profile before the next election. Horner won that battle with the help of Don Mazankowski, the deputy prime minister, but he paid a price. At first he was not given any of the parliamentary trips overseas. Then he was sent on a freebie to Yugoslavia. "I arrived the day the tanks started rolling down the streets," he joked, "and I knew right then and there that I was in the Whip's bad books."

Horner described himself as a moderate, common-sense kind of Conservative, who tried to bring "at least *some* level of sanity" to the caucus, but he considered Mulroney more a Liberal than a Tory, beholden to no principle or program beyond power. In January 1993, in fact, he publicly called for the prime minister to resign for the sake of the party's survival. A month later, after Mulroney had done precisely that, Bob Horner became one of Kim Campbell's earliest supporters.

"I admired her intellect," he said. "She listened well, she took advice well, she held meeting after meeting to get a consensus in the caucus. And I always found her a warm person. When I started putting on weight, she became afraid for my health and gave me a diet book. I liked her."

Her election as leader spurred him to seek one more term, which would take him past the retirement age of sixty-five. It also dramatically increased his chances of winning. For Campbell's summer popularity had brought the Progressive Conservatives neck and neck with the Liberals at around 35 per cent in the national polls, and even though the Grits were riding more than ten points ahead in Toronto, the Tories had shot up in the past few months and were expected to hold many of their suburban ridings. They had to, in fact, if they wanted to form another government.

"This will really offend some people," Senator Keith Davey remarked one morning over breakfast at his regular window table in the Prince Arthur Room of Toronto's Park Plaza Hotel. He hunched forward in his dark striped suit and lowered his voice as though to reveal a secret. "Many of my friends will resist what I'm going to say – except in a quiet corner – but it's a fact of life: what happens in national elections, in English Canada at least, begins in Toronto and happens from Toronto."

Davey, the legendary Liberal strategist, had often been accused of Metrocentricity. His political vision spans from sea to sea, even his friends joked, from the Humber River to the Don. But, like the baseball junkie he was, the "Rainmaker" understood the significance of a few key stats. Metropolitan Toronto had 23 of the 295 federal ridings, to which party organizers usually added another dozen in the satellite communities that arch Metro from Oshawa to Oakville. Those 35 seats, representing four million people, exceeded a third of Ontario's seats and all the seats in either British Columbia or Atlantic Canada. The Yorks North, West, Centre, and South-Weston alone had as many members of Parliament as Prince Edward Island. And the numbers were only a hint of the game in play.

"In the Liberal party, certainly, in both the Pearson and Trudeau years, Toronto was absolutely key," Senator Davey went on. "Elections were won or lost here. Policies were brought forward here. Communications were centred here. Programs, ideas, and campaigns were structured here. And that is essentially true in this year's campaign as it's unfolding."

Though John Tory adamantly denied that the city was as key to the Tories' campaign, the thirty-nine-year-old co-chair of the Conservatives' national campaign committee was pondering the needs and hopes of the Canadian people from the thirty-second floor of the IBM Tower in downtown Toronto. The photographs in his office attested to his twenty years of involvement in federal and provincial politics with the party's Big Blue Machine – many of whose luminaries, such as Allan Gregg and Paul Curley, were in control of the Tories' national election team. (Even Patrick Kinsella and David Camp, two of Kim Campbell's closest advisers from British Columbia, had strong personal ties to the Ontario machine.)

However bitter a truth, Canada's political class is centred – psychologically as well as physically – in just three cities: Ottawa as the seat of government, Montreal as the economic and cultural metropolis of French Canada, and Toronto as the financial and information powerhouse of the entire country. Of the three, Toronto usually predominates during a federal election because so many voters live within its orbit, so many of its ridings swing from one party to another, and so many bagmen and ad agencies operate from there. "And because so much of the national media – CBC News, CTV News, *Maclean's*, *Saturday Night*, the *Financial Post*, and so forth – is concentrated in Toronto," John Tory had to admit, "Toronto has more of a chance to set the agenda and momentum of the election. Some Toronto issues may get more attention than they deserve."

Still, most Toronto issues are the national issues. Rarely is there a Metro equivalent to the fate of the Hibernia oil project in Newfoundland or the subsidization of grain farmers in Saskatchewan, and flagrant attempts to buy Toronto's votes with a harbourfront park or an opera house have even been known to backfire. So, too, have attempts to build a national platform on trendy Toronto ideas such as economic protectionism and cultural nationalism. Under Brian Mulroney, indeed, campaigning against Toronto was considered more effective than campaigning in Toronto, because he built his two majorities upon the solid support of Quebec and the Prairies.

Now, in 1993, with Mulroney's bases threatened by the Bloc Québécois and the Reform party, the Progressive Conservative party was again looking covetously at Ontario's 99 seats – more than a third of the seats in the House of Commons – which in 1988 had split 46 for the Tories, 43 for the Grits, and 10 for the New Democratic Party. "Its natural constituency has always been Ontario," Dalton Camp observed, "where, even in the worst of times, it could count on enough support to maintain the party as a presence in Parliament." (It is a trait, shared by almost all members of the political class, that they would rather talk about numbers – riding numbers, voting numbers, poll numbers, deficit numbers, export numbers – than about policies or philosophies.)

And doing well in Ontario meant doing well in the 35 ridings of greater Toronto, of which the Conservatives held 18, the Liberals 14, and the New Democrats 3. No more than 10 of them were considered safe for their incumbents. That left at least 25 seats up for grabs – including Mississauga West. Its constituents, as a part of Mississauga, had swung Liberal in 1968, Conservative in 1972, and Liberal in 1974. Then, as a part of Mississauga North, they had swung Conservative in 1979, Liberal in 1980, and Conservative in 1984. And though, as Mississauga West, they had re-elected Bob Horner in 1988 by 4,548 votes, they turned around and voted Liberal in the provincial election of 1990.

To the Canadian political class, therefore, Mississauga West was more than an "instant city" of office buildings, subdivisions, highrises, industrial parks, and shopping malls, intersected by three major expressways, interrupted by the vestiges of nineteenth-century towns such as Streetsville and Cooksville, and surrounded by dairy farms and apple orchards. It was the homeland of those mysterious and some-what unpredictable folk known as Ordinary Canadians (suburban variety) and one of the most important battlefields on which a vast dominion would be gained or lost. Whichever party won Mississauga West in 1993 would likely win Canada.

The First Casualty of War

Bob Horner was one of 2,155 candidates representing fourteen parties in 295 ridings, all vying for the approval of eighteen and a half million Canadian voters on October 25, 1993. In theory a national election is a coincidence of local elections, with the majority of winners getting collective control of the government of Canada for several years. In practice party discipline, mass communications, and computer tech-nology have unified all the constituency contests into a single, cen-trally coordinated battle with a few regional variations. National strategists give detailed instructions to the candidates about where to erect signs, when to knock on doors, how to dress for canvassing, and what to say each day. The voters, meanwhile, focus almost all their attention on the party leaders criss-crossing the country on the TV news. In effect, though the success of the national campaign still depends on the results of the local campaigns, the results of the local campaigns largely depend on the success of the national campaign.

Bob Horner understood that his hopes had not rebounded in recent weeks because the good citizens of Mississauga West had sud-denly decided he was a truly admirable MP after all. He was benefiting from the plain fact that Kim Campbell had surpassed Jean Chrétien in popularity and respect in the opinion polls. Simply on the basis of being a woman and attending a bunch of picnics, it seemed, she had come to be perceived as superior in economic competence, leadership ability, and fresh ideas. But if the national trend had boosted Horner's campaign, he feared it could pull him down as easily as it had lifted him up.

The election was not two weeks old before Bob Horner began to worry. Not about Campbell – except that he thought she talked too fast for hearing-impaired seniors to follow – but about her chief orga-nizers. "There's got to be someone who can get her message across better than they've been doing so far," he grumbled. And he was not the only Tory grumbling. Lowell Murray himself had already turned to Jodi White in the middle of a back-room meeting and whispered, "I guess we're finding out which kind of campaign this is." Almost nothing was going right.

Out on the hustings, too, Jean Charest was coming across scores of Conservatives who were as bothered and bewildered as Bob Horner. "Our campaign was based at the outset on the issue of leadership, but it didn't say leadership for *what*, and that's where the public's mind was," he explained afterwards. "In 1988 our candidates could have summed up why they were running in two words – free trade. In 1993 I'd get off trains, planes, and automobiles and, sometimes several times a day, they would pull me aside and ask, 'What's the issue? What are we campaigning on?'"

No one at national headquarters seemed to know either. Just four days before the election call a senior government adviser, trying to throw together a last-minute policy brief to the cabinet from the dearth of material available, had asked John Tory those same questions and been rudely told to go phone Allan Gregg. Gregg was playing golf or at the movies all weekend, and did not answer the stack of urgent messages until late Sunday. ("Where's Waldo?" became a standard joke around the campaign offices.) The next day he breezed into Ottawa and, during a tense meeting in the Langevin Block with John Tory and other key strategists, was startled to discover that the working draft of Kim Campbell's opening statement made almost no mention of jobs. "There was a pretty severe strategic problem as to the understanding of what was important," Jodi White remembered. "It was frightening."

More frightening was that Campbell herself seemed blissfully unaware of the problem. She had rekindled the passion she had had on the Vancouver School Board for reducing government spending, and she was eager to lecture the voters on why they should share it. She felt, indeed, that the people were "miles out ahead of the traditional political punditry" on this issue and would respond with gratitude to her blunt talk. "I could say how many jobs I'd like to create," she announced at the very beginning of the campaign, "but I'm sorry – that's old politics."

She was off again, for the most part, dancing to the sound of her own voice. She rarely consulted with her cabinet, including Jean Charest, now her deputy prime minister. She seldom touched base with the network of party warhorses. She was not even in regular communication with John Tory. On the contrary, she was often shielded from her strategic advisers by a small retinue of travelling companions, Pat Kinsella in particular, who proved reluctant to transmit the danger signals and briefing notes coming out of Ottawa, Toronto, and Montreal. "At my first lunch with her," Jodi White recalled, "I was told that she felt hurt by some of the things we had done in the Charest camp during the leadership fight, and you pay a price when you bring in someone who doesn't fit your right hand like a glove. She had a big job, she was moving fast, and she needed someone who could hit the ground running with her. But we never got a chance to know each other very well. She was on the road, and she wasn't a telephone person."

That was in sharp contrast to the experience most of the Tory professionals had had with Brian Mulroney. "The problem with Mulroney was to get him *off* the phone," said Lowell Murray. "He'd come from the campaign trail as though back from the wars, and he'd summon us over to 24 Sussex to tell us the feel he was getting on the front. He was incredibly disciplined during an election. He understood why we were on a certain theme, why he had to stick with it, and what he had to say. But we didn't go through that exercise with Kim."

The consequence became apparent as soon as she strode out of Rideau Hall on September 8 to announce the election. Though some final revisions had been made to her statement at Gregg's insistence to beef up the message of hope, Campbell destroyed their intent during the press scrum that followed. "Realistically," she ad-libbed to a question about Canada's job prospects, "all the developed industrialized countries are expecting what I would consider to be an unacceptable high level of unemployment for the next two or three or four years. I would like to see, certainly by the turn of the century, a country where unemployment is way down."

To which the opposition and the media, focusing exclusively on the politics rather than the economics of what she had said, chanted in unison, "No jobs, no hope, till the year 2000!"

She had not intended to sound quite so callous, of course, but her matter-of-fact tone had the effect of relegating the desperate circumstances of Canada's unemployed to an OECD statistical curve. It also suggested that Kim Campbell was indeed an uncaring egghead whose definition of hardship had been her failure to become a concert cellist. Government experience and intellectual exhaustion had combined to produce nothing more original than staying the tough course and waiting for the invisible hand of the market to restore prosperity.

"Whoa! That was hardly on strategy," Gregg said. "Thematically we had to exploit what we were going to do to reverse the sense of diminished opportunity, and here she was telling people that they had to reduce their expectations. Perhaps we could have made a virtue out of her telling the truth, but it was deemed such a gaffe that we compounded it by cutting and running." Or, as the old master Keith Davey once put it, "The sad fact is that people vote for those who tell them what they want to hear. Voters reject short-term pain. It may be responsible to talk about the bad news, but it is not good politics."

Even in Mississauga West, a prosperous middle-class riding whose unemployment rate of less than 5 per cent was among the lowest in the country, jobs topped every survey of what concerned most people, not least because 41 per cent of all Canadians feared losing them. And, far from feeling like a magnanimous benefactor whom history and geography had made the wealth-producing centre of Canada, Ontario was feeling like every other have-not region with a long list of grievances and demands. Its unemployment rate had trebled to 10.8 per cent since the 1988 national election, and more than half of all the jobs lost in Canada since 1990 had been lost in the province. More ominously, beneath the cyclical problems lurked the structural problems that had been exacerbated by free trade, globalization, taxation, the breakdown of the east-west economy, and the shift from traditional resources and manufacturing to services and high technology. Companies were leaving, companies were consolidating, companies were downsizing, companies were going bankrupt, and not enough new ones were creating new work.

"The eighties' boom was based on hype and real estate, not as much on an underlying competitive strength as it needed to be," Premier Rae explained. "Our resource base was not expanding. Our pulp-and-paper industry was not reinvesting enough. Our automobile base needed to be strengthened and diversified. Add those things to the impact of the GST, to the recession in the United States and elsewhere, and the bottom just fell out."

Instead of riding to the rescue, the Mulroney government had chosen that moment to wrestle inflation with high interest rates and a high dollar and reduce its deficits by cutting back billions in transfer payments to the provinces. Ontario, as one of the three wealthiest, was especially hurt. Though a million Ontarians were now on social

assistance, the federal contribution to the province's health and education costs had dropped from 52 per cent to 31 per cent in the past
three years. Rae even came to believe that the federal Tories were
deliberately penalizing his people for political and ideological reasons.
The truth, he suspected, was that Brian Mulroney would rather have
spent a day in Cleveland than in Toronto.

"You know, Ottawa pays 50 per cent of Quebec's welfare benefits
and only 28 per cent of ours!" Rae said with an edge. "The industrial
heartland has been systematically ignored and neglected by the federal
government. The assumption is that they can inflict whatever punishment they want on Ontario." Nor did he consider Kim Campbell
much of an improvement. He was livid, in fact, that her cabinet
included only eight out of twenty-five members from a province
accounting for 40 per cent of Canada's population and 43 per cent of
the national tax revenues, none of them with a major economic portfolio. Metropolitian Toronto was represented by just one minister,
Pauline Browes, who was given charge of Indian Affairs and Northern
Development!

"Because the current recession has hit Toronto so hard, psychologically as well as economically," John Tory had recognized before the
campaign began, "Torontonians will be looking more than ever
before for something directed toward their specific problems. Not a
grant or a monument for short-term effects, but a plan to help them
adjust to inevitable global economic changes and to make the adjustment easier."

Campbell's ad-lib revealed, on the contrary, that the Tories had no
plan at all, and it opened the way for Jean Chrétien to roar into
Toronto the very next day and seize the number-one issue for the Liberals. "We want jobs! We want jobs!" some 1,500 partisans yelled in an
overcrowded restaurant located, for symbolic effect, in Michael Wilson's old riding. "Of course you want jobs," Chrétien responded.
"We have 226,000 people unemployed in Metro Toronto at this time,
172,000 people on welfare, and 162,000 people going to food banks
every month. The time has come to change these things. Our priority
is to create jobs."

A day later, in a union hall in suburban North York, Chrétien
announced a $6-billion infrastructure program to about five hundred
cheering construction workers. "None of you likes to be on welfare,
none of you likes to be on unemployment lists," he told them. "What
you want to do is go on the site every morning and build something

for the future." And when he talked about the human dignity of earning bread for the family table, he moved some of the middle-aged men to tears.

Kim Campbell, also in Toronto that morning, talked about her favourite "puberty music" and flirted with the traffic reporter on a local radio station. Then she dismissed Chrétien's job-creation plan as a cruel hoax. "We've got to stop buying people's votes with their own money," she declared. When pressed specifically to contribute $40 million toward the construction of a proposed trade centre, she categorically refused. "It is not a long-term solution to your problem," she told a few dozen union demonstrators, as though they should wait for the advent of high-paying jobs in computers.

In the past, those demonstrators would likely have been New Democrats. The NDP was promising to create more than half a million jobs in five years by spending even more than the Liberals, after all, and Audrey McLaughlin herself was in Toronto that day to escort the national media on a tour of several Metro plants that had been shut as a result of the Conservatives' free-trade deal. When McLaughlin was greeted by Premier Rae at a campaign office in Broadview-Greenwood, however, they both were greeted by union members protesting the Ontario government's public-service cutbacks. Even one of the three "human faces of unemployment" whom the party organizers had trotted out for the media was no longer sure about the New Democratic Party.

"We've got the NDP provincially and they're supposed to be for the working guy," Horst Huber, a laid-off plumber, told the *Toronto Star.* "But you look at what they've done and what can you say?"

In other words, while Audrey McLaughlin had yet to convince very many Canadians that she could bring better government to Ottawa, Bob Rae had indirectly convinced an awful lot of Ontarians that she wouldn't. And because the federal New Democrats – more than either the Conservatives or Liberals – have always been tarred by the economic misadventures and administrative follies of their provincial affiliates, they were running against their own record in Ontario, British Columbia, and Saskatchewan, as well as the Tories' record in Ottawa. In Ontario, as a result, the polls were showing a drop in support for the federal party from 20 per cent in 1988 to 8 per cent, even lower in relatively well-to-do constituencies like Mississauga West.

The Liberals were the presumed beneficiaries. In 1988 they had lost more than two dozen Ontario seats mainly because the anti-Tory vote had split two ways. "Our real opposition here is the Liberal party," said Jill Marzetti, provincial secretary of the Ontario NDP and chair of the party's Ontario Strategy and Election Planning Committee. "We don't think people will return to the Conservatives, but neither do we think there's a deep level of support for the Liberals in general, and Jean Chrétien in particular. It's not going to be easy, but our message will be that they're both the same tired old gang."

"Ottawa hasn't got the message – SEND IT!" barked the NDP's dramatic black-and-white TV ads, in which actors portrayed ordinary Canadians spewing forth their anger and frustration with a violent ugliness in their faces and voices. What came across most clearly, however, was that the NDP hadn't got the message. Among angry and frustrated voters, it too was part of the same tired old gang.

By the end of the first couple of weeks, the Liberals had taken firm control of the centre-left, traditionally the winning position on the political spectrum, and adopted the people's issue as their own. But the Conservative strategists chose to hold fast. They had convinced themselves, based on their principles and a skewed reading of the polls, that the public was in no mood for expensive election promises. "From this," Gregg wrote John Tory on September 17, "we might speculate that the Liberals' platform release might actually be hurting them! That is, considering the level of cynicism prevalent today, this initiative may be being interpreted as 'old politics' and 'posturing' rather than evidence of substance or a plan."

Gregg was not alone. For much of the political class, including much of the media, the deficit was a higher priority than jobs, not least because its players had very good jobs and all the skills, contacts, and confidence necessary for a reasonably secure future. They shared the gripes of middle-class taxpayers; they understood the workings of bond markets and the International Monetary Fund; they appreciated the way in which high deficits were linked to high interest rates and high unemployment. So reducing the deficit by reducing government spending was beyond debate. It was inevitable, just like the free-trade deal with the Americans and the need to recognize Quebec as a distinct society.

"Any politician who promises anything that has a significant price tag attached to it is lying," Peter C. Newman wrote in *Maclean's* at the start of the campaign. "We can't afford to maintain the social system we have, much less expand it. This country isn't just financially hard up; it's broke, bankrupt, insolvent."

Even the Liberals' infrastructure proposal seemed less an all-out declaration of war against unemployment than a subtle sort of image politics. It only promised to create between 50,000 and 65,000 jobs for the one and a half million people without work, after all, and Reform Leader Preston Manning was not wrong to joke that trying to stimulate the economy with $6 billion in public works was like trying to "start a 747 with a flashlight battery." Chrétien himself admitted that the program, whose federal funding would come from savings elsewhere, was primarily designed for the psychological boost in seeing construction trucks going up and down the streets again.

"We still thought the Liberals were foolish to be talking about spending public money on short-term jobs," said Michael Ferrabee, one of Campbell's inner circle. "We were going to let them barf their guts out, then watch them be picked apart. There seemed no need to panic."

Model Candidate

Carolyn Parrish, the Liberal candidate in Mississauga West, quickly discovered a secret method for assessing how well she was faring against Dr. Horner. After each of the all-candidates' debates, held a couple of times a week in a school gym or church hall, she bounded over to shake his hand. If it was dry, she knew she had done badly. If it was clammy, she figured she had whomped him.

"This morning it was yuck," she reported to her three key organizers during lunch at Zia's Ristorante, across from her campaign offices in a Victorian house on the main street of Streetsville, a hybrid community of quaint shops and monster homes located in the geographic centre of the riding. Parrish had just come from a debate at Loyola Catholic Secondary School. "And afterwards, when I sat down on the edge of the stage to talk to the kids, he copied me! He looked like a small Humpty Dumpty sitting there."

"Yeah," said George Carlson, her droll campaign chairman, "and he had his tie tucked into his pants too, which always reminds people of their weird Uncle Harry."

Carlson, who had nervously watched the debate from the sidelines, discounted its usefulness – he called it, in fact, "a symbolic sacrifice to democracy," because most of the kids either could not vote or would

automatically vote like their parents – but he was relieved that his candidate had garnered the loudest and longest applause. It confirmed what
the response at the doors, indeed the history of Canada, had already
suggested: the Roman Catholics, mostly first- or second-generation
immigrants and mostly new to Mississauga West, were leaning Liberal.

So were the Sikhs and the Greeks, the Somalis and the Bengalis,
the Ukrainians and the Iranians, the Koreans and the Caribbeans.
They were the principal instrument with which Carolyn Parrish, herself of Polish Catholic background, hoped to end Bob Horner's career
as a member of Parliament. "My name recognition is probably, in
places, higher than Horner's," she said. "He's been very low-key. If
you look at the parliamentary record, most times when he stood up
and sat down it was to second a patronage appointment."

"Or move adjournment," Carlson added.

Though Horner had seldom risen in the Commons and never risen
to the cabinet, he was recognized by many in Mississauga West as a
decent, hard-working constituency man. Since the 1988 election,
however, the community had changed so dramatically that he could
no longer rely on being recognized at all. Within five years its voting
population had increased about 50 per cent, from 93,000 to 140,000,
making Mississauga West the second most populous riding in Canada
(after York North). And, according to the 1991 census, 38 per cent of
the riding's population had not been born in Canada.

Fifty years earlier, when Toronto was predominantly WASP, this
would have been solid Tory territory. Mackenzie King always had to
rely on rural Grits, small-town Nonconformists, and Roman Catholics
for his Ontario seats. After him, as the chief executive officer of
Canada's postwar prosperity, Louis St. Laurent was able to take more
than half the Toronto ridings for a couple of elections, but his gains
were swept away by John Diefenbaker's upset in 1957. In the Conservative landslide of 1958, in fact, the Liberals could not elect a single
member from the eighteen ridings in what was known as Toronto and
York. Amid the ruins a gang of young reformers – known in legend as
Cell 13 – plotted the reconstruction of the Liberal Party of Canada.
They were, more than anything else, Torontonians.

Determined to create a modern, progressive, and democratic organization fixed upon firm urban bases, they set out to capture both their
party and their home town. And they succeeded with remarkable
speed. In 1961 one of the ringleaders, an advertising salesman named
Keith Davey, became national director of the party, and he brought

into its back rooms a host of campaign organizers, media consultants, strategic policies, and election ideas from Toronto. Lester Pearson, the new leader, was closely associated with Toronto; Walter Gordon, the campaign chairman, was a wealthy businessman from an old Toronto family; even the Toronto business community was giving up on the Tories under Diefenbaker's erratic, populist leadership. In 1962 the Liberals broke the ancient curse and carried off the lion's share of the Toronto ridings.

"We really did a great job," Davey crowed. "We were organized, we were systematic, and we kept most of Toronto Liberal from 1962 to 1984."

A key contribution to their achievement had been to lure the city's immigrant communities into the Liberal fold. While many had been drifting there anyway, drawn by the party's openness toward religious and linguistic minorities since Wilfrid Laurier's day, many others had been drawn toward Diefenbaker's rhetoric of human rights and anti-Communism in the 1950s. The economic recession of the early 1960s shook their commitment to the Conservatives, however, and Walter Gordon exploited the opportunity by connecting with community leaders to secure the immigrant vote for the Liberals. Subsequently, as Pearson and Trudeau opened Canada's doors to the world, the new arrivals attached themselves to the party that welcomed them and the next generations adhered to the party that honoured their traditions. Wherever they gathered, in Vancouver or Montreal, in Calgary or Halifax, they created a host of ridings that became reliable bases for the Liberal party. And those bases only kept increasing in number and importance as the proportion of immigrants kept increasing across the country.

The Tories and the NDP laboured diligently to attract their fair share of new Canadians. In government both parties were often generous in their immigration and cultural policies. In federal and provincial elections they managed to field some "ethnic" candidates and win a few "ethnic" ridings. But both parties were still seen as less friendly than the Liberals, and neither had been able to eradicate a strain of bigotry among its bourgeois or working-class members. "Mulroney didn't get enough credit for tripling the level of immigration since 1984 or appointing an Italian Canadian to the Supreme Court," said Senator Consiglio Di Nino, chairman of the Conservatives' election committee in Metro Toronto and himself an Italian immigrant. "But the second generation is taking another look at us, and those with real entrepreneurial drive – whether from Asia or Eastern Europe – don't want to have anything to do with the leftists. I'm an exception now, but there'll be more converts during the next ten years."

In the meantime, most of downtown Toronto's immigrant ridings remained the Liberals' strongest bastions. So, too, the new Canadians had begun transporting their Liberal allegiances to the white, Anglo-Saxon, Protestant, middle-class, and traditionally Tory suburbs such as Mississauga, where higher education, constant mobility, and mass communications were already shattering the old party loyalties.

"The ethnics voting Liberal is no more sheep-like than the wealthy voting Tory," Carolyn Parrish argued. "I've been to one or two Tory meetings, and though I can fake it as a regular old WASP" – she was a statuesque forty-seven-year-old with long, thick curls and big white teeth, resembling a former showgirl more than a former English teacher – "I just didn't feel comfortable there."

Both her father, a policeman, and her mother had been partisan Liberals, and Parrish herself had been inspired by her high school history teacher to work for "Red" Kelly, the hockey star whom Keith Davey had persuaded to run as a Liberal in 1963. But she took a long and circuitous route to becoming a candidate for the party. She marched in protests against the Vietnam War while at the University of Toronto in the late 1960s, flirted with the NDP, married an engineer, taught high school for four years, then quit to stay home and raise her two daughters. In 1984, when the elder girl was in Grade 3, Parrish got embroiled in a controversy over the school's sex-education program. Though no prude, Parrish was angered that a tacky American film, intended for the Grade 7 level, had been shown to a mixed class of eight-year-olds. She became angrier when the elected trustees of the Peel Board of Education suggested that they knew better than she did what was best for her child.

After a year of watching their board meetings, she concluded she not only *knew* better, she could *do* better. In 1985, and again in 1988, she won election as a trustee. That was where she discovered her passion for politics and her charm over people. Outspoken, gregarious, strong-willed, prone by her own admission to fury and tears, sometimes glib and often earthy, she soon became the de facto leader of a gang of reformers – including a young Tory organizer named George Carlson – who were determined to shake the old-timers out of a staid lethargy and give new energy and direction to the entire system. In 1989 she had patched together enough allies to win the chairmanship of the board, one of the largest in Canada, with 93,000 students under its authority and an annual budget of $650 million.

Whether fighting city hall to save a row of old trees on McLaughlin Road or defending the right of Sikh students to wear their ceremonial daggers in school, Carolyn Parrish attracted a lot of local publicity, a loyal following – and a great deal of hostility. She was, to her enemies, a flashy smartass on a colossal ego trip. (A feisty school board trustee often accused of being a loose cannon with an exaggerated opinion of her own qualities? That sounded familiar. "But the difference between Kim Campbell and me," said Parrish, "is that I have a heart.") Within months those who resented her activist agenda and brash style conspired to topple her from the chair. They succeeded when one of her closest friends betrayed her without warning. "It seemed the ultimate criticism of what I had been doing," Parrish said. "I spent six months afterwards in pain."

In 1991 she quit the board and turned her considerable energy toward a four-month campaign for a seat on the Mississauga city council. She lost what she considered a particularly filthy contest by only 3 per cent of the vote, not least because the Italian community had been mobilized to support her Italian opponent. "I was too naive to know about the mechanical side of politics," she said in retrospect. "I expected God to get out my vote."

"A tearful Parrish insisted she was through with politics," the *Mississauga News* reported at the time. Instead, she plunged almost immediately into one of the toughest political battles in Canadian history. Her work on the school board had convinced her that Ottawa was the seat of real power, if only because its transfer payments acted so tremendously on what the provinces could afford for education, and she had begun to fancy the "ultimate joy" of sitting some day in the House of Commons. So when the Liberal nomination in Mississauga West came open in the fall of 1991, she went after it even after being warned she had not a snowball's chance in hell.

Numbers Game

After decades of being mobilized to elect mainstream Liberals, the more political immigrant communities had come to realize they now had the numbers and skills to elect some of their own. The Jews got David Croll and Robert Kaplan into the House of Commons; the Italians got Charles Caccia and John Nunziata; the Greeks got Jim Karygiannis. Toronto Sikhs, the latest and perhaps most political of them all, had yet to elect a member of Parliament, but in December 1992 more than five thousand Liberals in turbans and saris turned out to secure the Liberal nomination in Bramalea-Gore-Malton for Gurban Singh Malhi – against three other Sikhs! "That meeting was like a visit to the Golden Temple in Amritsar," one witness recalled, though only 14 per cent of the constituency was Asian.

Carolyn Parrish, meanwhile, had had to take on a Sikh from England, a Muslim from Pakistan, a Christian from India, a woman from the Croatian community, and an Irish Catholic from Montreal. Together they signed up more than 15,000 members – some 3,500 Sikhs for the Sikh, 3,000 Muslims for the Muslim, 2,500 Indians for the Indian, 2,000 Croats for the Croat, and 4,000 all-sorts whom Parrish had gathered one by one in the wards where she had run for the school board and municipal council – creating the largest and perhaps wealthiest riding association in the country.

On November 22, 1992, almost six thousand of them showed up at a Lithuanian church hall in Mississauga, despite the cold rain and long queues. There were charges of false memberships and countercharges of vote buying. There were shouting matches and agonizing delays. "This process stinks, big time," Parrish complained in the midst of the fray. "This whole thing has been a charade, a three-ring circus." Eventually, however, after eleven hours and five ballots, she was declared the victor by a mere forty-seven votes.

"I made it, as a woman and with no help from the brass, so the system works," she said later, "but it was the most awful, exhausting, gruelling, mind-bending experience imaginable. For nine months, twenty-four hours a day, seven days a week, I had to stretch myself, my family, and my friendships to the breaking point. Even then, near the end, I thought I had lost. I'm a fighter and I wanted to run in my own riding, however tough the race, but I sure understand why people would grab an appointment from the top wherever they could get it."

She was referring to people like Art Eggleton, the former mayor of Toronto, who was parachuted into the Liberal nomination in York Centre under new party rules that had been intended to promote the representation of women and minorities as candidates. Since Eggleton was neither, his appointment was angrily interpreted within the immigrant communities as a way to avoid the nomination of yet another new Canadian. "Left to its own devices," an Old Guard Grit confided, "the party in Toronto would have twenty Italian candidates, seven Sikhs, seven Greeks, and a WASP in a pear tree."

"It looks like the old ethnic group has been threatened by some new ones, so it's changed the rules to stay in charge," another fumed privately. "Newer Canadians take politics seriously. If a lot of them want to get involved in deciding who their MP should be, and if the WASPs all prefer to stay home, well, too bad for the WASPs. It's an odd and not very healthy development to want to prevent thousands of citizens from coming out to support a Liberal candidate."

To which David Smith, chairman of the party's Ontario campaign, responded, "But is it healthy to hand over a riding to any machine, usually an ethnic group or single-issue bloc, that can hijack an executive or a nomination by a one-shot show of numbers? The leader needs some tools to put together an impressive team, and I'm not certain the Pearsons and Gordons of this world would get into this process if they had to spend a year of their lives dragging three thousand people out on one particular night."

For her part, despite her own terrible ordeal, Carolyn Parrish concluded that the greater effort had been worth the greater reward. "We put our candidate, our players, and our supporters through the pressure cooker," she said, "and we emerged with a united organization that's so strong it's scary."

She picked up something more important than an enormous list of potential voters and volunteers. This slim victory, coupled with her close defeat in the municipal election, had taught her the same humbling lesson that Kim Campbell had learned from the leadership race: No matter how strong the candidate, a good organization can make the crucial difference between victory and defeat. In the end, whatever Parrish's own efforts and attributes, if George Carlson hadn't set up an "absolutely scientific" system capable of monitoring her level of support during the day and mobilizing his network of more than 150 people to drag in an extra 345 votes during the last hour, she would have lost.

Canadian democracy would also have lost if not for the one hundred hours a week experienced volunteers such as George Carlson were willing to sacrifice to it. A plump man whose dark moustache and sly look made him seem older than his mid-thirties, he worked by day as an independent broker for a printing company in Streetsville, where he had been born into a family of diehard Tories. He had also been born with a love of politics in his blood. "It's like loving hockey or art," he said. "You just can't get enough of the strategies and what's happening inside."

Carlson followed the national flag debate when he was six. By the time he was ten, he used to delight in stopping on his *Telegram* delivery route – at the very same Victorian house, ironically, that now served as Parrish's campaign headquarters – to trade political scuttlebutt with Graydon Petty, a local councillor and the nephew of a former Tory premier no less, in exchange for reports on the condition of the sidewalks in Ward 2. He spent five years on the student council at Streetsville High and ended up its president. In 1982 he unsuccessfully sought a seat on the Mississauga municipal council. Three years later he won election as a school trustee, along with a "sweet and embarrassingly naive" neophyte named Carolyn Parrish.

Until then Carlson had helped the Progressive Conservatives in every federal and provincial election since the age of thirteen, when he canvassed for Premier Bill Davis in nearby Brampton during the 1971 Ontario election. But, after working to get Bob Horner elected in 1984, he became increasingly unhappy with what he saw as the party's swing to the right. "I was always more progressive than conservative," he explained. "My ideological home is somewhere between big labour and big cigar smoking, and I'm a bit of a nationalist in that I believe a country is more than a corporation."

Carlson's unhappiness peaked in 1985 when he expected to be a delegate to the Ontario PC leadership convention, but was pushed aside by the crudest sort of back-room politics. His hurt and disgust were only fuelled by the defeat of his candidate, Dennis Timbrell, by a right-wing car salesman from Muskoka named Frank Miller. At the federal level, too, Mulroney's broken promises and gross patronage had made George Carlson embarrassed to be a member of the Conservative party. "Mulroney had all the talents of a labour lawyer," he said, "but I never thought he had the best interests of the people at heart."

Though he did a small bit for Horner in 1988, Carlson grew more comfortable among his middle-of-the-road Liberal friends, not least because he had always had a high regard for the decency and patriotism of Jean Chrétien. He was ready, in other words, when Carolyn Parrish asked him to manage her nomination fight and election campaign. Though he had done neither job before, he could draw upon almost a lifetime of experience in the lower echelons of the political class. He knew, like every other constituency organizer, that the local campaign was nothing but a short-term frenzy designed to achieve only two basic goals: find your voters, and get them to the polling booth on election day. The score of charts in the back rooms, the hundreds of handshakes in the malls, the thousands of signs on the lawns, the tens of thousands of pamphlets on the doorsteps – or where the candidate goes when, which volunteer does what, how much money is raised by whom – each and everything was directed toward one or the other purpose.

"That's the only point of canvassing," Carlson explained. "You can have all the polite and interesting conversations you want, but if you get bad body language within three seconds and the guy has a Rotary Club sticker on his big car, you get the hell out of there." If, on the other hand, the Parrish team found a Liberal, they noted the name, got the phone number, asked for help and permission to put up a sign, and relayed the data to one of the four computers at her Streetsville headquarters.

Parrish knew she had only won the nomination because she had had "a stronger and better army." And if organization had meant so much when the numbers were relatively small and the candidates known to everyone, it meant that much more in the national election. For the past year, between taking care of her family and visiting her father in the hospital each day for almost three months before his death in March, she had knocked on more than five thousand doors, and now was vowing to knock on as many in the next few weeks. Her ambition, indeed, was to draw up a list of sixty thousand Liberal supporters – more than the total vote of most ridings – and get every single one out on E-day.

"If I didn't have a natural aversion to losing, I could become complacent," Parrish said in week two. "But I will run and work my tail off until election day because I'm terrified of losing. I want to win so badly. This is the epitome of my whole life."

Yesterday's Man

On September 28, 1993, the end of week three of the campaign, Carolyn Parrish bought a new red dress and went to the Sheraton Centre in downtown Toronto to eat Alberta roast beef (at $500 a plate) and hear Jean Chrétien address thirteen hundred corporate sponsors at the Liberal party's annual fund-raising dinner. "I'm here as a guest of St. Lawrence Cement," she teased, "but I'm worried they want to fit me for shoes." Though profoundly tired as the campaign approached its halfway mark, she remained upbeat about her prospects, and her mood was in no small measure a reflection of the confidence of her leader.

Chrétien's confidence was based, more than anything else, upon simple arithmetic. As long as the Liberals remained near 40 per cent in the polls, he assured the "nervous Nellies" around him, the split in the rest of the vote among the four other parties almost guaranteed him a majority government. Even in August, with Kim Campbell riding high, Chrétien had been predicting that the Liberals would take 25 seats or more in Atlantic Canada, 20 seats in Quebec, at least 75 seats in Ontario, and between 25 and 30 seats in the West. Now, with the Tories slipping in every region according to the most recent polls, he was expecting to do even better.

"He may not be pretty," Parrish observed from the back of the huge hall, "but it's time this country stopped looking for glitz. I'm not one of those who adored him from the beginning. I've slowly grown to admire him." It was, in fact, an enormous relief for a self-confessed "control queen" like Parrish to see him doing so well. "I don't like putting myself in other people's hands, and I hate the idea of working my heart out and losing simply because someone in the national campaign screws up."

Parrish knew the rule of thumb: After the national leaders and the national parties and the national issues, the merit of a local candidate is generally worth about five points. "You can't totally discount a good candidate," she had heard George Carlson say often enough, "because many ridings are won by less than 5 per cent of the vote. But at the door it usually doesn't matter, you can run anybody."

That was especially true in an urban riding as enormous as Mississauga West, where pathetically few citizens turned out for the all-candidates' meetings and the local newspaper was so bad (the joke went) that it came *inside* the K-Mart flier. The sheer size of the constituency made it impossible to greet more than a smattering of the population. There was certainly no time to explain the intricacies of deficit reduction or job creation. As a result, the local candidates had almost no power of persuasion other than to show they cared enough to say hello. Most decideds had made up their minds out of habit or in reaction to the national campaigns; most undecideds were waiting for the televised leaders' debates.

In the early days of the campaign, Parrish had been distressed to hear people on the street parroting the media's line that Jean Chrétien was nothing but a fifty-nine-year-old has-been, a second-rate leftover from the Trudeau era, yesterday's man. The consensus in the press gallery – as reflected in the *Toronto Sun*'s early prediction of 127 Liberals, 121 Tories, 25 *bloquistes,* 16 New Democrats, and 6 Reformers – was that he would be lucky to win a minority in an Italian-style parliament.

"He is getting good press in most of English Canada, but not in the major Toronto media," Keith Davey observed before the election began. "That's a problem we'll have to deal with." An even tougher problem was that much of the French-language press loathed him. So, while Canadians saw Prime Minister Campbell doing the twist on their front pages and nightly news all summer, few knew that the leader of the Opposition was out perfecting his campaign pitch in almost one hundred cities and villages across the country. "There was only one occasion when an Ottawa-based reporter attended one of these functions, just one," he later complained. "Everybody back here was saying, 'Chrétien's not doing anything.'"

All at once, however, after years of either underestimating or ignoring him, reporters discovered Jean Chrétien as though for the first time. They had assumed that his fractured English would make him an object of general derision. Instead, they saw how his folksy rhetoric, moving skilfully from partisan ridicule to national pride, usually inspired trust and good feeling. They had assumed, too, that his thirty years in the public eye would make him the very sort of old-style politician with whom Canadians were apparently fed up. Instead, even though preliminary polls ranked experience less than twentieth on a list of voter priorities, many people began turning to him – as Chrétien himself phrased it – as the most experienced sailor in a boat rocked by rough seas and violent storms, imploring him, "Take us to shore, we want to survive."

In 1963, when Chrétien was first elected to Parliament, Kim Campbell was elected president of her high school council. In 1967, when he first entered the federal cabinet, she received what she later called a "sense of the tensions in the country between English and French" during a trip to the Montreal world's fair. More pertinently, perhaps, Chrétien had spent three decades fighting populists such as Preston Manning and separatists such as Lucien Bouchard. No matter how lofty he became as a cabinet minister, no matter how many times he dined with tycoons and heads of state, he remained proud of his working-class roots and close to his working-class constituents. He deliberately laced his speeches with slang and emotion; he scrupulously avoided any cause for scandal in his personal and professional life; he shrewdly considered what sort of district to live in and why he should not own a Cadillac Seville.

"Since I had to fight populists," he wrote in his autobiography, "I learned from them and even tried to outdo them. That has often shocked and annoyed the intellectuals, who exaggerate my humble beginnings or conclude I am not educated."

He did indeed pay a heavy price among the intellectuals for his colloquial speech and unpretentious manner – as well as for his Canadian patriotism – but that usually irritated him more than it harmed him. Even in temporary retirement after 1986, he remained one of the most popular politicians in Canada, as the unprecedented sales of his memoirs demonstrated. "A successful politician must not only be able to read the mood of the public, he must have the skill to get the public on his side," he wrote in *Straight from the Heart*. "The public is moved by mood more than logic, by instinct more than reason, and that is something that every politician must make use of or guard against."

For a while, after becoming leader of the Liberal party in 1990, he seemed to lose his instinctual bond with the public and, with it, his own sure-footedness. As he stumbled from mistake to confusion, more and more people bought the media's line that he was not "prime ministerial" enough, that he spoke too roughly and looked too raw, that he would be an embarrassment on the world stage and an incompetent at home. In his darkest hour Chrétien himself wondered if he had the right stuff for the top job.

He decided he did, of course, and almost everyone who now saw him on the road noted how relaxed he looked, without seeming either cocky or complacent. After Brian Mulroney, too, it was refreshing to see a leader who looked natural in a denim shirt and a baseball cap – more natural than Preston Manning, in fact. Even the most jaded reporters found him remarkably accessible and good-humoured, to the point where Chrétien and his wife joined them for a spontaneous dance up and down the aisle of the campaign bus. Consciously or not, the Liberal leader's relentless optimism seeped into their coverage, and he was forgiven a lot more slips of the tongue and gaps in policy than Kim Campbell.

"Thus," the editors at the *Globe* noted, "the Tories have taken a proper lashing for suggesting social spending would have to be cut, without saying where or how much. But what has Mr. Chrétien said? He has said nothing on pensions. He has said nothing on unemployment insurance. He has said nothing on social assistance, except to muse publicly about forcing those on welfare to work for their benefits – a 'gaffe' that would have caused weeks of hysterics had the Prime Minister uttered it."

He was also helped by a smart – but dangerous – initiative his Liberal strategists had taken. According to a conventional rule of the game, opposition parties aren't elected: governments are defeated. The opposition normally launches a savage assault against the government's record while trying to avoid policies and promises that would inevitably disappoint some voters and alienate others. When policies and promises become unavoidable, goes a second rule, they are best revealed like a striptease, item by item, to build a fever of excitement and feed the media's insatiable need for hot news. In this election, however, the Liberals decided to break both rules by issuing a 112-page platform, including specific programs and projected costs, on the eighth day of the campaign.

Creating Opportunity: The Liberal Plan for Canada, better known as the Red Book, had evolved from the thinkers' conference the party held in 1991, the policy resolutions a party convention passed in 1992, the consultations of a roving committee co-chaired by Paul Martin and Chaviva Hosek, and the results of extensive polling. More significantly, it had sprung from the public's skepticism about electoral politics and the Liberals' negative reputation as the party of 1960s ideologues and reckless spendthrifts. "It had to be fiscally responsible; it had to avoid exaggerated promises; and it had to create hope," Chrétien said afterwards. "If its priorities were the right ones and offered light at the end of the tunnel, then we felt it would overcome the cynicism."

The Red Book sought a feasible, affordable balance between an active government and a free market, between job creation and deficit reduction, between social assistance and individual motivation, between national sovereignty and global integration. It promised to invest $2 billion in the infrastructure program, but it also promised to cut the deficit from 5.2 per cent to 3 per cent of Canada's Gross Domestic Product within three years. It promised to protect free access to health care, but it also promised to improve the efficiency of

Canada's welfare system. It promised to renegotiate parts of the North American Free Trade Agreement, but it also promised to promote exports and trade. "Liberals," it declared in a statement of principle, "unlike Conservatives, fundamentally believe that government can be a force for good in society. Economic growth is not a matter for market forces alone. Jobs, health care, a safe and sustainable environment, equality for women and men, care for the very young and the aged, and the alleviation of poverty are societal issues that cannot be addressed simply by having each individual aggressively pursue immediate, narrow self-interest."

Whatever the merits of its message, the Red Book had the extra benefit of freeing Jean Chrétien from the need to make the dull policy speeches he seldom delivered well. Whatever the issue, from free trade to the GST, from day care to manpower training, he simply had to wave it in the air. "You can come to me with this book every week after I'm prime minister," he repeated at every stop, including the Sheraton Centre dinner that Carolyn Parrish attended, "and say, 'Where are you in your promises, Mr. Chrétien?' This is a realistic plan to create realistic hope." Then he would hold up the Tories' plan – an empty blue binder – and get a big laugh from the crowds.

"I was stunned that the Tories had nothing," said Chaviva Hosek, the smart and charming dynamo who had gone from Ontario politics to Chrétien's office as his policy adviser. "The mistake they made was that they believed we were the complete idiots they said we were, that we hadn't learned anything, that we hadn't figured out where the public was, that we hadn't changed. The Red Book was supposed to demonstrate that we had done a lot of thinking and show what we could do as a government in a fiscally responsible way. No Liberal platform has ever been 'owned' by more people, and we did a better job because we talked to so many people."

At a deeper level, the Red Book became a totemic device, like Chrétien's denim shirt and his bus tour. Relatively few voters studied it or even read its synopsis in the newspapers. Its detailed arguments and qualified proposals were soon reduced to a few pat promises. (When John Tory tried to pin down a Liberal consultant about GST reform during a TV panel discussion, for instance, he was curtly told, "It's in the plan, John. Page 117. Read the damn thing." Tory did not realize at the time that the document was only 112 pages long.) So the Conservative strategists, it could be argued, had not been entirely misguided in plotting to emphasize style over substance. They had merely

missed the point that, for many people, substance had become a crucial component of style.

"The Red Book was way smarter than we ever thought," Allan
Gregg conceded. "Not because it made people say that the Liberals
have *the* answer, but because it made them say that the Liberals have *an*
answer – which was a recognition that there were problems to be
solved. It was a tremendous counterpoint to the unearned self-satisfac-
tion that was oozing from the Tories."

Lost Weekend

"On opening day, the Progressive Conservative party boasted a new
leader and not much else," David McLaughlin, a senior adviser to
both Brian Mulroney and Kim Campbell, confessed in his account of
the election campaign, *Poisoned Chalice*. "There was no strategy –
except what the polling said; no platform – except what Kim Campbell said; no communications strategy – except for unscripted town
hall events; no media management strategy – except the admonition
not to talk to journalists; and no tour plan, just a bus schedule for the
next few days. Taken together, they boil down to a complete lack of
focus, theme, or message to Campbell's events."

It had not taken the Tories long to realize, with growing alarm and
confusion, that they would not be able to coast to victory on the
strength of Campbell's personality and the mirage of a new politics.
Both were proving dysfunctional. There was, for example, the decision to replace orthodox campaign rallies with "town hall" meetings.
Instead of delivering a fiery stump speech from behind a podium to
several hundred delirious partisans, Campbell was to sit on a stool and
field unrehearsed questions from random groups of "average" citizens
in schools, factories, and other "locations of the new Canadian reality." Not only had Bill Clinton used the technique with considerable
success during the 1992 American election, it satisfied Campbell's
desire to conduct quasi-intellectual seminars on public issues and Allan
Gregg's wish for a stylistic device that would reinforce her image as
just folks.

The new politics was unconquered territory for the political class,
however, with uncharted possibilities and risks. The party professionals

had yet to master how to run a campaign that did not look like it was being run by party professionals – without, at the same time, making it look like it was being run by a bunch of rank amateurs. And though the first public forums went well enough as a kind of political science tutorial, with Campbell earnestly scribbling notes and expounding at length on macroeconomics, the Tories sacrificed the important advantages that had made the stump speech so orthodox in the first place: the ability to control the agenda, orchestrate an unveiling of policies, energize the volunteers, and stage-manage a sense of momentum. No matter how polite and impressed the people in the room may have been with Kim Campbell, she appeared under constant barrage. No matter how soft and routine their questions, she was ever ready to wrestle with each one until the crowd begged for mercy.

"Her form of word and concept association amounted to an ongoing Rorschach test to divine hidden meanings as well as search out the core message," David McLaughlin observed. "She disliked set-piece speeches and resisted shorter, simpler messages when a longer would do. That awareness led to the campaign and her staff going to the other extreme: providing her with the barest outline of speaking notes which she invariably found unsuitable or insufficient. The result was a high level of frustration."

The media, in particular, were frustrated, because Campbell often neglected to toss them the thirty-second clip or quotable headline they needed in order to do their job and justify their enormous travel expenses to their editors. "Her instincts were not the instincts of a person who had been in a national campaign before," Senator Murray noted. "She thought that if she went out and did something, and it was covered by the media, that should suffice. At one point, I remember, she was going to make a big speech attacking the Liberal platform. We told her that she should be setting it up beforehand, testing out lines and so on. She didn't do any of it because she didn't think the audience was appropriate. Who the hell cares about the audience! She was talking through the media to the general public. She never understood that."

"What we were doing wasn't, by the media's definition, news, so they functionally killed it," Gregg added. "Reporters would say, 'Look, you've got to start kicking shit out of Chrétien, for *us*, because that's good television. Hanging around Crayola factories talking to workers isn't good television, and we're not going to cover it any more. We're going to start saying that this is a boring campaign, with no life or substance. If Campbell would get up and call Chrétien a cocksucker, we'll guarantee you tomorrow's headline.' That wasn't a conspiracy. They just needed their daily Gainesburger.''

The press corps found plenty else to grouse about. The Tories' two media buses were like crowded slums compared to the luxurious newsroom-on-wheels that the Liberals provided. And, compared to the high-spirited organization surrounding Chrétien, Campbell's team had all the gaiety of undertakers. Time and again the journalists on the Tory deathwatch were hampered by logistical errors, technical glitches, inadequate briefings, and a lack of time between events to file their stories. Relations between the prime minister and the media became so testy during the first week – "Maybe you need a hearing aid!" she snapped in reply to one reporter's question – that she was kept away from them for several days.

"When the poll came out showing that I had the highest approval rating since Pearson," Campbell later commented, "I got a sense that that was a psychological turning point for some in the media, who decided I was getting some kind of free ride." As a result, she believed, they decided to give Jean Chrétien and Preston Manning free rides. "New politics, old media" was how she explained it. And though there was plenty of truth in her explanation, whenever the pack got ready to go after Chrétien and Manning, it was diverted by yet another of her screw-ups. ("I just go to bed and have a good night's sleep," Jean Chrétien joked. "Then I read the paper in the morning about Ms. Campbell's latest statements, and I have enough for the whole day.")

The worst damage to the Conservatives' campaign was inflicted by an off-the-cuff comment she made during a press scrum in St. Bruno, Quebec, at the start of week three. It arose from her persistent refusal to be specific about how she planned to keep her promise to slash the deficit to zero in just five years. Campbell's reluctance was understandable. A cut of that size would undoubtedly require a severe reduction in Ottawa's social-assistance payments and its fiscal transfers to the provinces for their health, welfare, and education programs. "In the end," she had blurted out in French during her first day on the campaign trail, "there are going to have to be cuts in the social programs." Just as obvious were the perils of saying so. "Maybe," she quickly added. After that near miss, she would only admit that some changes might become necessary if Ottawa's revenue projections proved wrong. The voters would just have to trust her to make the right changes.

But whatever trust had once existed was shaken on Thursday, September 23, when the *Globe and Mail* bannered a front-page headline: "Social policy plan kept under wraps – UI, welfare, pensions could pay for Tory pledge to end deficit." Campbell's strategists immediately advised her to dismiss the so-called plan as an incomplete and unapproved proposal from the bureaucracy – which was technically true – and to reaffirm her determination to protect Canada's social safety net. Instead, when confronted by the media about the report, Campbell only left the impression that she did not want to discuss something so politically hot during the election campaign – which was also true.

"I think it takes longer than forty-seven days to tackle an issue that's that serious," she said. A moment later she dug herself deeper into the hole by adding, "This is not the time, I don't think, to get involved in a debate on very, very serious issues."

There went the credit Campbell had been earning for her candour and courage. There went the hopes she had raised for the politics of inclusion. Her remark reminded Canadians of Brian Mulroney's deadliest sin, duplicity, and it played into the doubts many people were harbouring about why they should even bother to vote if the political class was going to do what it was already secretly plotting to do anyway. Tory fortunes immediately plunged ten points in its wake. So did the spirits of the Tories' campaign team. Not only had Campbell ignored their initial advice, she ignored their pleas for a fast retraction, partly because her own staff was divided about how fast and self-flagellating the retraction should be, partly because the earliest press reports missed the full significance of what she had said, partly because she was too proud and too stubborn.

"Later we tried to explain to her why it had been such a disaster that she didn't retract instantly," Jodi White remembered. "She said she had never done national-level damage control with the media before, that she would have done it if it had been explained to her. She apologized, but the fact is she wasn't a good listener and hadn't listened at the time of the problem."

Nor could the problem have hit at a worse time. The Tories were in the desperate throes of trying to regain the agenda – and at least some momentum – by finally pulling together their own booklet of policies for the start of the following week. On Friday afternoon, after issuing a belated clarification of her remarks, Campbell flew to Vancouver to recuperate from an illness that had been sapping her energy and concentration. (It was what a male informer described as "one of those female plumbing things," serious enough for a doctor to advise Campbell to take a break from the campaign. She refused, apparently worried it would be taken as evidence that women cannot compete in a man's game.) She rested on Saturday – and *not*, she later made a point of telling anyone who might have heard the rumour to the contrary, *not* in the arms of her Russian boyfriend – and on Sunday she walked in an AIDS fund-raiser. Between one thing and another, she failed to meet with the two PMO officials who had been sent from Ottawa to brief her on the Tories' long-awaited deficit reduction proposal.

On Monday, September 27, she seemed as perplexed by the plan's coloured charts and technical arguments as the five hundred high school students she was addressing. And when she roared into Toronto the next day to unveil *A Taxpayer's Agenda* before a PC Business Association luncheon at the Marriott just a few hours before Jean Chrétien's Sheraton Centre speech, the party faithful were urged to greet their leader with a standing ovation, then forced to sit down again in bemused silence because the prime minister was still on the bus writing last-minute additions to her speech.

As it turned out, neither a better buildup by her advance staff nor a more adequate preparation on Campbell's part would have saved the so-called Blue Book from its own inherent weaknesses. The paucity of ideas coming out of the Conservative government was made more apparent, not less, by their being gathered together in just thirty-six pages. "It said things like, we will flush the toilet after using and not wear blue socks with brown shoes," Allan Gregg recalled, "and that's how it was received by the electorate. You cannot just get up there and say, 'Elect me, we will do nothing.'"

On the broad themes, in fact, Campbell was saying, "Elect me, we will do everything." Whereas the Liberals were promising jobs and social programs at the cost of rapid deficit reduction, and the Reformers were promising rapid deficit reduction at the cost of jobs and social programs, the Tories returned to the old-style politics of promising rapid deficit reduction *and* jobs *and* social programs. "I'll throw myself across the railway tracks" to preserve Canada's health-care system, Kim Campbell now declared – which, as Chrétien joked at dinner that night, wasn't much of a promise considering that the Tories had cancelled all the trains.

Her speech, like the Blue Book itself, was a humiliating admission by the party pros that they were being whipped at their own game.

The Liberals had a man with a plan, they controlled the centre-left ground, they possessed the number-one issue, and they were playing well as a team. The Tories, on the other hand, lacked the internal discipline necessary to stick with either their old devices or their new style. "We had our own people being quoted in the press that the Tory campaign was brain dead," Gregg said. "That just scared the shit out of those in the decision-making positions. Rather than showing any courage, we went back to doing what we had always done before – which only added to the perception that we didn't know what we were doing or had been deceitful about the new stuff."

So Kim Campbell was put back behind a rostrum, before a partisan crowd and the national media, with a specific set of "sound bites" and "attack lines," to report on what she had learned from the town hall meetings. "First," she said, "people want government to help restore economic opportunity by creating lasting and meaningful jobs for Canadians. Second, they want government to take action that will preserve and sustain our precious Canadian quality of life. Canadians want continued access to universal health care, income-support programs that work, and a justice system that leads to safe streets and safe communities. And third, Canadians want to get government working again for *all* Canadians."

Deficit reduction had slipped into third place as a priority, or so Campbell's speechwriters now suggested, and the Conservatives could not even demonstrate a credible means of achieving it without raising taxes or cutting programs. After her speech, indeed, Campbell was deeply embarrassed during a meeting with the *Globe*'s editorial board when she was caught in a substantial misunderstanding of her own fiscal projections. "She launched into an explanation that business subsidies would be cut by $750 million in the fifth year of the program," the newspaper later reported. "A chorus of 'Nos' stopped her. After some discussion, she admitted she was wrong. One of her top advisers says her lack of preparation for newspaper sessions 'falls in the incomprehensible category.'"

The next day, September 29, Dalton Camp went public with the seriousness of the Conservatives' troubles. Their slogan – "It's Time" – was wrong. Their advertising – "Eyeball-to-eyeball polispeak" – was wrong. Their issue – the federal deficit – was wrong. "As manager Casey Stengel once said, looking out at his foundering baseball team from the dugout, 'Can't anyone here play this game?'" Camp wrote in his *Toronto Star* column. "In the living memory of all involved, there has never been a national campaign quite like this one where no one is truly satisfied with the way things are going but no one seems able to talk about it in a coherent, constructive way. The Prime Minister is herself to blame for the lack of communication. If she lacks confidence in the people who are running her campaign, it's not too late to replace them. Otherwise, she should start calling every day, if only to become reacquainted with those she left behind when she set out to sweep the country. They might even help."

Possibly, but even if the tactical screw ups were overcome, the strategic conundrum would remain. In trying to regain the ground they were losing to the Liberals, the Conservatives were in danger of losing even more ground to Reform. "While Ms. Campbell vows to make deeper cuts if the deficit does not decline as hoped," the editors at the *Globe* declared the very morning of Camp's column, "the Liberals are quite content to see $30-billion deficits linger on into the future. There you have it: a party that thinks the deficit's a problem, but still hopes we can grow out of it, and a party that knows we can't grow out of it, but doesn't think it's a problem. There is, of course, a third alternative, a party that both acknowledges the problem and proposes real solutions: Reform."

Not only had the Conservative strategists underestimated Reform's potential to steal significant support from the right, they now had no idea what to do about it. "We have been outmanoeuvred on two fronts simultaneously," a confidential memo from "Allan (The Vague One) Gregg" to "John (The Brain Dead One) Tory" admitted the day after the attacks in the *Star* and the *Globe*. "The Liberals have gained ground as the party with 'a plan' whose priority is jobs. Reform have done a better job as to selling themselves as the party of 'change' whose priority is the deficit." Some Tories were even whispering of an impending debacle in which they might hold on to only eighty-five seats!

In Mississauga West, certainly, there was a perceptible flight of disenchanted voters toward the Reform party that week. Bob Horner had already met the full force of their disenchantment while canvassing one evening in tony Credit Pointe. At three homes with Reform signs on the lawn, he got the roughest reception of his life. "They called me everything they could lay their tongue to," he said, visibly shaken by the memory, "ordered me off their property, swore at me in front of their children, called Kim Campbell a blonde slut and whore. It was really nasty."

What hurt, besides the insults, was that he never had a chance to show his sympathy with the roots of their anger. Here was a Tory, after all, who had persuaded the House of Commons to pass his private member's bill outlawing drug paraphernalia in Canada. Here was a Tory who had attracted national attention the previous year by suggesting that the members of the Bloc Québécois be tried for treason. Here was a Tory who had railed as loudly as any Reformer against lazy MPs feeding at the public trough and excessive party discipline.

"Bob is almost ideologically matched to the Reform party's philosophy," said Jeff Knoll, his campaign manager. "Reformers are Conservatives who just can't wait. But Canada is facing a lot of big problems that aren't going to be solved overnight by a bunch of reactionary rednecks with simple doctrinaire solutions. We tell them, if you want Jean Chrétien to win, then go ahead and vote Reform. Because Preston Manning is Jean Chrétien's best volunteer."

Over in Carolyn Parrish's headquarters, George Carlson agreed. Though Reform was only attracting 4 per cent of Metro Toronto's voters at the start of the campaign, compared to 11 per cent in Ontario as a whole, it was expected to get between two-thirds and three-quarters of its support from disgruntled Conservatives. And that was true not just in Mississauga West, but in every province west of the Ottawa River. "Whenever we find Reformers," Carlson said, after characterizing them as cranky and mean-minded white people, "we thank them for their interest in democracy and ask if they need a ride to the polls."

Mad As Hell

Charles Conn, the unfortunately named Reform candidate in Mississauga West, was not going to speak badly of any man who had once served with the RCMP. Instead, he saw Bob Horner as just one more victim of the old party system gone mad.

"In a parliamentary democracy," Conn explained with the smooth voice and confident patter of the advertising executive he had once been, "you ought to be able to elect a representative to look after your interests and then forget about it. It's like belonging to a golf club where the members elect an executive to deliver the services they expect, from clean towels to hot water. If the executive runs amok and starts piling up debts for things which the members never approved of, and every member now owes a ton of money, you'd throw the bums out. And if the new executive pushes you even further into a hole, would you go back and elect the first set again?"

That was the Reform party's basic pitch to the voters of Mississauga West. In shopping malls and seniors' residences, on doorsteps and cable TV, Conn expounded at length about the "black dagger of debt" the Liberals and Tories had manufactured over the past twenty years. ("Why *black?*" asked the NDP candidate, Paul Simon, an immigrant from Guyana. "Isn't debt usually red?") He produced charts to show how Reform would eliminate the national deficit in three years. He distributed reams of material to tell why Reform wanted to reduce the immigration quotas and revamp the unemployment insurance system. But his clearest message was trumpeted in two bold sentences on a party broadsheet: "SO YOU DON'T TRUST POLITICIANS. NEITHER DO WE."

Charles Conn may have looked like a prototypical politician as he campaigned around Mississauga West with his business suit and charming smile, but he insisted he was not a politician at all. "I'm a *representative*," he said, "of a bunch of people who finally got tired of being told what to do, who are 'as mad as hell and ain't going to take it any more,' and who have gathered around a set of principles and policies that make sense. And it's not surprising that they make sense, because they were drawn over the years from what the people felt ought to be done."

Born in Toronto in 1938, Conn had graduated in commerce from Queen's University and worked for more than a dozen years as an account executive for a couple of major advertising agencies in Toronto, New York, and Vancouver before he was fired in 1977. He did contract work for a few years, supplemented by some university teaching and training seminars, but the devastating recession on the West Coast in the early 1980s sent him back to Ontario, where he became the marketing director for Brights Wines. In 1988 he went out on his own again, trying among other things to develop a taste for Ontario ice wine in the Far East. But the financing "walked away" from that particular venture, as he phrased it, and Conn had been "scrambling" from one thing to another ever since. And though he considered himself an engaged citizen – former president of Arts '62 at Queen's, former president of Junior Achievement in Vancouver, former treasurer of his evangelical church – he had never joined a political party until September 1991 when he joined the Reform Party of Canada.

"I voted for the Conservatives in 1984 and 1988, and they didn't deliver," Conn said. "I track the whole problem back to Trudeau's second administration, when he made his unholy marriage with the NDP. That's when the deficits started to mount. We threw him out in 1979 for his irresponsibility and arrogance, but he got back in because of Clark's incompetence. Then Mulroney came along and promised change, and did nothing. The Tories just bought into the Liberal-NDP structure where the sun revolves around the government, where a top-down autocracy determines the issues and the solutions, where heads of interest groups get together to discuss everything and make the deals. Humans instinctively understand that there ain't no free lunch, but when someone's shovelling it down your throat, it's tough to say no. So we have to stand up in front of people and tell the truth: Canadians have to pay for their services. There's no magic fairy, there's no money tree."

But the country's economic problems could not be remedied, Conn added, until the political class was forced to pay attention to Canadians and the matters that affected their lives. "This feeling of alienation from their governors is extremely strong," he said. "It's a real anger and distrust."

The anger and distrust were greatest, not among those who had despised Brian Mulroney for slashing social programs and implementing free trade, but among those white, middle-class, English-speaking tax-payers in the hinterlands and the suburbs who had voted for the Tories in order to reduce the role of government and put an end to "French Power" in Ottawa. For they were not alienated from a particular policy or even an entire set of policies. They were alienated from the prevailing consensus – indeed, the very idea of consensus – that most of the political class in Toronto, Montreal, and Ottawa had come to share.

That consensus was basically the traditional winning formula: lean to the centre-left and hold Quebec. The first meant government activism and entitlement programs for every citizen; the second meant official bilingualism and catch-up policies for French-speaking Canadians. Though the Liberal party had monopolized that formula since Laurier's day, both the Conservatives and the New Democrats had come to accept that they could only break its hegemony by becoming modern, moderate, multicultural, and bilingual themselves.

To that purpose, the Tories had to undergo a long march from the political wilderness of the 1960s, when John Diefenbaker ruled over a rump of knee-jerk reactionaries and anti-French monarchists. Robert

Stanfield and Joe Clark, one a patrician from Nova Scotia and the other a small-town Albertan, struggled at enormous personal cost to drag their party into the big cities, into French Canada, into the immigrant communities, and into the late twentieth century. And nowhere did they meet greater resistance than in Western Canada.

Though each of the four western provinces had developed its own political culture based on the particular conditions of settlement – with Manitoba more like Ontario, Saskatchewan more a wheat pool, Alberta more the American frontier, and British Columbia some utopian fantasy – the Canadian West was marked by the trek of strong-willed individualists who chose to distance themselves from the traditions and institutions back east, by the flood of immigrant groups who were neither English nor French, and by the practical and psychological effects of its having been bought by Ottawa from the Hudson's Bay Company in 1868 or, in the case of British Columbia, separated by a couple of thousand miles and a wall of mountains. As a result, many westerners did not buy the political class's definition of Canada as an interventionist national state anchored in a historic entente between two European peoples. On the contrary, they tend to see that definition as part of the conspiracy by which Ontario and Quebec maintain domination over them.

For more than a hundred years Western Canada gathered the evidence. Land grants, freight costs, grain markets, tariff regulations, time zones, bank rates, gas exports, oil prices, industrial strategies, government contracts, there was no end to the grievances. Politically, too, westerners fumed about how Parliament was weighted toward the populations of the two largest provinces and influence tilted toward the business and media circles of Toronto and Montreal. It was, as Keith Davey explained, mostly a matter of numbers.

"The main lessons of folk history are similar across the West," Don Braid and Sydney Sharpe wrote in their book *Breakup*. "Ottawa can't be trusted. Your best friend, if you send him to Ottawa as an MP, can't be trusted. The prime minister might seem friendly for a while, but Ontario or Quebec will always yank his leash before he gets carried away. Official bilingualism is an expensive policy that matters only to Quebec and Ontario. Quebec and its eternal worries are more important to Ottawa than all four western provinces together."

For much of its history, the West has sought some sort of redress. It produced Louis Riel, the Manitoban Métis who led an armed rebellion against the government of Canada before Ottawa hanged him in

1885. It sent dozens of Progressives to Parliament in 1921 on a platform of free trade and direct democracy. In every election since the Great Depression, it elected a radical contingent of CCFers and New Democrats to defend western agriculture against the exploitation of the eastern banks and the Canadian Pacific Railway. It was the mainstay of the federal Social Credit party for almost three decades. It was the bedrock of John Diefenbaker's Tory populism. It was the wellspring of countless angry premiers, from W. A. C. Bennett to Ross Thatcher, from Peter Lougheed to Howard Pawley, all of whom transcended their party affiliations and provincial boundaries to battle the imperial arrogance of Central Canada.

Neither the protest parties nor the provincial powerbrokers succeeded, however, in breaking the West's profound sense of inferiority and alienation. Though Lougheed, for one, argued that the "only way there can be a fair deal for the citizens of the outlying parts of Canada is for the elected provincial governments of these parts to be sufficiently strong to offset the political power in the House of Commons of the populated centres," he ended up at Pierre Trudeau's side lifting a glass of champagne to both the National Energy Program and the Charter of Rights.

"Why do you westerners let five little pip-squeaks from Quebec run the country?" Trudeau once asked. "Why don't you take it over and throw us out?" In 1984, as if heeding that astute advice, they went beyond their regional leaders and protest parties and gave fifty-eight of their seventy-seven seats to Brian Mulroney's Tories. They had decided, in effect, to change strategy and place their hopes on riding a mainstream winner to Ottawa.

Western Canada proved just one half of Mulroney's grand design, however. The other was to build on the labours of Stanfield and Clark, add his own attributes as a fluently bilingual Quebecker, and make the Conservative party a welcome home for French Canadians. With the West *and* Quebec onside, he calculated, the Tories could win majority governments for eternity. "I've always thought that Western Canada's needs were in harmony with the aspirations of Quebec" was how he pitched it. "They both suffered by comparison with Ontario."

But the root of Mulroney's triumph became, paradoxically, the cause of his party's downfall. Since the Conservatives already had a strong base in the West, Mulroney concentrated on capturing Quebec, which also happened to be the political culture he knew and loved best. But where was he to find Tory voters, not to mention Tory organizers and Tory bagmen, in a province that had not elected almost any Conservative MPs in twenty years? The obvious answer was among those Quebeckers who most hated the federal Liberals: the separatists, the nationalists, and the rural remnants of Maurice Duplessis's Union Nationale. Though Mulroney had long been a passionate defender of Trudeau's federalist vision in the swankier bars of Montreal, he climbed into bed with Trudeau's arch-enemies, gambling the unity of Canada for personal power.

Nothing demonstrated the limits of elite accommodation and brokerage politics more dramatically than the utter failure of Mulroney's all-too-clever scheme. As Trudeau had discovered, there was no appeasing the appetite of Quebec nationalists for power. By the time Mulroney learned it, the Bloc Québécois had been formed by unsatiated renegades from his own caucus. Meanwhile, if westerners had been irritated by the clout of French-speaking ministers under Trudeau, they were shocked by the presence of Parti Québécois sympathizers in the Conservative government. And if they had been embittered by the Official Languages Act, they were enraged by the Meech Lake and Charlottetown accords.

Don Mazankowski, Joe Clark, Harvie Andre, Jake Epp, Pat Carney, and several other westerners became important cabinet ministers; but so did Marcel Masse, Benoît Bouchard, Roch LaSalle, and (after moving from the back rooms to the front bench) Lucien Bouchard. The West got the deputy prime minister, the governor general, the head of the Federal-Provincial Relations Office, the dismantlement of the National Energy Program, and the Western Diversification Initiative; but Quebec got the clerk of the Privy Council Office, the chief of staff in the Prime Minister's Office, the distinct-society clause, the CF-18 aircraft maintenance contract, and an expensive new prison in Mulroney's riding. Even free trade and the retrenchment of Ottawa were seen more as sops to Quebec than victories for Western Canada.

"If these western ministers really had influence," asked one Albertan, "why didn't Senate reform move to the top of the government's constitutional agenda? Why wasn't the government rethinking the objectionable aspects of the Liberal approach to language and cultural policy? Why were western MPs from Conservative ridings unable to exert more effective pressure to curtail public spending?" The problem, he suggested, was that the "western ministers used their 'influence' primarily to represent unacceptable Ottawa positions to their western constituents, rather than to represent legitimate western concerns and aspirations to Ottawa."

Presto!

That Albertan was a slight, middle-aged man with a squeaky voice and righteous demeanour named Preston Manning. A son of Ernest Manning, the popular radio evangelist who ruled as the Social Credit premier of Alberta from 1943 to 1968, he had been born just a year before his father's victory and had grown up in the back rooms of party politics. He wrote influential policy papers for the Alberta government while barely out of university (where he studied physics and economics); he ran as the Social Credit candidate in Edmonton East in the 1965 federal election; and he was seriously considered as a possible successor to his father at the age of twenty-six. So he had "already had a long whack at the provincial thing," as he put it, "and it didn't seem to advance the interests of the West."

Instead, he decided, westerners had to achieve effective representation at the locus of national power in Ottawa. That meant certain institutional changes such as an elected upper house, similar to the American Senate, made up of an equal number of members from each of the ten provinces. More importantly it meant, as Preston Manning told a Vancouver conference on Canada's economic and political future in May 1987, that "the West needs a party which makes western concerns and western aspirations its number-one priority." For twenty years, in fact, he had been studying the possibilities of forming a new political vehicle that would, as he and his father had written in 1967, "harness the energies of a free enterprise-private economic sector to the task of attaining many of the social goals which humanitarian socialists have long advocated."

The structural problem remained, of course, that the four western provinces only had eighty-six seats in total, less than a third of the House of Commons and thirteen fewer than Ontario alone. But Manning had a two-step solution. In the immediate term, he argued, "a new party that captured thirty to forty seats across the West would have a better than fifty-fifty chance of holding the balance of power," like the NDP had done to its great advantage between 1972 and 1974.

In the long term, the new party could "draw support from across the political spectrum, using the strength of its positions on constitutional and parliamentary reform" in order to capture the government of Canada.

"Preston seldom lies, he's remarkably candid, but he has a way of stating his true intentions that makes people hear something else," observed Tom Flanagan, a mild-mannered, American-born political scientist at the University of Calgary who would serve as Manning's research director, then policy adviser from 1991 to 1993. "So, while it's on the record that he wanted a non-ideological national party, I'm sure that most of the people in that hall in Vancouver heard a manifesto for a conservative western party. That's what the Reform party became in its first incarnation – and may always be – but that's not what Preston said and it's not what he was aiming at."

Six months later, on October 30, 1987, while Mulroney was still beaming with pride at having got the ten premiers to sign the Meech Lake Accord in June, many of the three hundred people at the Vancouver meeting regathered in Winnipeg and created the Reform Party of Canada under the banner "The West Wants In." They also elected Preston Manning as their first leader, even though he was no ad agency's dream candidate and had never held public office. He even turned those liabilities into assets. Despite his lifelong involvement with the political class, he sprang as though from nowhere as a plain man of the people, a humble vessel of God's work, Mr. Smith Goes to Ottawa.

In politics as in comedy, timing is crucial, and both the Reform party and Manning's style could not have been better timed. Not only were disgruntled westerners yearning for a political alternative, but Canadians in general were becoming increasingly contemptuous of the political class because of its economic mismanagement and all the scandals in Ottawa. Manning did not just react to their contempt: he helped incite it. He liked to entertain his rallies with descriptions of the disease he called Ottawa Fever. "First of all," he said with his high-pitched drawl, "the hearing starts to go. You have trouble hearing. Then the memory starts to go. You forget things you said two months before. Then the tongue gets very loose. There's a lot of talking. And sometimes the head swells to abnormal proportions."

Reform, apparently, had inoculated itself against this fever by its populist organization and grassroots agenda. It did not even like to consider itself a party. It was more like a crusade, in the tradition of the protest movements and evangelical sects that had swept up from the United States and across Western Canada at the turn of the century. Its platform was said to come up from the members, not down from the executives. The will of the people was supposed to prevail through the loosening of party discipline in the House of Commons and the introduction of citizen-initiated referenda.

Exactly as Preston Manning had hoped and helped, the wave of popular dissatisfaction washed Reform of its western identity. People in other regions, particularly in the suburbs and hinterlands of English Canada, began to respond to select aspects of its agenda – some to its tough stand against deficits and the GST, some to its hard line toward Quebec and immigration, some to its derisive critique of Parliament and politicians. By October 1990, Manning was able to carry his message into the very heart of the beast, Ontario, and be greeted by one thousand cheering supporters at the Opera House in Orillia. A few months later, in April 1991, the Reform party voted to become a national party and seek votes in every province except Quebec. At the same time and for the same reason, as Manning admitted afterwards, it voted "to move away from positions that could be interpreted as extreme or parochial."

"Easterners hold a stereotype of the West as a region with a chip on its shoulder and a massive inferiority complex," said Rick Anderson, the boyish-looking Ottawa lobbyist who leapt from the back rooms of the Liberal party to the inner councils of Reform. "But I see the 'big' West playing itself out in the party, with a great big heart and a great big set of ideas about how to make Canada work better. And a lot of the thinking coming out of the Reform party, as well as from western academics and western journalists, has found common cause with the concerns of people elsewhere."

Anderson, who had done everything from distributing flyers in the 1974 federal election as an eighteen-year-old university student to managing Donald Johnston's campaign for the Liberal leadership ten years later, had been alienated by the centralization of power in the PMO under Pierre Trudeau and what he saw as the lack of important policy discussion under John Turner and Jean Chrétien. In the fall of 1990, after watching Manning endure an aggressive four-hour grilling at an Ottawa dinner, Anderson warmed to him as a genuine agent of change. A friendly correspondence followed, and Manning was soon telling his staff that Rick Anderson was precisely the kind of person Reform had to accommodate if it was ever to win Ontario.

"When expansion came," Sydney Sharpe and Don Braid observed in *Storming Babylon*, their account of Reform's rise, "Manning's rhetoric about regionalism and western power ceased (actually he had shrewdly toned it down several months before the final decision was made). He no longer talks about Ontario's domination of the country. Manning began to focus far more on his 'national' issues: New Canada versus Old Canada, Quebec, and fiscal responsibility. He started to fight more strenuously against charges of racism that might hurt him in big urban areas like Toronto."

Before too long, in fact, Manning seemed as concerned about doing well in Ontario as every other party leader except Lucien Bouchard. He regularly campaigned throughout the province. He methodically courted the Toronto-based media. He deliberately played up the concerns of suburbanites, like those in Mississauga West, about the dramatic increase in crime, immigration, and taxes. He fervently prayed that at least a few of the four-way races would split in Reform's favour, as he often explained, "so we can't be just dismissed as some regional rump party."

He was helped, too, by the backlash that developed in English Canada during 1992 against any special status for Quebec. At first he resisted exploiting the issue, partly because he felt that the people were sick and tired of hearing about the Constitution after the failure of the Meech Lake Accord, partly because he was sensitive about Reform's image as a haven for anti-French bigots. Indeed, while Rick Anderson was pushing him to support the Charlottetown Accord, Manning's own instinct was to stay out of the debate altogether. But after conducting a series of town meetings and opening up the phone lines, he became persuaded that his membership wanted him to speak up – with a loud "No."

"In some ways Preston is a very conventional politician, in his emphasis on communications and timing, in his willingness to use calculated ambiguity," Tom Flanagan said. "But what's unique about him, what constitutes his political genius, is that he listens to people whom most politicians ignore. We used to joke that he was always off in some town called River – Peace River, High River, Dog River – paying close attention to the people who disagreed with the various dogmas around which the three main parties had converged. There was a political opening there, and though he's a cautious man, he had the daring to articulate their views. Unlike most politicians, he was willing to risk speaking the unspeakable. That may be his undoing some day, but you don't break into the system unless you're willing to take risks."

The Do-It-Yourself Campaign

In June 1991, Charles Conn was taken along to a Reform meeting in the Toronto suburb of Markham. Impressed to find a party that had the guts to put his kind of principles and policies in writing, he joined up in his own riding of Mississauga West a few months later and was immediately put on a committee that met every other week around a dining-room table to discuss policy resolutions for the party's 1992 national assembly. By the following April he was encouraged to seek the nomination as the Reform candidate in the federal election, a rigorous procedure in which he and the other two contenders had to survive an interview with the riding association, debate each other three times in front of the membership, and reveal themselves in a forty-two-page questionnaire.

"I believe in the worth of the individual," was the first of Conn's ten-point reply to the question about what values he held most dear, "and that the well-being of a community is the sum of the well-being felt by each of its individual members." He also believed that the only race is the human race, that free will is greater than a person's genetic or environmental inheritance, that there is satisfaction in work itself, that life itself depends on the bonding of a man and a woman, that love is positive and hate is negative, and that God is within each of us. Finally, for good measure, he threw in honesty, integrity, hard work, thrift, respect, deference, knowledge of history, actions based on principles, creativity, and boundless enthusiasm about the potential future of this great land and the world.

With all that going for him, Conn easily won the three-way contest on September 26, 1992, then set about to learn how to run a campaign based on little more than a handful of inexperienced volunteers and a sense of divine mission. He attended a series of candidate courses. He solicited money from his Christmas card list and a few wealthy constituents. He organized weekly town halls at which he honed his public speaking in front of an average of fourteen people. He got thick manuals with step-by-step instructions and administrative charts –

arranged in circles, not tiers, of authority – from party headquarters in Calgary.

For the most part, however, party headquarters was as limited in its expertise and resources as he was. Only two of Reform's 194 candidates held elected office – or, as Conn expressed it, "Only two are at the public trough, all the rest of us are making things work in the real world" – and only a few of its staff had ever been active in a national campaign at any level in any party. The manuals and courses were composed of bits and pieces borrowed from how-to books, political science texts, the history of protest movements, someone's memory of how things used to be done by the Tories or Social Credit, reports of an interesting NDP technique or a useful Republican device, the members' own instincts, and Preston Manning's personal knowledge of the ways of the political class.

"They studied campaigning like they studied fiscal, social, and defence policy," said Rick Anderson, who became actively involved with Reform in the summer of 1991 when Manning invited him to meet the party brass in Calgary and share his professional ideas about how they should prepare for the election. Following the party's decision to expand beyond the West, Manning assumed that Reform would wage a standard campaign – the leader's tour, the tracking polls, the media advertising, the targeted mailings – much like every other national party. Even Anderson's most innovative ideas, from town hall meetings to denim shirts, were just the latest trends among the political class in Washington and Ottawa, little different from what the back-room pros were planning for Kim Campbell and Jean Chrétien. To the greenhorns in Calgary, they were doubly attractive for seeming unheard-of.

Unfortunately for its plans, Reform found itself without the cash to compete with the traditional parties on their own terms. Its "Save Canada" fund-raising drive, which had been expected to raise $12 million, raised only $2 million, and the party's war chest at the start of the election campaign was estimated around $150,000. (Ultimately Reform spent $1.5 million, including $587,000 on advertising, while the Conservatives spent $10.4 million, two-thirds of it on advertising, and the Liberals spent $9.9 million.) "So the question became," said Anderson, "how do we do a grassroots campaign and an issues-oriented campaign more successfully than they have ever been done before?"

It was a question, as it turned out, that suited both Manning and his party very well. "Preston used to say that we had to master modern technology, polling, advertising, and all that stuff," said Tom Flanagan, "but he was always ambivalent about using them. And his instinct was sound, if not in the abstract for everyone, at least for Reform under his leadership. He had his own ways of sensing what the people wanted, which probably would have conflicted with the polling data. He would have felt he had to control a big advertising program, which probably would have led to some big errors. And if you're going to do all that, you have to build a strong organization of experts, consultants, strategists, and pollsters and let them do their work. If Reform had had $10 million, the mistakes would have been suicidal and it would have conflicted with Reform's basis as a leader-focused, populist party. So Reform stumbled into running the only kind of campaign that could have worked for it."

By luck and necessity, the party discovered that spending a lot of money on sophisticated TV ads was not as important as having an eager army of volunteers and a platform that spoke to the concerns of enough people. It also chanced upon the effectiveness of its wordy broadsheets, produced on crude newsprint with few pictures and minimal design. "That was largely for budget reasons," Anderson admitted, "but it also emphasized our message that the content is more important than the look. And the grassroots kept pushing us in that direction: this is what our neighbours want, give us more. We eventually distributed seventeen *million* pieces of literature during the campaign."

"It's not the glossy candy fluff that the others are handing out," Charles Conn boasted. "It's real, it's important." So, without Horner's money or Parrish's machine to conduct a door-to-door campaign based on computer lists, polling data, hired managers, and expensive signs, he resorted to broadcasting Reform's "Blue Sheet" of policies throughout Mississauga West and riding the national campaign of the national leader on the national media.

Unlike Kim Campbell, Preston Manning had had plenty of rehearsal with the town hall format and knew how to orchestrate it. Nor was he handicapped by the excessive expectations of the public and the intense scrutiny of the press. It was his further good fortune, indeed, that the media had neither the money nor the interest in covering him for the first couple of weeks. While Campbell staked her early claim to the deficit issue, Manning was engaged in a disconcertingly empty exercise of letting the people "say first what they consider important rather than having the politicians tell them what this election is about" — as though the Blue Sheet had not already gone to the printers. It looked exactly like the public-relations gimmick it was. Worse, in the eyes of many conservative Reformers, it looked as though Manning was hesitating to articulate the party's right-wing agenda in case it jeopardized his hopes for electoral success.

"Reform did as well as it did by playing to the right," Flanagan said afterwards, "but I don't think that was Preston's original intention. There were all kinds of signs in the pre-election planning that he was going to stay away from the right. But whenever he feels under pressure, he goes back to basics — basics being the sort of hard-right ideology of most Reform members."

Manning later denied any such coyness. But, with his party stuck around 10 per cent in the polls, his instincts could not have been better when he charged more boldly toward the right on September 20. Just as the Tories were beginning to surrender under siege from the Liberals and the media, Manning fanfared Reform's proposal to eliminate the deficit within three years, specifically by cutting $5 billion from unemployment insurance, $3.5 billion from old-age pensions, $5 billion from government operations, $4 billion from subsidies to business and special-interest groups, and $1.5 billion from transfer payments to the provinces (primarily in the areas of health and education). By the end of the third week of the campaign, as a result, though Campbell and Chrétien still enjoyed twice as much support as Manning in terms of personal popularity, he had been the only one to make significant gains in the polls — all at the expense of Kim Campbell.

"Reform is the one party to date to trust Canadians with the truth," the editorialists at the *Globe and Mail* soon declared. "Indeed, if there is one candidate in this election who is truly offering 'hope,' that much-advertised elixir, it is Mr. Manning: hope that the economy might one day break out of the death spiral of high debt and higher taxes, as much as the hope that Canadian politics might climb out of the slough of cynicism and deception."

Charles Conn could certainly feel a shift in Mississauga West. "I think 80 per cent are still undecided," he said, "and if the Liberals and Conservatives continue to throw shit and derision at each other, people are going to look for an alternative. Anyone who pretends to call the outcome of this election at this stage is smoking something strange."

New Shoes, Old Politics

Wednesday evening, October 6, 1993. Week five. By now the Tories were down more than a dozen points and Bob Horner had dropped about twenty-five pounds. But that only seemed to add some spring to his step as he set out to conquer Poll 238, a typical suburban neighbourhood of brick bungalows and some fancier split-levels, most with a two-car garage and a basketball hoop, where dads raked the leaves on Chokeberry Crescent, moms came to the door drying their hands on their aprons, and tots rode their bicycles up and down Hornby Street in the cool autumn twilight. "I'm wearing $640 worth of new orthopaedic shoes," Horner announced, "and I'm really ready to move."

It was not long before he was stopped dead in his tracks. "I'd vote for you if you weren't a Tory," said the occupant of the very first house Horner canvassed. "You're 100 per cent. I liked it when you called Lucien Bouchard a traitor, that was bloody good. But I can't stand Kim Campbell, and you're stuck with her."

Horner wrote him off as a Grit – the guy had a Parrish sign on his lawn, after all – and went on to the second house, the home of a friend and supporter. "The last time you came here, you said you guys were going to cut the deficit," the lifelong Conservative said. "So what's the story this time, Bob?"

Horner laughed, knowing the fellow was good for a vote and a sign location anyway, but he could not hide the wounded look in his eyes and the pitiful tone in his voice. Unlike a true politician, Dr. Bob had never developed a thick hide, nor had he ever got over his shyness about going up to strangers and begging for their help. Rather than risk rejection, he preferred to ask if they would *consider* supporting him. Given that he had won about half the vote in the last election, the likelihood was that every other person would say no. The reality was turning out to be closer to three out of four. Horner was visibly relieved to come to the third house. One of his sons lived there, and the beleaguered candidate could look forward to tackling nothing worse than a hug from his grandson.

Judging from what Bob Horner was hearing at the doors, a good many people in Mississauga West had watched the leaders' English-language debate on television two nights earlier, and most of them had been put off by Campbell's performance. They particularly resented her refusal to answer Bouchard's direct question about the final figure for the 1992-93 deficit. "What is the real deficit?" he asked her. "Normally we know it in August or September. We are in October and we still don't know it. You have an obligation to tell the public."

It was an important question. If the actual number was much greater than the last budget estimate – and everyone assumed it was at least $5 billion greater – then the Tories' deficit reduction plan was already off the rails and deeper cuts would be coming down the line. But Campbell, who later claimed to have known neither the number nor the fact that the reporting date had been shifted to November, tried to cover her ignorance with some diversionary blather. Bouchard persisted, throwing one punch after another, until he landed a knockout blow. "You are hiding the truth, madam!" he shouted. "You are hiding this figure!"

Though Horner had received a few messages the next morning from irate voters demanding the answer, he didn't think that the debate had changed anyone's mind. The first reaction of most TV pundits and headline writers, too, was that there had been no "defining moment" like there had been between Brian Mulroney and John Turner in the 1984 and 1988 debates. Perhaps because the key exchange had been with Bouchard, not Chrétien, or thanks to the emergency "spin-doctoring" Campbell and her team had done in the press room immediately afterwards, the media were slow to pick up how much further damage Campbell's credibility had just suffered in the living rooms of the nation. Jeff Knoll, however, had immediately turned to his wife and said, "We've just lost the election."

"Why wouldn't she tell us the number?" Horner was now being asked by a woman who became so absorbed with grilling him in her front hall about military helicopters, capital punishment, and abortion that she ignored the onions burning on the stove and the children screeching in the bath. "We should have known it in August."

"Where'd you read that?" Horner countered.

"The *Star*."

"There you are!" he replied with a triumphant twinkle. It was her own fault, he seemed to imply, if she believed anything she read in that Liberal rag.

People in the News

In truth, whatever the origins and orientations of Canada's major media, the day of the truly partisan press had long passed. The *Toronto Star*'s Ottawa columnist, Carol Goar, had even led a front-page account of Monday's debate by declaring that "Prime Minister Kim Campbell showed poise under fire," while dismissing some of Jean Chrétien's arguments as "simplistic and unconvincing." And hadn't it been a supposedly Conservative rag, the *Globe and Mail*, that first raised the devastating news of a secret Tory plan to slash Canada's social programs?

Bob Horner's jibe was rooted less in the sins of the *Star* than in the frustration all politicians feel about their inability to control the media. A free press is considered more sacrosanct than a free market, after all, and its power to raise up celebrities and issues – for no better reason, it often seems, than to pull them down – has become the most effective check to the abuse of public office. The *Star*, for example, had just launched a series of investigative stories about the Mulroney government's deal to privatize the terminals at Toronto's Pearson International Airport. Not only did it put Bob Horner on the defensive in Mississauga West, where many people had a professional or parochial interest in the nearby airport, but it triggered a hot debate across the country, pitting the economic benefits of privatization against the Tory record of patronage and corruption.

"Our real power is our ability to set an agenda," said the *Star*'s John Honderich. "If we decide that we want to make an issue, then we'll go ahead and do it. And because we're the biggest daily in Toronto, the TV and radio outlets in this city get on to what we're doing and make it part of the national agenda. The Pearson story was important, I think, because it was the issue that brought Brian Mulroney back into the campaign. It was a metaphor for the kind of sleazy dealings that people didn't like about him, and Campbell put her imprimatur on it by pushing it through."

However much the parliamentary gallery may pride itself on being a kind of disloyal opposition, made up of free-thinking outsiders ever ready to battle arbitrary measures on behalf of the people, it remains as integral a part of the political class as the Loyal Opposition. They are players, not spectators, and they generally abide by the conventional rules of a game that has given them such remarkable clout. Nor are they, despite their pretensions, any more representative of the Canadian people than the politicians and bureaucrats in Ottawa.

There was a time when the press, along with the rest of the political class, spoke more authentically for the grassroots. As journalism gained in influence and prestige, however, it attracted people with better education, paid them higher salaries, elevated them into more rarefied circles, and isolated them from the daily realities confronting the majority of Canadians. The lives of the powerless became economic abstractions and social trends, often based upon the same polling data and focus-group surveys the politicians were relying upon to know the public's mind. And the resulting conservatism was then compounded by a period of hiring freezes, layoffs, and buyouts in the communications industry.

"Eighty-eight per cent of our newsroom is between the ages of thirty and fifty-five," Honderich noted. "That means you don't get the verve and energy you need from the younger generation. You get a lot of complacent, middle-class people with two-income families and big mortgages."

Many reporters, indeed, slipped comfortably into supporting the political class's agenda during the free-trade election in 1988, the Meech Lake debate in 1990, and the constitutional negotiations in 1992. "I supported the Charlottetown Accord fervently," Susan Delacourt, one of the *Globe*'s Ottawa correspondents, later confessed in her book *United We Fall* (which she dedicated to "the Honourable Men and Women of Politics"), "and during the referendum I had a very hard time listening to the views of No campaigners."

"We were unprepared for the ferocity of the referendum and the viciousness with which most people lumped the media in with the elites' management of the issue," said Elly Alboim, former chief of CBC-TV's parliamentary bureau, now an Ottawa lobbyist. "And it coincided with the tremendous competitive pressures we were all experiencing, the financial squeeze, the alienation of our viewers and readers. I think, therefore, that the media saw the popular revulsion with normal elite accommodation as an opportunity to reconnect by 'empowering people' and 'letting the people speak.' It was less a democratic impulse than a commercial repositioning."

Bill Thorsell, the *Globe*'s editor, did not believe that the public had been terribly angry with the media – "Where were the data that this public attitude toward the so-called elites had now consumed everybody in a fire of resentment?" he asked – or that his newspaper had redesigned its editorial product in an attempt to buy back advertisers and readers. But he did admit that cash, not principle, had been the inspiration behind some new features of the 1993 campaign. "The best way to report public opinion is to have a really good polling program," he said. "But most of us did not have a lot of money during this election for that, so we supplemented what polling we did have with panels of readers, for example."

Whatever the cause, the result was an outbreak of journalistic experiments similar to the town halls and 1-800 tactics the political parties were trying. CBC's "Prime Time News" televised several forums in which "the people" were allowed to confront contending politicians about the major issues. CTV's "Canada A.M." introduced a weekly phone-in item. The *Globe and Mail* began a series called "Vox Populi" in which voters in several cities were asked for their opinions. The *Toronto Sun* assembled an eleven-member "People's Panel" to comment on the campaign and predict its result. The *Star* expanded its space for letters, ran a "Voices of the Voters" feature, and invited everyone to call the StarPhone poll and vote on the most important issue.

"It wasn't as if we all sat down and agreed to do town halls," John Honderich said. "There was just a lot of soul-searching after Charlottetown. We had missed part of the story, we hadn't been sufficiently informed, and we bloody well had to take steps to be better informed. One could see a pattern where the media had aligned themselves with the power elites, and by so doing, we hadn't given the disenfranchised enough space."

Though the fad did not catch on in the French-language media, except with the ever-popular open-line shows, it wasn't confined to Toronto. From St. John's to Victoria, in fact, it was hard not to open a newspaper, turn on a radio, or switch to the TV news without being exposed to the latest thoughts of the man or woman on the street. Or *off* the street: the *Globe* devoted most of a page one Saturday to the views of eight inmates at the Mimico Correctional Complex.

"That broad, what's her name," Steve Szabo (two years, possession of narcotics and trafficking) said of Kim Campbell, "she's full of shit." Leslie Bruce Brown (ten months, dangerous driving and simple assault) expressed the hope that "Chrétien dies and Trudeau comes back," though he had a poor impression of all politicians – "picky, snobbish, and they don't bring you out ice-cold drinks" – based on some personal experiences as a house roofer. "Prisoners are very undecided, skeptical," mused Mike Burnside (fifteen months, fraud). "Maybe because they are from the criminal element, their distrust is a little more finely tuned than the average citizen." But Bryan Burke (eight months, breaking and entering) conceded more generously that politicians are just "people" like him. "They do their jobs," he said. "Ya gotta fib. That's what I tell my kids: 'Don't tell lies, tell a fib.'"

The very randomness of the process suggested the obvious question: Did these people speak for anybody but themselves? Polling, for all its flaws, earns its authority by sampling hundreds or even thousands of people in order to get a representative snapshot of the public's views. Its raw numbers are then analysed in light of historic patterns and the socio-economic variables. Without that sort of methodology or interpretation, the haphazard musings of convicts and truckers were more a public-relations gimmick than an exercise in responsible journalism. "It was a well-motivated effort," Thorsell himself conceded, "but it wasn't very successful because of all its statistical limitations."

There was a subtler and more serious problem. Having missed much of the popular anger and cynicism during the 1992 referendum and been late in recognizing the potential strength of the Reform party, the press went searching for the angry and the cynical during the election. When it found them, it usually indulged them. "The People's Panel is made up of ordinary readers who reflect this region's ethnic, racial, and economic makeup," the *Toronto Sun* announced. "Panel members are young, old, rich, and poor. The one thing that they have in common is frustration with the political system."

That also happened to be the case with the fifty undecideds, "picked with the help of a professional research company," whom "Prime Time News" gathered to attack Jean Charest (PC), Paul Martin (Liberal), Dave Barrett (NDP), Preston Manning (Reform), and Gilles Duceppe (BQ) during a televised "town hall" about jobs. The five politicians talked for an hour about community-venture capital funds, free trade with Mexico, value-added jobs, and taxes. They answered questions about the deficit, the GST, the power of multinational corporations, apprenticeship programs, and job retraining. But "the people" remained stubbornly unimpressed.

"It was badly done, and I blame the CBC," Jean Charest said afterwards. "The mind-set, whether deliberate or unconscious, was more entertainment than information, and it was not presented in a constructive way. And if those people weren't encouraged to do it constructively, they only saw that they had a thirty-second opportunity to take a run at us. So we were very, very vulnerable, because the viewers just remembered the image, not the substance of what we said."

But substance wasn't the purpose. The purpose was to boost the show's ratings by catering to the kind of titillation that once drew vast crowds to bear-baiting and public hangings. "Everything that's been said here was said in the 1930s," one woman complained. "We need some new ideas." The owner of a trucking outfit felt "an increasing level of frustration" with the whole exercise. An airline employee thought the politicians' answers were "removed from the everyday reality of a person not working." A businessman wanted more guidance about where he should invest his money. An agricultural worker wanted better solutions for the problems of agriculture. A medical trainee wanted action against provincial trade barriers. "I'm afraid it was just a lot of rhetoric," another man sighed.

"Was there *no one* in this whole hall who liked *anything* they heard tonight from *any* of the candidates?" Peter Mansbridge, the host, finally asked.

Evidently not. Yet neither Mansbridge nor any of the panellists threw any further questions back at the undecideds. What exactly did they expect from their politicians? More jobs, lower deficits, fewer taxes, and better services, no doubt, but how precisely did they propose getting them? If all five parties, ranging from Reform to the NDP, seemed to lack new ideas and credible solutions, why was that? And if none of them would do, what about all the other options available: the Green party or the National party, the Marxist-Leninists or the Libertarians, the Christian Heritage party or the Natural Law party, which was promising to end unemployment within a year, eradicate the deficit within three years, get rid of the GST immediately, create "a Perfect Government that Will Prevent All Problems and Satisfy Everyone," and launch seven thousand transcendental meditators into yogic flight above Ottawa?

"I've never before seen anyone get such absolute, unbridled access to our television screen," Elly Alboim said. "I mean, if you don't give it to expert opinion, why the hell would you give it to uninformed opinion? There was an unwillingness to mediate the debate between the politicians and the people. There was an unwillingness to pit the opposing opinions of the 'ordinaries' against each other."

That unwillingness stemmed less from an awed respect for the *vox populi* than from a condescending assumption on the part of the political class: The common people cannot stand up to the harrowing inquisition that politicians and every other public figure must bear from professional journalism. It stemmed, too, from cowardice. Politicians and reporters seldom challenge the public to think more clearly and act more responsibly in case they meet Kim Campbell's fate and get branded as arrogant elitists.

Rarely, as a result, did the political class find any defenders, while the airwaves and tabloids were full of grassroots spleen. "Hope, fear leave voters stressed out." "Politicians find voters in a grim mood." "Canadians are alienated, but the politicians 'just don't get it.'" It was certainly a fresh and interesting angle, which nicely suited both the media's commercial strategy and adversarial mentality. Less certain was whether it was accurate. A COMPAS poll, for instance, found voters feeling more frustrated (31 per cent) and worried (28 per cent) than angry (a mere 5 per cent), and that very much matched what Bob Horner was finding on his rounds.

"Furthermore," Alboim observed, "as the campaign goes on and you continue to hunt out the undecideds, who become increasingly a smaller and smaller fraction of the electorate, you end up with an unbalanced view of how most people are regarding the election. I don't think the media understood the structural and political implications of allowing this egregious hostility to wash day after day after day. It's not as if they were deconstructing in order to reconstruct. They were simply allowing this sort of anarchical or nihilist tendencies in people to express itself."

That was strange, one might suppose, given the media's own identification with the political class. But when the pack is possessed by the exigencies of competitive journalism, the dogs rarely pause to consider if they are running toward a cliff. Nor do most journalists like to be reminded, contrary to their romantic and often naive self-image as crusading renegades, that they have either the power or the duty to defend the virtues of parliamentary democracy – the very virtues for which Russians were risking their lives on the streets of Moscow while Bob Horner was seeking votes on Chokeberry Crescent.

In responding to the charges of irresponsibility, moreover, many editors and reporters simply dismissed all the soapbox nihilism as irrelevant bits of human colour and an unsuccessful experiment. "We went overboard," John Honderich admitted. "Instead of writing riding profiles in terms of the candidates and the issues, we used the voice of a voter. I wouldn't do that again. Everybody had the same complaints about jobs and the GST, and all the whining didn't add anything. I got tired of it."

Playing the Horses

"No election passes without a lecture that the voting public would be better served if we were to spend more time analysing the issues instead of calculating the point-spread," wrote the Montreal *Gazette*'s political reporter Hubert Bauch in defence of his colleagues in the press. "This is a noble concept, and in a better world, it would sell a lot of papers. But on planet Earth, the first thing any member of the voting public will unfailingly ask a political reporter during an election campaign is: So who's gonna win?"

Certainly the press gallery had been widely criticized – often from within their own ranks – for not providing Canadians with enough objective information or detailed analysis about the Free Trade Agreement, the Meech Lake Accord, and the Charlottetown deal, as well as for putting the personalities, tactics, melodramas, and gotchas of the Tory leadership race ahead of the policies and problems facing the country. So, for the same reasons that the parties felt pressured to produce their Red books and Blue books, the media started producing full-page synopses of the different platforms, television specials about the economic situation, "reality checks" on the facts behind the rhetoric, and a plethora of "media watch" items to evaluate their own performance before the public.

In the first few weeks of the campaign, the 1993 election carried refrains from the free-trade election of 1988, in which policy differences became translated into ideological disputes about the role of the state in Canada and the fundamental values of the Canadian people. Even Kim Campbell's current gaffes – unlike the ones upon which the press had pounced during the leadership campaign for evidence of her true personality – were connected to substantive questions about job creation, deficit reduction, and the fate of the social safety net. The mere presence of Reform and the Bloc Québécois as influential players also meant that neither the brokerage politicians nor the gutter press could as easily obfuscate the great conflicts about government activism and national unity seething beneath the traditional consensus of the Canadian political class.

"These people are very informed, very tuned in," Bob Horner noted as he darted from house to house before the sun set and his constituents became nervous about opening their doors to a stranger. "A few years ago they wouldn't even have known that an election was happening."

But it was equally apparent that they were better informed about the problems than the solutions. Most remained convinced that balancing the nation's books was simply a matter of trimming bureaucratic waste, for example, and even those who understood the dimensions of the issue did not have much practical advice about how to solve it. One man suggested inheritance taxes. Another suggested selling British Columbia to the Chinese. "I don't know what to do about it," a woman confessed. "All I know is, whoever I vote for, big business will still make all the decisions."

Most Canadians had only started to pay attention to the election with the TV debates, and so had missed the vigorous policy arguments that occurred in the first half of the campaign. By the midway mark, the parties had published their platforms; the leaders had honed their speeches; the editorialists had exhausted their arguments. There seemed nothing more for the political class to say about jobs, deficits, or social programs that had not already been said at least once a day for a month. Now, indeed, the standard rule was to keep repeating the safest ideas and surest lines until E-day. So the leaders' debates had more to do with image than information – which the fact of their being seen on television only reinforced, of course – while the local candidates did not have any time to deal with all the questions and concerns that the debates had left unanswered. ("Avoid long-winded talkers, arguments, or philosophical discussions," Carolyn Parrish's canvassers were instructed. "Win votes, not arguments!")

"My impression," concluded Bill Thorsell, "is that the media has got better, on balance, in laying out the issues, providing the background, checking out the truth of things. The question is when – and whether – people sit down and absorb it. You have to time your explanatory work and expostulatory background to when people say they're interested and need the information."

No sooner were the debates over, however, than the media's attention clearly shifted from policies to politics. Would the Liberals get a majority? Would Reform slip past the Tories? Would the Bloc Québécois displace the New Democrats? Analysing the polls replaced analysing the platforms, with some bizarre effects. Liberals considered voting NDP to counteract the right-wing pressure from the Reform party in the House of Commons. Reformers considered voting Liberal to prevent the Bloc Québécois from holding the balance of power. Conservatives considered voting Reform to keep the Liberals from winning a majority. The *Globe and Mail* studied the trends and urged "voters who share our concerns at the Liberals being given a 'blank cheque' to vote tactically, Tory or Reform, depending on which party's candidate is best placed to defeat a Liberal."

Oddly enough, given the power it invested in the polls, the *Globe* continued to crusade against the recent electoral law banning the distribution of new opinion surveys in the last two days of the campaign. "For sheer goofiness," its editors fulminated, "there has never been anything to match this breathtaking assault on the public's right to know in all the long history of harebrained paternalist schemes their 'betters' have concocted." Yet what else would prevent the media from reporting, by design or error, a set of false results – not an uncommon weapon in the arsenal of back-room manipulators – which could subsequently sway a lot of votes before anyone had the occasion to refute them?

As if to destroy its own argument, the *Globe* itself published a front-page story on October 8, based on reports from Liberal party sources, boldly declaring that the newest Angus Reid poll put the Reform party in second place, for the first time, ahead of the Tories. The story created a palpable sense of momentum among Reformers, and an equally palpable sense of despair among the Tories, until it was revealed to be a mistake. "We regret the inconvenience," Bill Thorsell announced to his readers the next day. The *inconvenience*!

It certainly would have been inconvenient if the mistake had been made when it was too late for a correction and the newspaper's loyal subscribers were already heading off to the ballot stations with the editors' "vote tactically" ringing in their ears. In fact, the *Globe*'s election-day headline, building upon a week-old CROP poll in *La Presse*, was "Chrétien faces loss of own seat." Not only did the poll prove totally wrong, it might well have been deliberately skewed (as some senior Liberals charged) in order to discourage Quebec voters from leaping on to his bandwagon. Instead, it only aroused the Liberals of Saint-Maurice to work even harder for their leader's victory and, by the by, proved the *Globe*'s argument against banning polls the sheerest goofiness.

As Bob Horner headed into the last stretch of the media's horse race, meanwhile, he knew he could no longer place any hopes in the popularity of Kim Campbell or her little Blue Book. Yet the bounce in his step was not entirely due to his brand-new shoes and his weight loss. "When this election started," he now confided, "I wouldn't have given a plugged nickel for my chances of re-election. But things have changed."

According to the unscientific survey Jeff Knoll was conducting each day by telephone, the Tory slide appeared to be levelling off in Mississauga West, while Reform was growing so quickly – almost doubling its Ontario support to 20 per cent since the start of the election – that it had begun to take votes from the Liberals too. If that trend continued, Horner would be in a close three-way race. And since his computers were showing more than a third of the voters as firmly committed Tories, he saw a chance to squeak back into Parliament. "So I'm going to leave Reform alone," he said, "and focus my attack on the Liberals."

Hail Mary Time

Following Preston Manning's satisfactory performance in the television debates and his party's steady climb in the polls, the Conservatives, the Liberals, the NDP, and the media all decided it was time to turn their guns on the Reform party. "They are cruel and they are heartless," Kim Campbell said of Manning's hack-and-slash policies, "and they would destroy the very things that we think define us as a society." Jean Chrétien predicted that Reform's deficit-reduction program would destroy health care, jeopardize old-age pensions, and send unemployment soaring to 25 per cent. "Preston Manning calls himself a non-politician," Audrey McLaughlin told her audiences. "Let's make sure he stays that way."

But it was the media who landed the most damaging blow. On October 13, while the pros of the local and national press were presumably busy ferreting out the opinions of the average voter, York University's student newspaper exposed the Reform candidate in the suburban Toronto riding of York Centre as an out-and-out racist. As a result of the ensuing controversy, Manning forced John Beck to withdraw from the race, but that didn't prevent many of the Liberals – and not a few New Democrats – who had been drawn toward the Reform party as a means of sending a protest message to Ottawa from quickly pulling away.

The disenchanted Tories, however, were still "clinging like barnacles to the side of the Reform barge," as Jeff Knoll put it. So Bob Horner's campaign had to change direction again and attempt to pry them off. To do so, Knoll was counting on all the advantages of money, experience, and organization. Without them, he knew, Charles Conn was reduced to addressing a series of sparsely attended public meetings, erecting a smatter of cheap-looking signs, and casting a stack of unreadable pamphlets as though to the wind. Most Reform supporters, for all their fury and zeal, remained armchair spectators, so far as Knoll could see, and the majority of them probably could not recognize their candidate's name.

"The hard fact is that the tax-and-spend Liberals are about to elect a larger number of MPs than their voting numbers warrant," Horner soon warned in an open letter to the identified Reform supporters on his computer lists. "A vote motivated only by protest for the Reform candidate in Mississauga West will likely help to elect the Liberal candidate. *Together* we could send an MP with a *conservative agenda* to Ottawa. . . . Please, *think twice.*"

As a computer consultant by trade and a semiprofessional political manager, Jeff Knoll had an enduring faith in the classic techniques and advanced technology – not to mention moolah – of the political class. Perhaps because his great-grandfather had been some kind of assistant to Sir John A. Macdonald and his mother used to canvass for Conservative candidates, Knoll had become a PC Youth at the age of thirteen and knocked on doors in the 1979 federal election when he was only fifteen. "I really loved the stuff," he said. "It was like a way of life." He studied poli sci at university, of course, and even married into politics. (His wife is the daughter of Dennis Timbrell, the former Ontario cabinet minister whom George Carlson had once hoped would succeed Tory Premier Bill Davis.)

In 1988 Knoll served as Patrick Boyer's campaign manager in the nearby constituency of Etobicoke-Lakeshore. It was a tight race, made tighter because the Liberal candidate suddenly dropped out in the middle of it, pitting Boyer against an undivided opposition to free trade, and Knoll was able to claim a good deal of credit for the 763 votes by which the Conservative party won the riding. He was unable to do as well for himself, however. He lost as a Tory candidate in the

1990 Ontario election, and then he lost two bids for a seat on the Metropolitan Toronto council. "It was an investment in the future," he shrugged. "My goal is to be premier of Ontario some day."

He seemed, in style, more likely to become one of the "good old boys" who populate the back rooms and the Canadian Senate. Even Bob Rae, the socialist premier, was a smooth-looking lawyer with a wardrobe of blue suits, whereas Jeff Knoll was a rather slovenly young man – just "an average guy," according to his own description – with a languid manner, a beer belly, and the doughy face of someone who watches too much television, eats too much junk food, and needs a good night's sleep. He had, in fact, worked for a couple of years as a full-time organizer for the Ontario Conservatives before striking out on his own as a consultant.

In December 1992, he was hired by Bob Horner. He assembled the campaign team, developed the public-relations strategy, and set up the high-tech canvassing system in which trained volunteers (who had been more accustomed to addressing envelopes and licking stamps) recited a list of questions over the phone, entered Tory supporters into the computers, and targeted the undecideds to receive a letter or call from the candidate about the issues that most concerned them. ("It's like a telemarketing program for each individual voter," Knoll boasted.) He had Horner photographed in "kindly veterinarian" poses for the glossy brochures. He hustled local businessmen for a contribution. He wrung endorsements from the Catholic Women's League, the Canadian Police Association, the Mississauga Fire Fighters Association, and the Don Rowing Club.

"The back room is the perfect place for an organization junkie," he said. "You can see your concepts develop into reality almost immediately, and you have only forty-five days to make them work."

Though an organization junkie, Knoll was not absolutely indifferent to the substance of a campaign. The 1988 election had taught him how a policy debate could have a significant impact, and his phone banks and targeted mail were designed to deal with the issues. Knoll himself believed that the real call of politics remained the desire to do some good. But, in his day-to-day labours, the party platform hardly mattered. "I'll read the Blue Book when I've got time after the election," he joked. His talent – and, one sensed, his pleasure – had more to do with the mere playing of the game.

"I am fascinated by what infects people with the germ of wanting to work in a campaign," said Mary McGowan, Knoll's counterpart over in Carolyn Parrish's camp, a former teacher who had caught the bug during the 1979 election and subsequently become a professional organizer for both the federal and Ontario Liberal parties. "There's nothing intrinsically interesting about the tasks – most of them are no fun at all – but some people just seem to love the whole atmosphere. It gives you an immediate way to get involved. It gives you a great feeling of community. It gives you a huge network of contacts. And I call it the best dating service in the world: I met my husband in the 1980 election!"

"There's a definite kinship among political operators," Knoll agreed. "My best friend, for example, is managing the Liberal campaign in Trinity-Spadina, and I'd support him if he ever runs for office. We share stories and techniques, and we share the fact that there are a lot of circles where we're both pariahs."

Long before Machiavelli, of course, behind-the-scenes advisers have been viewed with contempt and suspicion. They are portrayed, almost by definition, as anonymous, conspiratorial, sly, and wholly without heart or scruples. They serve, at the same time, as useful scapegoats for unpopular but still powerful rulers. And there has been enough evidence, from the counsels of Rasputin to the dirty tricks of the Watergate burglars, to justify the assumption that they would do *anything* to win power. "The campaign managers' job is to win elections, not public esteem," John Laschinger and Geoffrey Stevens stated bluntly in their book on back-room politics in Canada. "They all bend the rules when they consider it expedient to do so. And, in truth, bending the rules, and getting away with it, gives back-room politicians more fun than anything short of actually winning a convention or an election."

In recent decades, too, the more sinister ways of the political class have become entwined with people's suspicions about mass communications and modern technology. Advertising seems a form of subconscious brainwashing. Computer-generated mail seems an Orwellian device for lies and deception. Polling, instead of giving citizens the power of a daily plebiscite, seems a clever manipulation of public opinion. (Which, according to Patrick Kinsella, Campbell's grey eminence, it is. By means of its results, he once bragged, "We can change your mind, we can move you to do something that you may not have agreed on is the logical thing to do.") And everywhere, invisibly, lurks the corrupting influence of money.

A popular backlash resulted, adding to the growing tension between the political class and the people. Political advertising came to be viewed with the same skepticism as any other commercial hyperbole. The personalized letter from the candidate went as quickly into the trash-can as every other piece of junk mail. So many people began refusing to answer the telephone surveys that pollsters worry about the statistical validity of their results. More effective yet, the voter was increasingly likely to promote – or punish – politicians according to the openness and integrity of their politics. The losers were more likely to be those for whom winning meant everything and spending money the way to do it.

"Is this how the old parties seek to bind the nation together, with cords of fear?" asked the *Globe* on October 13, with regard to the concerted attacks on the Reform party. "In the Tories' case, indeed, this is precisely why they have blown this election. The party has not fallen so low because it has not been negative enough. Without a platform, rather, it has not given Canadians a single positive reason to vote for it. Neither have the Grits, of course, but this is the point that eludes Tory strategists: there's only room for one smarmy opportunistic party in Canadian politics today."

The issue exploded like a nuclear device the next day, Thursday, October 14: a few seconds of light and heat, followed by weeks and perhaps years of fallout. It was triggered by the despair into which the Tories' national organizers had been falling with each passing week. In that darkness, Allan Gregg decided it was time to resurrect the ultimate weapon that had succeeded so well for the Tories in 1988, when they suffered a mounting opposition to the Free Trade Agreement after John Turner's vigorous performance in the TV debates. The solution had been to attack Turner's credibility – never very strong in the first place – through a series of negative ads. In Gregg's famous phrase, they simply bombed the bridge. Now, his numbers told him, that again might be their only hope.

"We were so far down by this point, it was 'Hail Mary' time," he said, "and the only way we had any chance was by creating a sense of momentum with a quick, hard hit. If we were able to do only *one* thing, what would give us maximum effect? Suppressing the Liberal vote. And the weakest link in Liberal support was Jean Chrétien, specifically his perceived economic incompetence."

As early as September 30, in fact, Gregg had sent a memo – "RE: THE LOW ROAD" – to the campaign's advertising director, Tom Scott, listing "some concepts we should be exploring with your creative team" in order to nail Chrétien. First and foremost, besides being an out-of-date politician with out-of-date policies, he was "*an embarrass-ment.*" "Would you have him working for you," the memo suggested as the line of attack, "let alone representing you at the G7, the UN, or federal-provincial conferences? He clearly has neither the intellect nor the competence to lead Canada in these trying and complicated times."

Scott subsequently prepared two thirty-second television spots to illustrate that message. Against a series of still photographs that high-lighted Chrétien's facial paralysis and made him look moronic, the voices of "ordinary" Canadians asked, "Is this a prime minister?" and answered, "I personally would be very embarrassed if he were to become the prime minister of Canada."

"They were real photographs, pulled from the middle range of attractiveness," Gregg explained, "and they were used not to make fun of his face, but to put in question his leadership ability and eco-nomic competence. That could obviously be driven home with more salience by a picture of him than by a picture of a wheat field or Parlia-ment Hill. So the pictures were just a communications device, not the object of what we were doing. And when we showed them to focus groups, they changed perceptions among people leaning toward the Liberals and away from the Tories, enough to make a difference."

The ads certainly did make an enormous difference, but not exactly the one Gregg had intended. Liberals, as well as the many Canadians who liked Chrétien in spite of his party affiliation, were disgusted and angry. Even some of the journalists who pursued him for his reaction grew teary when he said of his physical defect, "God gave it to me – when I was a kid, people were laughing at me – but I accepted that because God gave me other qualities and I'm grateful." But the most dramatic reaction came from Conservatives, some of them the very people who had been ridiculing Chrétien's handicap in private. The commercials served as a kind of mirror in which the ugli-ness of their partisanship, the vulgarity of their prejudice, were reflected back to them – and the sight was a great deal more répugnant than Chrétien's paralysis. Indeed, the whole concept of the ads was as much an insult to the intelligence of the Canadian people as it was to the intelligence of Jean Chrétien.

Across Canada, even in Campbell's own riding offices, Conserva-tive voters and volunteers sought to distance themselves from what the back-room organizers had done. ("They bombed the bridge, all right," said one, "but it was full of Tories.") Some wept openly. Some got into screaming matches. Some vowed never, ever, to vote for the Progressive Conservative party again. In Mississauga West, Bob Horner immediately issued an apology to the Liberal leader, while scores of new supporters poured into Carolyn Parrish's campaign offices.

Battle Fatigue

The next evening, in a Quebec City hotel room, Kim Campbell cried, too, but for other reasons. The new firestorm had pushed the Reform party's troubles off the front pages and completed the demolition of her credibility as a new-style politician different from Brian Mulroney. Though she argued that she had not approved the ads – or even known they were in the works – she had to accept responsibility for them, and she implicitly admitted their wrongness by ordering them pulled from the air. "Pulling them," said Allan Gregg, "reinforced the notion that, not only were we completely self-satisfied and self-absorbed, we were sleazy, unethical, and prepared to do absolutely anything to cling to undeserved power."

He had argued, instead, that the Tories could not possibly suffer more by leaving the ads on, and might even gain some yards. But neither he nor the other party pros could withstand the outrage directed against them personally by the media, the public, and many from their own party. The ads provided the excuse that permitted Conservative candidates and workers to vent almost two months of frustration and unhappiness with their national campaign. Gregg, in particular, was savaged for his presumption in turning his job as party pollster into a position of strategic command, then contenting himself with a handful of ambiguous memos that he rarely showed up to explain or develop in person with his colleagues at campaign headquarters. Instead of reining in Gregg's propensity for the grand apocalyptic gesture or forcing him back to the drawing boards, John Tory seemed cowed by him, to the point where he told a couple of dozen senior strategists that they *would not be allowed to leave the room* until they all agreed with Gregg's negative offensive. "It was like being trapped in an EST meeting," one participant recalled. "After a while everyone just gave up. What was the point of arguing?"

Gregg was preoccupied with his wife's gruelling fight against cancer, and at the ripe old age of forty-one he was bone-weary from waging more than forty-five campaigns in fifteen years. Even before the election was called, he later admitted, he had had enough and should not have taken on one battle too many. He was talked into it – not least by his own ego – because there did not seem to have been anyone else who could have done the job. "That created a tiredness," he said, "and because we all had been through so many campaigns and talked the code, we never spent the time teaching Kim Campbell to make sure she understood the game. She may have been insensitive to many things, but stupid she wasn't."

Indeed, she was smart enough to notice that one of the stage sets Gregg and Tory had prepared for a commercial – oak desk, Canadian flag, pretentious bookcase – was all wrong. "That's not me," she barked at them. "That's Brian Mulroney!" But it was too late to do anything about it: the train was well down the track, heading for the wall, with everyone on board.

The professionals had undoubtedly screwed up, in other words, but they had only been allowed to screw up so badly because of Campbell's amateurism. She could not provide them with the real and psychological support that a leader must provide. She could not communicate her goals to them. She could not inspire them to go the extra mile or bully them into singing from the same hymn-book like Mulroney used to do. On the contrary, she regularly undermined their *esprit de corps* with her blundering and insularity. She did not know them well enough. She did not know their needs. Worst of all, she did not know how much she did not know.

"She had a media image and not much more," was David McLaughlin's own conclusion. "When that disintegrated she had nothing else to fall back on." As a result, she lost the support of many who had backed her during the leadership campaign; she lost the confidence of many who had worked for her in the PMO and on the bus; she even lost the enthusiasm of thousands of friends and fans who had been going flat out day and night to get her re-elected in Vancouver Centre. "Not once during the campaign," McLaughlin cited by way of explanation, "did she stop by Campaign Headquarters to boost morale. Indeed, when one such visit was scheduled and headquarters filled with expectant volunteers and workers, particularly youth, it ended up being cancelled at the last minute. Posters that had been put up only hours before in anticipation of the event were literally ripped down."

Despite the enormous obstacles the Tories faced in their bid for a third mandate, they had had the momentum and some good numbers going into the campaign. When those began to collapse, many of the party pros and volunteers just stopped giving their best. And so, like the Grand Old Duke of York, Kim Campbell just marched them up to the top of the hill, then marched them down again.

The Party's Over

"This being a swing riding," Jeff Knoll conceded in the wake of the ads, "Mississauga West will swing in the direction of the party most likely to form the next government, which now looks like the Liberals. So, with our national party in free fall, our campaign is in danger, and we will have to look at alternative strategies for the last week."

His own "Hail Mary" strategy came to him like a vision in the middle of the night, and it was so bold that when he proposed it to Horner the next morning, Knoll prefaced it by asking, "Are you brave?" At noon that day, Monday, October 18, exactly a week before the vote, Kim Campbell would be coming into Mississauga West during her final blitz of more than thirty Ontario ridings. The Horner campaign had arranged for her to address a hundred local Tories during lunch at the Delta Meadowvale, and though she was no longer the asset she had been in September, she would have the national media in her wake. And the media were at the heart of Jeff Knoll's scheme.

The previous August, Bob Horner had attracted attention by suggesting that members of the Bloc Québécois should be tried for treason. His remarks played very well at home and still earned Horner frequent praise on the street. English-Canadian resentment toward the notion of Quebec separatists in the House of Commons, enjoying the privileges of the British parliamentary system and accepting federal tax dollars in order to help break up the country, was building with every new poll. Support for the Bloc, instead of melting away as had been generally predicted, had grown to around 50 per cent in Quebec. That was expected to translate into as many as fifty of the province's seventy-five seats – enough to give it the balance of power in a minority government or even make it Her Majesty's Loyal Opposition.

Horner was speaking for a lot of Mississaugans when he said, "The idea of Lucien Bouchard in Stornoway just burns my ass!"

Knoll's plan was to exploit that resentment by getting his candidate on the network TV news, the only news to which most voters pay any attention. And that required doing something sensational. "The national strategists are probably going to have a kitten," Knoll said, "but we're in a riding-by-riding fight, and I'll do whatever's necessary to get Bob back in Ottawa."

Just before Campbell's arrival, Horner spiced up his introductory remarks with some news for her, the luncheon crowd, and the dozens of reporters at the back of the Mississauga Heritage Room. On the grounds that "Mr. Bouchard and his crew cannot bear true allegiance to the queen of Canada while at the same time attempting to dismember our beloved country," he announced his intention, if re-elected, to table a private member's bill to *expel* any separatist members of Parliament from the House of Commons. "I love this country," he said, "and I'll be damned if I am going to sit by idly while a bunch of traitors plot its very demise."

His statement sounded like yet another nail being hammered into Kim Campbell's coffin. It was likely to knock whatever she said out of the headlines, and it would certainly make her uphill struggle even more difficult in Quebec. If she felt betrayed by the self-serving action of a colleague and friend, she showed no sign of it as she stormed into the room, grinning and waving, amid the usual pandemonium of TV cameramen, party handlers, and security officers. She even gave Dr. Bob a kiss on the cheek.

There was nothing in the confidence of her manner or the zing of her speech, indeed, to indicate that her chief Quebec organizer had already publicly conceded a Liberal victory (or that her own pollster, without telling her, was privately predicting that the Tories might win fewer than twenty seats). She sped through her file cards at a mile a minute, full of happy talk about her "activist agenda" for a national fiscal plan, parliamentary reforms, budget consultations, small-business loans, trade and technology, the modernization of social programs, and other changes to the status quo. "And," she promised, using a native expression that had become current among the political class, "I will walk my talk."

In the seven months since her entry into the leadership race, however, she had been a lot more talk than walk. The politics of inclusion had come to nothing; the real choices she had hoped to present to

Canadians had failed to materialize. As the going got tougher, she herself got more isolated and less likeable. Even her admirable strength in the face of adversity only contributed to the sense of a self-satisfied person too proud to need anybody else. "I'm always the calm in the eye of the storm," she bragged openly, "even when all hell is breaking loose." Yet the hell was usually of her own making. By blowing her own horn in *La Presse* a couple of days before her visit to Mississauga, for example, she had managed to offend Brian Mulroney, Jean Charest, a number of her most important Quebec organizers, and every Canadian who did not share her happy fortune in coming from British Columbia.

"The important thing isn't popularity, but respect," she had said during the summer. "People know they can't agree with you on everything, because issues are too complex, but if they feel they know where you're coming from, that you'll deliver the straight goods, that you're fair-minded and open, that you come to decisions from listening and not from reacting in some knee-jerk way or an excessively partisan way, based on personal loyalties or inappropriate motivations, then you can win their respect. That would be my goal."

She failed to achieve even that. For all her brainy expositions and West Coast candour, she connected intellectually and emotionally with almost no one. That explained, more than anything else, why she could not duplicate what Pierre Trudeau had done in 1968. Trudeau had also inherited an unpopular party. He too had had little political experience, little interest in political gamesmanship, and little familiarity with the political class upon whom his victory depended. He too could appear isolated, unlikeable, self-satisfied, and proud. But the more people saw of Trudeau during the campaign, the more intriguing he became and the more respect he earned. Love him or hate him, he had a depth of mind and complexity of character that were at the root of his charisma. Kim Campbell had neither. Beneath the conflicting personas and the flurry of words, there was remarkably little substance.

Nor did she have the firmness of vision and purpose that had pushed Trudeau into power. For all Campbell's idealistic posturings about standing up to the political class or slashing the deficit for the sake of future generations, she succumbed with remarkable ease to the old pros in the party, the bureaucracy, the lobbies, and the media – only to bungle what they taught her and end up the subject of their scorn. The true parallel, in fact, was with Trudeau in the 1972 election, when his political agenda was exhausted, his charismatic authority seemed rather shopworn, his personal instinct was to conduct a series of low-key "conversations with Canadians," and his party machine careened without direction from despondency to despair. In 1972 Trudeau had been headed, if not for the Liberals' base in Quebec, where Kim Campbell would soon end up.

All at once, within a half-hour of finishing her speech, she dashed from the room to board her campaign bus for the next event in downtown Toronto. She had had occasion to meet only a very few supporters. She had had time to listen to hardly anyone. Then she had vanished amid the same confusion of media lights and party officials in which she had appeared at the stomp 'n' chomp fund-raiser a mere six months earlier, leaving the people to finish their lunch and wonder what the hell all that had been about.

"Kim Campbell wasn't *about* anything," a senior civil servant remarked at a dinner party a few weeks afterwards. "She was just plain incompetent." It was the political class's final judgement. Jean Charest – even Brian Mulroney, for God's sake! – with their instincts for the game and their hold in Quebec, would have done much better than she did. They certainly could not have done any worse. "In 1984," Mulroney himself commented afterwards in an indirect swipe at his successor's performance, "I started the campaign fourteen points behind and we won 211 seats. In 1988, we started twenty-three points behind six months earlier and we won another majority. So don't exclude campaigns, don't exclude campaigners and campaigning."

Far from excluding either, Bob Horner was putting all his hope in them. He got his flash moment on TV that night and a lot of congratulatory calls the next morning. "I might have cost us a couple of seats in Quebec," he boasted, "but I've earned us at least twice as many in the rest of Canada." By week's end, the *Mississauga News* endorsed him – "Voters can sleep well voting for Horner" went its peculiar line of argument – and the *Toronto Sun* declared that he would win "by the skin of his teeth." Horner himself, now down thirty-five pounds and still trailing the Liberals, thought he had recovered enough ground to be able to overtake Carolyn Parrish. He was out before six every morning, handing out his literature at the GO train stations, and more and more people were saying that they were behind him all the way.

The Curse Is Lifted

On Saturday, October 23, two days before the election, Carolyn Parrish was felled by a particularly severe migraine, induced by tension and accompanied by vomiting. It caused her to miss Jean Chrétien's farewell rally with all his area candidates in the Metro riding of York West, where a couple of thousand pepped-up Grits crowded into a windowless banquet hall on a gorgeous autumn morning to wave placards and chant "Chré-tien! Chré-tien! Chré-tien!" Toronto, significantly, was the Liberal leader's last campaign stop before he returned to his own riding for the vote.

The campaign had turned out to be a variation on *Beauty and the Beast*, in which the grotesque monster was transformed into a charming prince while the blonde heroine, exposed as a vain and miserly witch, was exiled from the magic castle to wander by herself through a night forest full of wolves. And, in a completely surprising twist, the Beast was even bestowed with Beauty's female virtues of empathy, openness, and compassion. A few months after the election, on a brilliant winter's night, Chrétien and his wife were enjoying a very romantic ride in a horse-drawn sleigh through the Quebec countryside. Suddenly a dazzling shooting star flashed across the sky and vanished. "Kim Campbell," Aline Chrétien said.

Though a well-run election campaign may have little bearing on how effectively the winner will govern – Canadians need look no further than 1984 and 1988 for proof of that – it does serve as a kind of rite of passage. If a party cannot mobilize a network of partisan supporters to accomplish a specific goal under defined conditions in a limited period of time, it is unlikely to do better in the face of conflicting interests, unexpected crises, new circumstances, and long-term problems. And if a leader does not demonstrate an ability to listen and respond to the concerns of the people during the very process of currying their favour, he or she almost certainly will not discover a passion to do so in high office. The Conservatives had obviously fallen short on both counts during the 1993 campaign. The Liberals had unquestionably earned "the gold star" that Campbell herself awarded their campaign.

The well-prepared efficiency of the Liberal organization helped put to rest many of the doubts about Jean Chrétien's competence. His dignified demeanour "above the fray" of the television debates belied the cartoon image of him as a crude hick from Shawinigan. Despite his oversimplifications and wisecracks, more and more Canadians found themselves attracted to the power of his optimism and the pleasure of his company. He seemed to have found the right balance between populism and leadership, and in an era when politicians are supposed to look and sound like television stars, he was able to turn his physical handicap and fractured syntax to his advantage. They made him authentic, a down-to-earth person with whom people could identify, exactly what many people were seeking after the packaged slickness of Brian Mulroney.

Chrétien's style, in other words, worked as an antidote to his decades of power and prominence in the political class, connecting him vicariously to the lives of ordinary people. Even when he was not completely convincing about the promises in the Red Book, he seemed utterly sincere about his good intentions and his resolve not to disappoint – which, in a skeptical and uncertain age, may be the most that any politician can promise anyway. "Canadians don't expect miracles," he said. "They expect judgement, integrity, and hard work. If I can create that atmosphere of confidence, then we will feel good about ourselves again."

When election day finally arrived, Carolyn Parrish did not get up until after ten. October 25, 1993, was going to be a long, anxious day, and she figured she had better pace herself for whatever it was going to bring. She had also been up half the night, cruising around town with George Carlson, to check that her signs were not being uprooted by any overzealous opponents and to make sure that the Tories were not out in the dark distributing a scurrilous and illegal flyer she had recently discovered by accident.

Produced by an anonymous group called the "Parrish the Thought!" Committee, it pulled together a bunch of unflattering and sometimes distorted quotes by or about Parrish, from her approval of a 39-per-cent pay increase for school trustees in 1990 to right-wing columnist Diane Francis describing her in the *Financial Post* as "undistinguished" and "lacklustre." It was clearly the dirty work of some Horner supporters – Parrish's prime suspect was Jeff Knoll – but Horner himself denied any hand in it and even demanded that it be killed when he learned about it on Sunday evening.

"Bob has to live in this community, whatever happens," Knoll explained the next morning, as another contingent of his three hundred volunteers set out to get the computer's identified Tories to the polls or wave Horner placards at several major intersections, "and he didn't want to be a part of a negative campaign. Even though" – and here his air of regret seemed to lend evidence to Parrish's suspicion – "this thing might have helped him if it had got around."

Knoll, after only an hour's sleep, looked ill and irritable, and he had his own grievances: Tory signs pulled down by Liberal and Reform workers, Liberal and Reform signs put up around the polling stations in contravention to the electoral law, Liberal "assholes" spreading rumours that Dr. Bob had terminal cancer, Reform "brownshirts" calling Horner a fat pig. He still believed that his man had a good chance of winning, even if his party only got the fifty-four seats that Knoll was now predicting, but the game had clearly lost its fun. "I used to feel that all of us in politics were cut from the same cloth, but I've come not to like these people," he said with a sour expression.

"These people" were over at Carolyn Parrish's house on Oneida Crescent, and so was the fun. Her six hundred volunteers had already blitzed some eighteen thousand households with a message reading, "Urgent! I need *your* vote *today!*" Dozens of kids in red Parrish sweatshirts arrived to collect the lists of those supporters who had voted, and pausing only to devour the Pizza Pizzas, left to pull out those supporters who had not. In the midst of the commotion the candidate herself rushed in and yelled, "Yes! We're going to win this sucker!" But her ambition now reached beyond winning: she wanted to win *big*. She wanted to know she would have beaten Horner even if Reform had not split his vote. She wanted to create a solid majority, based primarily on the immigrant population, that would make Mississauga West (and the two new ridings that would be carved out of it before the next election) Liberal bastions forever.

Her head told her it was possible. The national trends looked positive, she had forty-five thousand identified Liberals on her computers, and various multicultural organizations had supplied more than twenty thousand names as "best guess" Liberals. But her guts still warned her that she could lose. "If you've ever lost," she said, remembering her tearful defeat in Ward 7 and her close call during the nomination, "you lose your self-confidence." In fact, she confessed, she was "scared shitless."

The worst was the hour and a half before the polls closed. At a quarter to eight, Carolyn Parrish huddled in an armchair in her campaign office, shivering under a heavy blanket from exhaustion and nerves.

She had been running for public office almost constantly for two and a half years. She had begged at tens of thousands of doors, raised and spent more than $100,000, mortgaged her home, imposed upon her friends, and brought chaos to her family. She had nursed and buried her father just seven months before – oh, how she wished he was with her tonight! – and her body was shaking uncontrollably with fear.

Half an hour later the first polls came in from Hurondale – a fifty-fifty area in the past – and she was way ahead. Ten minutes after that, six polls reported from Meadowvale – heavy Tory country – and she took them all. "We're on our way!" Carolyn Parrish whooped. The roars rocked the old house in Streetsville. The champagne began to flow at the victory party in the legion hall. And when the last numbers were added up, she had won 53,567 votes, or about 56 per cent of the total cast, which was just slightly higher than the percentage by which Ontario gave the Liberals ninety-eight of its ninety-nine seats and a majority government in Ottawa.

One More Chance

Such was the force of the national campaign, driving veteran ministers into oblivion, lifting unknown candidates into office, that more than a few Liberal organizers were left wondering why they had bothered to work so hard. "I could have gone on vacation for seven weeks," said one, "and still won a stunning upset." Halfway through the election, Liberal insiders learned that their candidate in the Toronto riding of Markham-Whitchurch-Stouffville had once sent a letter wishing his former employers dead for not giving him a promotion. Nothing was done about it, however, partly because no one wanted to interrupt Chrétien's momentum going into the TV debates, mostly because no one expected Jag Bhaduria to win anyway. To everyone's immediate shock and later regret (including Jean Chrétien's), he took the riding by more than fifteen thousand votes.

If this was the sort of top-down phenomenon that caused Preston Manning to deride the party system, he was in a weak position to draw attention to it. Few of Reform's winning candidates – perhaps, only Manning himself – had been wafted to victory on the strength of their own qualities and efforts. Most people who voted Reform did so because of the party's policies and its leader. Certainly Charles Conn did not place second in Mississauga West because 20,218 people had studied his CV and wanted *him* to be their personal representative in Ottawa. Most of them probably didn't even know his name before they went into the voting booth.

Nor could Preston Manning and Lucien Bouchard continue to argue from the results that Canadian democracy was a mere sham. With six years of effort, a well-formulated set of ideas, and some fortuitous timing to compensate for its lack of money, organization, and experience, Reform went from one seat to fifty-two, doubled its national support during the campaign to 19 per cent, and displaced the Tories and the New Democrats as the voice of fiscal responsibility and grassroots protest in the House of Commons. The Bloc Québécois, meanwhile, went from eight MPs to fifty-four and became the official Opposition in Parliament. Their ascendency demonstrated the very opposite of what they usually claimed: If enough people stopped whining about politics or the federal system and got involved in the process instead, they could make a quick and very real contribution.

Beneath all their euphoria and dismay, however, both of them lost the election. The Bloc clearly failed to give Quebeckers the "real power" it had promised. Reform similarly failed to meet its stated ambitions to empower westerners by holding a minority government to ransom and win more than two seats east of Saskatchewan (one in Manitoba and one in Ontario). Exactly as Bob Horner had predicted, the greatest effect of the regional protest parties was to assist the election of a Liberal majority – which the TV networks were able to announce, much to the chagrin of westerners and Quebeckers, based on the early returns from Atlantic Canada and Ontario.

In his postmortem, Dalton Camp even attributed a significant part of the Tories' rout to the fact that "its power base had shifted from its traditional Ontario axis and moved west," where concern about the Reform party had "brought a new and different political realignment to the Conservative party." That did more than jeopardize a crucial number of Ontario seats such as Mississauga West. It alienated moderate Canadians *in every region of the country* who still looked to the central government for help and leadership, who still honoured the historic entente between anglophones and francophones, who still valued instruments of national unity and Canadian identity such as medicare and the CBC, and who still believed in the virtues of tolerance, compromise, generosity, and pragmatism. "Conservatives, for the first time in memory," Camp concluded, "were out of touch with the political culture they themselves had created."

Out of touch, too, were most of the media. So ashamed were they about missing the revolt against the Charlottetown Accord, so embarrassed were they about underestimating the strength of Reform or the Bloc at the outset of the campaign, so excited were they about the unusual copy provided by Preston Manning and Lucien Bouchard, they went to the opposite extreme and misjudged the mood of the nation in 1993 as badly as they had done in 1992. Certainly no foreigner, subject to the barrage of TV clips and newspaper reports about Canada's cynical electorate – "disgusted, angry, fed-up, worn-out, exploited, ignored and bitter" was how the *Toronto Star* described Canadians the day before the election – could have guessed that the turn-out rate would be over 70 per cent or that almost two-thirds of the voters would cast their ballots for the three "old-style" parties.

The real upset was the startling resurrection of the Liberal party and – by implication – of the political class. Not only had the Liberals been thought in serious trouble when the campaign began, there were doubts even on election day about whether Chrétien could win either a majority government or his own riding. He did both, of course, in a romp, and he did it according to most of the conventions of a classic, left-leaning, Ontario-centred, Quebec-sensitive strategy. He even thought he would have done better if Campbell had been stronger, because the anti-Liberal vote would then have been split in half in many western ridings and many moderate Tories would not have felt compelled to vote Reform to help prevent the Bloc Québécois from becoming the second largest party in the Commons.

But, as Chrétien headed toward Ottawa and long afterwards, there raged a debate about the true mandate he had received from the people beyond good intentions and honest character. Had he earned any mandate, indeed, or simply succeeded by default? Had people voted *for* him and his Red Book, or merely *against* Kim Campbell and the Mulroney record? Had the election really been a victory of ideas or a triumph of sophisticated organization? The answer was further complicated by the fact that he won his majority with only 41 per cent of the national vote and a minority of seats in both Quebec and the West (though the addition of New Democrats, Red Tories, and left-wing *bloquistes* suggested that Canadians were still predominantly liberal in their political orientation).

In fact, the 1993 campaign had been marked by an unusually clear choice in the direction of public policy and the role of the state. No leader, with the possible exception of Lucien Bouchard, rose or fell primarily because of his or her personality; Chrétien and Manning overthrew the modern myth that political success is mostly a matter of looking and sounding good on TV. And though some academics and editorialists complained that the first-past-the-post electoral system seriously distorted the meaning of the result, there was no widespread quarrel about its legitimacy. Some thought the Tories should have obtained more than two seats for their 16 per cent of the vote, representing some two million people, especially since the NDP had won nine seats with only 7 per cent of the vote. Many more thought the Bloc Québécois should not have formed the official Opposition with only 14 per cent of the vote, all concentrated in one province. But most people, including those who hated the result, agreed with the *Globe* that "the Liberals have won the keys to 24 Sussex Dr., fair and square."

Why? At the superficial level, because the vast majority of Canadians got what they wanted: a humiliating come-uppance for the Conservatives. Liberals and Reformers, *bloquistes* and New Democrats – all could share a feeling of enormous relief, made sweeter by a dose of cold vengeance. Perhaps the greatest virtue of electoral politics, for all its faults, is its ability to give people both a strong government and a regular, orderly way of overthrowing it. Canadians seem willing to put up with years of arrogance and abuse, content in the knowledge that some day they will enjoy the delectable pleasure of booting the bums out.

More profound, and of crucial importance, was the sense of rightness. Democracies can only survive if there is a fundamental conviction that the decision of the people, as expressed by a legal and equitable system, is always right. Without that conviction, the door is ajar for would-be tyrants from the right or left to argue that the people are too ignorant or misguided to be trusted with authority. And though there are plenty of examples in history where majorities have made short-sighted and even tragic choices, Canadians have shown themselves remarkably astute and fair. More often than not, their respect for common sense, social justice, political caution, and public education has caused them to do whatever seemed, at the time, most appropriate.

Consider, for example, three of the most controversial and consequential elections in recent times: the victory of the Parti Québécois in Quebec in 1976 with only 41 per cent of the vote, the victory of the Progressive Conservatives in Ottawa in 1988 with only 43 per cent, and the victory of the New Democratic Party in Ontario in 1990 with only 37 per cent. Given the huge stakes and high emotions involved, any one of them could have precipitated a cry of foul play – and an agitation for proportional representation – from the majority whose will had apparently been thwarted. That did not happen, not because most voters were indifferent, but because they understood the appropriateness of the results. The Quebec Liberals had not deserved a third term in 1976; the federal Liberals had not earned a return to power in 1988; and neither the Liberals nor the Conservatives had merited success in Ontario in 1990. Similarly, in the autumn of 1993, most people wanted to punish the Tories and New Democrats for their errors and hypocrisies – and if the punishment happened to be more severe than intended, few showed any regret.

It seemed only appropriate, as well, to give almost exactly equal say to the "two solitudes" of Canadian politics – western conservatives and Quebec ultra-nationalists – whose views had often gone unarticulated in the House of Commons. (Not that there weren't grounds to debate the true nature of *their* mandates. According to campaign polls, 55 per cent of the Reform vote was merely a negative expression of protest, not a positive affirmation of policy, and 57 per cent of the Bloc's support considered it a no-risk defence of Quebec's interests while only 29 per cent wanted sovereignty.) However odious the views of Reform and the BQ to many Canadians, however exaggerated their number of seats in relation to their national support, the airing of their ambitions and grievances was probably an accurate reflection of the tensions within Canadian society and perhaps even a healthy development for the future of Canadian democracy. And, in its instinctual wisdom, the electorate rejected all the appeals to give either the Reform party or the Bloc Québécois the critical balance of power.

Most Canadians appreciated, it seemed, why a majority government would be better placed to face the economic and political problems ahead. And the only party capable of forming a majority government – with the added legitimacy of having at least some representation from every region – was the Liberal party. Its platform and its leader may have been far from ideal, but after considering the alternatives and assessing the polls, the people judged the Red Book and Jean Chrétien to be – well, appropriate.

If there had been anger across the land, it turned out not to have been blind anger, ready to pull down the structure of traditional politics. Traditional politics had done an acceptable job of forcing the politicians to heed the people's agenda during the election. The question was whether they would – or even could – heed it in government. Canadians seemed willing to give the Liberals a new, and perhaps last, chance. "We, the political class," was how Chrétien himself described his essential mandate, "have to gain back the confidence of the people."

Bob Horner guessed that the public would now just get angry at someone else. "The sad part is that people must have been lying to me all along," he said, with more bitterness than sadness in his voice, after going to Carolyn Parrish's victory party – against the rather sour advice of Jeff Knoll – and shaking her hand. He had finished a humiliating third in Mississauga West, as his party had in Ontario. "I would rather they had told me the truth."

CHAPTER THREE

A Great Fall

Initiation Rites

E ARLY on the morning of November 9, 1993, Carolyn Parrish
and her husband David walked up to Parliament Hill from the
Chateau Laurier Hotel – a short distance, but the last leg of her
long and arduous journey to reach the House of Commons. She felt as
grey as the cold drizzle that was falling on Ottawa that morning. Not
completely recovered from the vicious bug that had struck the day
after her election victory (as though it had been waiting a couple of
years, with increasing fury, for her to have a moment to indulge it),
she had been kept awake for much of the night by David's hacking
cough. "I nearly became the first MP to be found guilty of smothering
her husband to death with a pillow," she grumped. But as she passed
the eternal flame and approached the main doors at the base of the
famous Peace Tower, her spirits were lifted by the glory and excitement of it all. Today she was going to be sworn in as an official member of Canada's thirty-fifth Parliament.

First, however, she and David had to attend an orientation session
for the Liberal caucus: how to set up offices in the capital and in the
riding, when to be at what meetings, where to find the washrooms. It
seemed, from the mood of intimidating strangeness to the smell of the
floor wax, like the first day of school, though another rookie compared it to the feeling Margaret Mead must have had on her first day in
Samoa. Then, at noon, with Parrish carrying her father-in-law's Bible
and David carrying the thicker (and perhaps more commanding) orientation binder, they proceeded along a marble corridor in the Centre

151

Block to Room 216N, the Speaker's Salon, an ornate but sparsely furnished reception room with blue brocade on the walls, a carved wooden door, an elaborate stone fireplace, a photographer with his lights, and a clerk in black robes.

Parrish swore the oath of allegiance, the photographer yelled "Beautiful!" and that was that – except for a quick trip to the basement, to pose for a mug shot and pick up her Via Rail pass, and a brief stop at the sergeant-at-arms' office to collect her gold MP's pin. It earned her a salute from the security guard when she left the Parliament Buildings a few minutes later for lunch at the National Press Club. As she stepped out under the neo-Gothic portico, she saw the prime minister's limousine and RCMP escort speed away from the west entrance to take Jean Chrétien to the launching of Pierre Trudeau's memoirs at the National Archives. If it was hard for any Canadian not to be slightly dazzled by the power and history that enveloped the Hill as palpably as the fog, it was harder still for Carolyn Parrish to believe she had become a part of it all.

Later, after she had become a familiar face among the movers and shakers exchanging gossip and intrigue over the lasagna at Mamma Teresa's, Parrish described her first couple of months in Ottawa as hectic, tiring, and very confusing. "I'm used to setting my own agenda and controlling my own destiny," she said, "but here I was constantly overwhelmed by the twenty-seven places I *had* to be and the forty-seven things I *had* to know. And the separation from my family was really tough at first. There were a lot of nights when I'd find myself working late in the office, and I'd realize I hadn't eaten anything since lunch but wouldn't feel like going to sit in some restaurant by myself, so I'd just go back to my small apartment and throw together a tuna sandwich at midnight."

The glamour of the job had proven surprisingly short-lived. It was lost in Bob Horner's old routine of fifteen-hour days, up to Ottawa on an early flight every Monday morning (often with her face in a vomit bag because she's prone to air sickness), caucus meetings, Question Period, committee meetings, House duty, office meetings, speech preparation, staff meetings, a stack of correspondence, then back to Toronto most Thursday nights to work Friday and Saturday in her constituency headquarters and show up at a round of riding events. "They deliberately keep us busy," one of Parrish's exhausted caucus colleagues speculated, "to prevent us from thinking."

Even her maiden speech in Parliament was an anticlimax. She got ten minutes just before the supper break to rail against cruise-missile testing – "I always thought that was the Liberal position," she explained – only to discover herself preceded by eight "warmongers" from her own party. The cabinet, it turned out, had decided to extend the tests for another year. But at least she had been able to say what she thought: government backbenchers were often pressed into reciting speeches written by back-room officials or anonymous bureaucrats, whether they agreed with the content or not.

And if Carolyn Parrish's head ever swelled as she strode from her seat in the House into the corridors of power, it was invariably deflated by the blank look in the eyes of the parliamentary reporters as they searched for someone important to scrum. Contrary to Trudeau's infamous crack that MPs are just a bunch of nobodies as soon as they leave the Hill, Parrish usually felt like a nobody on the Hill. "Back in Mississauga people are always approaching me for a word," she laughed. "Here it's, 'Excuse me, lady, you're in my way.'"

Most times she was relieved that the press gallery had not turned its harsh lights in her direction and jabbed its microphones into her face. She was still apprenticing, and she instinctively understood how the media could nail someone who was "just off the turnip truck" – as happened in January 1994, when the hunting pack, frenzied by the smell of blood, went after the Liberal rookie from Markham-Whitchurch-Stouffville, Jag Bhaduria. First they publicized the intimidating letters he had sent to officials at the Metro Toronto School Board in 1989 for not promoting him to vice-principal. Then they questioned the legitimacy of the law credential he had boasted on his campaign literature. In the ensuing furore, Bhaduria was forced to stand in the Commons and beg the public's forgiveness, expelled from the Liberal caucus by the prime minister, vilified by the *Markham Economist and Sun* (which had not cared to examine his life *before* the election), and presented with a petition from twenty-five thousand outraged voters demanding his resignation.

To many people, especially Reformers, the Bhaduria incident demonstrated the very reason Canadians need a mechanism by which a majority of constituents can fire – or, euphemistically, "recall" – their MP without having to wait until the next election. According to one poll, 75 per cent of the population wanted just such "a chain you can yank if your MP constantly votes against your interests," as Preston Manning once described it. To most of the political class, however, the result was liable to be a perpetual series of witch-hunts in which the momentary heat generated by every unpopular issue would be exploited for partisan purposes. Few MPs win by a majority of votes in the first place, after all, and no government remains in constant favour. Reform itself put three significant conditions on its recall proposal to reduce the obvious opportunities for abuse: it required a very high number of petitioners; it could not be triggered until eighteen months after the election; and it could only be used once against any particular MP during the life of a parliament.

"However principled and well intentioned the law," warned John Conway, a political sociologist at the University of Regina, "it will be used by vested interests to harass premiers, prime ministers, cabinet ministers, or any elected legislator who dares not to bow before the demands of the rich, or the powerful, or the well organized." In 1937, he noted, William Aberhart's Social Credit government repealed the recall legislation it had put into effect in Alberta just the year before, because his political opponents almost succeeded in getting Aberhart himself recalled.

"I don't condone what Jag did, it's sad," Parrish said, "but I think he has been subjected to a lot of racial pressure. When you look at his opponents on the TV screen, they all have white hair and white skin, and you can tell from their comments that a lot of them are Reformers. So are they really going after Jag because of what he did, or because they want another shot at getting a Reform MP elected? None of us arrived immaculate from the forehead of Zeus on to the Hill. We're human beings, and if we weren't, we wouldn't be representing the country very well."

The Old Boys' Association

Justly or unjustly, Bhaduria paid a price for the Chrétien government's determination to restore the integrity and credibility of the political class. The restoration began partly by fulfilling the promises to kill the Tories' helicopter and airport deals, but mostly by careful management. The merest hint of scandal was enough to bring a lightning response from the PMO, as was the case when the new minister of revenue was advised to drop a legitimate suit he had begun against the federal government as a private citizen. And the slightest evidence of extravagance earned a scowl from the prime minister himself. When one minister complained about being restricted to only twelve staff members (some of Mulroney's ministers had used seven times as many), Chrétien curtly reminded him that there were plenty of talented Liberal backbenchers "from the B team" ready and eager for a place in the cabinet, no matter how small the staff.

Though the Liberals' first Speech from the Throne, on January 18, 1994, promised the appointment of an ethics counsellor, adjustments to the pensions for MPs, and a stricter regulation of lobbyists, the best press and most favourable mail came from image changes, not institutional reforms – Mulroney's armoured Cadillac was replaced with a Chevrolet Caprice, his brand-new $53-million "Air Farce One" was put up for sale, and his wife Mila's office in the Langevin Block was closed down. Each gesture represented only a minuscule saving to the annual deficit, but together they reaped enormous political profit. Most Canadians were still convinced that the deficit was rooted in such extravagancies, and the Reform party kept fostering that illusion through its puritanical obsession with the subsidized price of haircuts and shoe shines on the Hill.

"Reformers, bless their souls, are either grasping on to things that are too grandiose to do or going after the nickels and dimes," said Parrish, who soon got into the frugal spirit of the times by discovering a technical trick by which the federal government might save as much as $6 million a year on the cost of MPs' airline tickets, even though she had mocked the Tories during the election for making the deficit "a bogeyman that was going to strangle us." "Reform always reminds me of the year when the Peel Board of Education brought in a budget that was so humongous and overpowering, we felt so helpless, that we spent three and a half hours debating a lamp for the director's office."

Backbenchers, as a result, soon found themselves with fewer privileges and perks – yet almost no compensating increase in power. Carolyn Parrish could help a constituent get access to ministers and bureaucrats or speed up a limited number of immigration cases. From time to time she could make a pitch to the entire cabinet at the weekly caucus meeting or attract a bit of media attention for a pet issue. She could exert some influence by means of her participation on the Industry committee, with a question in the House, or through a private member's bill. But the procedural reforms the Liberals announced in February 1994 did not really address her deep sense of frustration, despite Chrétien's joke that he had given so much power to MPs that no one would want to become a cabinet minister.

"It's still driven from a centre," she said. "The Whip whips you into voting with the party, and that gives intense power to the ministers. They don't have to convince the rest of the caucus of something, they just have to present it."

One day, for example, they presented a bill to build a fixed link between Prince Edward Island and the mainland. Everything Parrish knew about the project distressed her: it would threaten the island's special culture, it would damage the fishing bank, it would be costly to maintain, and it would suck capital from Ontario. Her inclination, therefore, was to absent herself from the vote. But when Liberal Whip Alfonso Gagliano caught wind of her little rebellion, he called her into his office for a chat. "He's a man of few words," Parrish said, "but he explained the importance of party solidarity to me and suggested, if I did this now, five or fifty others might do the same thing the next time. If I had answered that I was a heavy-duty environmentalist and this thing went against my conscience, I think he would have left me alone. But my reasons weren't based on an ethical position, and it was possible that greater minds than mine knew all the details. So I thought about it for half an hour" – during which she consulted George Carlson, who sarcastically advised her to go ahead and destroy her hard-earned political career for the sake of some goddamn bridge in the middle of frigging nowhere – "then I went and voted as I was supposed to."

Then there was her government's decision to slash tobacco taxes as a way of eradicating the lucrative underworld trade in contraband cigarettes from the United States. As an award-winning activist against drugs, alcohol, and smoking during her years as a school trustee, Parrish was incensed by the proposal – as was Bob Rae, who launched a vitriolic attack against Ottawa for failing to consider Ontario's interests in the rush to solve what was really only an issue in Quebec. But she was again persuaded to reconsider her stance, in this case, because a heated caucus discussion had pushed the cabinet to come up with a broader scheme to curtail smoking as well as smuggling.

"Normally it's easy to vote with the party," she said, "and I don't feel like a sheep because I can really speak out in caucus. In another time I probably would have been nailed for some of the stuff I've pulled, but there's a degree of openness that comes right from the top." Still, she had to admit, Chrétien was very much in charge. "I've seen him stand up and just say that this is something we *all* will have to support, the implication being that we're either with him or 'agin' him. He expects loyalty."

Loyalty remains the moral and practical foundation upon which parliamentary democracy stands. Modern parties arose in the nineteenth century when individual representatives coalesced around certain leaders and ideals, then offered themselves to the public as loyal to both. And the very legitimacy of the government is grounded in its maintaining the loyalty of the group with the largest number of elected members, whose election – as the 1993 campaign again demonstrated – was more a matter of group affiliation than of personal attributes. If MPs were to vote as they wish on everything, neither their leaders *nor their voters* could rely from day to day on anything, and the pressure would be on them to divide according to language, region, and economic interest rather than come to a consensus by necessity. The Commons would revert, in other words, to the anarchy that had caused political parties – and the party Whip – to be invented in the first place.

Over time, no doubt, the discipline became stricter than efficient or responsible government required. Where once the idea of loyalty conjured up public-spirited men and women subordinating their petty purposes to some nobler duty, it came to evoke faceless cowards raising their hands as one in order to satisfy the whims of some ruthless autocrat. Even within the political class, a growing number of voices called for Ottawa to adopt Westminster's three-tier rule, in which each vote is graded according to whether it is a question of confidence upon which the government may fall, an issue of secondary importance, or a matter of personal conscience.

Jean Chrétien himself worried about the pull toward presidential government in Canada. "In my judgement," he wrote in his memoirs, "maybe no more than fifty MPs make a personal difference in the outcome of their elections. The rest tend to rely on the appeal of their leader and the luck of belonging to the winning party. The risk is that MPs will become more marginal, more expendable, and at the mercy of the leadership. Certainly few back-benchers will be prepared to give their leaders frank advice or tell them to go to hell if they know they can be replaced. This is a danger for our system because we don't have the same checks and balances that are built into the American presidency."

But Carolyn Parrish had cause to suspect that the Chrétien government was only moving "slowly and lugubriously" toward the Red Book's promise of more free votes. In April 1995, she watched as three Liberal MPs were tossed off their committees for voting against the gun-control bill, and two months later Warren Allmand nearly lost his chairmanship of the Justice committee for voting against his party's budget. "I see why people in power don't want to let go of their power," Parrish said. "In the hands of a benevolent leader like Jean Chrétien, that's maybe okay, but in the hands of a Brian Mulroney, the whole democratic process can be abused."

Because of Mulroney, indeed, the Reform party had been able to make a national issue out of the arcane topic of parliamentary reform. It seized on the popular belief that representatives are sent to Parliament in order to defend the interests of their communities and articulate the views of their constituents – and invariably end up bought or brainwashed by the system. Out west, goes the story, a crowd of supporters escorted their new MP to the airport for his first flight to Ottawa. No sooner had the plane headed out of sight than they all started shouting, "The son of a bitch, he's sold out to Central Canada!" Maritimers would have said Upper Canada. Quebeckers would have said English Canada. Ontarians would have said Quebec.

Members of Parliament, however, have another – sometimes contradictory, often overriding – responsibility: to seek solutions among divergent interests and sell the resulting compromise to their ridings. If it was normal for Bob Rae to play to the sentiment that Ontario was again being shafted by Ottawa, this time with the shameful complicity of the province's ninety-eight Liberal members, it was equally predictable for Carolyn Parrish to have broadened her Mississauga perspective. In caucus, in committee, and in the Commons, she grew to understand the problems the other regions were experiencing and the quandaries every cabinet minister faced. That, in turn, mitigated her desire to make trouble.

"If I had voted against the fixed link," she said in hindsight, "I would have caused a lot of problems for my Maritime colleagues without having had the cabinet's long-range view. So maybe the system works after all, in that it channels the little fishies in the right direction until they're big fishies and know what they're doing."

Parrish even applauded when Transport Minister Doug Young arbitrarily overruled the objections of many Toronto-area MPs in the Liberal caucus to his proposal to commercialize the operation of Pearson Airport. "They freaked," she said, "but he did what was right: he put the national interest ahead of their parochial interests." And she reversed her own campaign rhetoric against the construction of new runways at Pearson after immersing herself in data and arguments that had not been available to her as an opposition candidate.

"I know I can't do that too often without looking like the flip-flop queen," she said, "but I learned a couple of valuable lessons. One, if you don't have all the information, you can make a rash decision. Two, though it would have been easy to stick to my original position, I had to be true to my own integrity. Part of my job is to give my constituents the information that they don't have, so they'll know why I've made a certain decision."

She learned a third lesson as well. Even if every vote were free, political survival and peer pressure would prove as tyrannical as the party Whip. Suppose that she could regularly vote against the cabinet's recommendations without bringing down the government. Why would the party brass help either her career or her riding when she did not deign to help them? Even if she were able to secure the Liberal nomination a second time and win another election, would her victory signify approval for her independent spirit or for her party's record? And if her vote were crucial for the passage of a bill, would she likely resist – any better than the average American congressman, say – some boondoggle for Mississauga West in exchange for her support or the promise of a lucrative reward from some moneyed interest?

"The brightest stars," she observed, "always behave, they always vote the way they're supposed to, they always speak when they're asked to, because there's always the carrot of a cabinet shuffle being dangled in front of them. The odd bodkin can get away with bucking party discipline once or twice, but if you're a maverick, you'd have to be an idiot not to notice you're not going anywhere."

Ultimately it is this human factor, rather than any rule, that accounts for the consistent behaviour of Canada's political class, despite the high turnover in the House of Commons. (The new Parliament set a record, in fact, with 204 newcomers out of 295 members.) While Mitchell Sharp may have been technically correct when he noted in his memoirs that Canadians have "no governing class, very few professional politicians, no body of people who spend a lifetime in active politics either as MPs or as MPs-in-waiting," he downplayed the influence of continuing players such as himself: a powerful mandarin in the 1940s and 1950s, a senior minister in the 1960s and 1970s, the head of a government agency in the 1980s, and, in 1993, at the age of eighty-two, a dollar-a-year adviser in Prime Minister Chrétien's office.

"It really is an old boys' association up here," Parrish concluded. "Those who've been around for a million years tend to pat the rookies on the head and say, 'There, there, we'll teach you to play the game.'

After I bashed into that wall four or five times, with injuries, I stopped whining and figured out how to work around it."

Manning the Barricades

For Preston Manning, working around the old boys' association was no solution to the frustrations that drive good men and women out of Parliament. Whatever their hopes and intentions, he observed, "they find themselves reduced to the role of glorified clerks, dispensing prepackaged information on government programs and handling complaints, while major decisions on policy and direction are made elsewhere and presented to them for rubber stamping." And precisely because of the human factor operating to perpetuate the political class, he argued, the solution was "to recruit and train a new kind of politician for the twenty-first century, whose mission is to change the federal political system itself rather than to conform to it."

At one point during the campaign, when he was challenged about his lack of experience in elected office, Manning replied, "Experience in what? Making a jackass of yourself in Parliament?"

The remark reflected the best and worst of him. The best, because it spoke to his sincere belief that political debate could be conducted with a great deal less partisanship and acrimony than generally seen in the House of Commons. The worst, because it hinted at the smug and sanctimonious air with which he often dismissed all those who had gone before him into public life, with the possible exception of his father. "What's the difference between a politician and a catfish?" was one of his election jokes. "One's a slimy, wide-mouthed bottom-feeder and the other's a fish." And both the best and worst were based on Manning's presumption that he would be a different – and undoubtedly superior – sort of politician because his politics flowed from his evangelical Christian faith.

In this faith, as he described it in his autobiography, "God is portrayed as sending, not another lawgiver, but a unique and divine mediator to restore our relationships to him and to one another" – Jesus Christ. Christ's mediating techniques, which resolved conflict not by coercion but by "restoring communication between the alienated parties" and asking them "to accept his sacrifice as payment of the price of reconciling with each other," became the model by which everyone, not least politicians, should seek to repair the strained and broken relationships of ordinary life.

"Leaders of a government find themselves mediating between public service unions who want higher pay and more job security, and taxpayers who refuse to pay higher taxes," Manning offered as an example. "They must reconcile both to the idea of receiving less (less service for the taxpayers and less money and job security for the unions). The only possible way for those mediating such a dispute to gain a hearing from the disputants is for government leaders to visibly take less themselves (lower pay, fewer benefits). Visible sacrifice by the mediator is essential to credibility and gaining a hearing if one wants others to make sacrifices for the sake of better relations."

It was not simple political gimmickry, then, that caused him to arrive in Ottawa and, before a horde of television cameras and newspaper photographers, place a For Sale sign on the 1988 Pontiac Bonneville the government had provided for his use as a party leader – a "visible sacrifice," including driver, worth an estimated $60,000 a year. At the same time he urged his Reform MPs to give up their right to cheap picture frames and discount meals, surrender their opportunities for exotic trips and attractive pensions, and volunteer a 10-percent cut in their annual salary of $64,400. And, lest some caucus members were tempted from the paths of righteousness by the rouged face of power, he even proposed setting up an ethics committee to investigate and advise them on what it termed, with deliberate vagueness, "matters affecting their public reputations."

Within the Commons, too, Manning tried to project himself as a new kind of leader in charge of a new breed of MPs. He sat in the second row, rather than on the front bench, and vowed to bring a calm and constructive approach to Question Period and the debates. He commissioned his caucus to explore inventive ways of involving their constituents in the decision-making process, such as town halls and electronic referenda, in keeping with Reform's principle that the wishes of the people should take precedence over the wishes of the political class. Whether on the budget or the future of Quebec, his first instinct was to go out and consult the voters about what he should think and do. "We don't want to be the same as the people we're replacing," he insisted from the very start.

He also encountered from the start – as Carolyn Parrish had – the realities that have made MPs and parties so constant in their ways.

Suddenly, for example, many Reform MPs who had railed against the salaries and perks of parliamentarians began to realize the heavy cost of maintaining two residences, two offices, and all the other financial demands of public service. "You can't automatically assume that just because someone is elected here that they're wealthy," Ian McClelland, the Reform member from Edmonton Southwest, was soon explaining in the press to justify why some of his colleagues might refuse to share Manning's visible sacrifice. "It could be that some people have had a significant reduction in pay already and have a mortgage and kids in school."

By April, indeed, Manning himself was on the defensive, trying to spin the startling news that his party (and indirectly, therefore, the taxpayer) had been slipping him an extra $31,000 a year, no receipts required, for clothes, trips, dry cleaning – and the use of a car! The media, of course, were delighted to play up the hypocrisy of Manning's position, but many ordinary Reformers and party notables also expressed disappointment and anger. Rarely has a Canadian politician been so neatly hoisted with his own petard. And the more he complained that his main reasons for being in politics were "completely wiped out by this type of stuff," the more he sounded like all the politicians he had been so glibly slandering for years.

Nor was that the end of Manning's troubles. The controversy merely exposed the political and ideological currents swirling beneath the placid surface of his leadership. Its very placidity had begun to disturb a lot of Reformers who now felt that their party was not being aggressive enough in the House, in the media, or in the minds of the electorate, as a result of which its popularity was slipping in relation to the Liberals' in every part of the country. Manning's reluctance to react to the February 1994 budget until he had finished two weeks of public consultations cost Reform an invaluable opportunity to berate the government's policies on live television and the front page, and his unorthodox efforts to lower the heat in the Commons made Lucien Bouchard the leader of the Opposition in practice as well as title.

"I'm not good myself at manufacturing emotion for emotion's sake," Manning had to admit. "The other thing is we're often on fiscal issues, clinical numbers. This is one of the contrasts between ourselves and the Bloc: issues of interest to them are a lot more emotional." And, he came to recognize, the press gallery has certain operational biases that he could not ignore: the short run is more newsworthy than the long run, emotion is more newsworthy than reason, the negative is more newsworthy than the positive, the destructive is more newsworthy than the constructive, and action is more newsworthy than failure to act.

"Some Canadians probably like Reform's new gentility," the *Globe*'s editors complained when their own patience with it had been exhausted by the spring of 1994, "as though politeness were the cure to anything significantly wrong with Parliament or the country. But the bottom line (if we may use so bald a phrase) is that some of the issues that desperately need to be illuminated in Parliament are not getting the attention they deserve, and the Liberal government is coasting when it should be bouncing."

And so, while the Reform caucus was discovering that not all MPs are mere swine at the trough, it came to see why the distance across the floor of the Commons is measured by sword lengths and how the news is structured by conflict and colour. By the time the House reopened after the 1994 summer recess, the party had decided to move Manning to the front bench and make each of its MPs an expert "critic" in a specific area of government, in order to bring more punch to its arguments. On a more puerile level, the Reformers began heckling and hissing the Liberals and holding up numbers from one to ten, like the Olympic judges do, to score the ministers' answers in Question Period.

That was just show biz compared to the real problem, which remained rooted in Preston Manning's ideal of a leader as a Christlike mediator. He wanted Reform to be a populist party driven by its constituents' wishes rather than by any particular ideology. "In rejecting the state-imposed policies of the welfare state," he once explained, "we have to be careful we don't simply replace those values with other state-imposed values more to our liking but still imposed top-down."

"Though most of his personal views would be conservative," Tom Flanagan noted, "Preston avoids calling himself a conservative and wants to construct a movement that transcends ideological differences. So, in some ways, he's trying to subvert the party he made because it's not what he envisaged. I remember him telling me once that populism isn't an ideology, it's a methodology. It isn't to push an agenda, it's to overcome tensions and reconcile differences. That's why he puts so much more emphasis on representation than on policy A, B, or C."

In April 1994, for example, in what was billed as "the party's first major experiment with direct democracy," Manning devoted inordinate time and resources to producing an hour-long "electronic town hall" on a Calgary cable station. He and four panellists, all Reform MPs, introduced the issue of assisted suicide, interacted with a studio audience, and invited eight hundred previously selected party members as well as the general public to phone in their responses to a series of questions. The results were then calibrated with the results of public meetings, mail surveys, and public-opinion polls in order to determine the thinking of the people, which was then supposed to instruct the Calgary-area MPs how to vote whenever the matter arose in Parliament.

There was certainly nothing wrong with it as an exercise in participatory democracy. Thousands of viewers had a chance to learn about a complex problem; hundreds had a chance to register their opinions. But, as a democratic exercise, it had serious problems. Given that all the panellists and most of the respondents were Reformers, had the findings been manipulated by narrow interests or did they really reflect the will of the people of Calgary? What would the MPs do if most Albertans, most westerners, or most Canadians were found to have an opposite will? And even if the will of the people could be discerned with a reasonable amount of precision, should members of Parliament be rendered incapable of making responsible judgements on their own? Manning certainly implied so, at least in the mind of many Reform voters.

"The real test of a populist is not how many times or how loudly he or she invokes the name of 'the grassroots' in pushing his or her own agenda," he often argued, "but in whether or not he or she is prepared to abide by the majority decision of a democratically constituted assembly or decision-making process, when that decision conflicts with his or her personal preference."

That was easy enough to comprehend in theory, especially on a black-and-white issue and from the vantage of an opposition bench. It was harder to imagine how any party – or any government – could survive if the 295 MPs had no room to negotiate, compromise, or determine the collective interest. In truth, Manning's position did not reduce MPs to mere voting machines or the national interest to the sum of 295 local interests. He saw "the real art of representation" as a balance among the party line, the member's judgement, and the views of the constituents – which was no different from what every parliamentarian would say, except for his caveat that if the three conflict, the discernible will of the majority should prevail over the other two. "If your constituents clearly tell you to do something, you ought to be free to do it," Manning said, "and, secondly, the defeat of a government motion should not necessarily bring down the government."

That still left some tricky questions. What would happen in the field of energy policy, for instance, if the oil-consuming ridings consistently demanded lower prices from the oil-producing ridings? What if, in the area of fiscal policy, those who wanted immediate job creation adamantly overruled those who wanted drastic deficit reduction? What, indeed, would happen to the essential principle of cabinet solidarity? On the important issues, Manning maintained, with enough information and explanation, the public could arrive at a general consensus as it did during the Charlottetown referendum. "The elites think they can distinguish between the local and the national interest," he said, "but they never concede that the people can too. In fact, the people in my riding are more capable than most of the parliamentary committees in Ottawa of thinking nationally and internationally." Yet on gun control, assuming he was accurately reflecting the will of his constituents to oppose it, both the national polls and the national interest put him on the defensive, forcing him to resort to the strange argument that the broad support for it would go down some day, "which makes it a bad law."

Manning's very notion of a popular will arose from a small, relatively homogeneous society – Alberta – with a predominant political culture based upon a unique history of American pioneers and a natural-resources economy. His political philosophy was shaped by the assumption that most Canadians – men and women, anglophones and francophones, WASPs and aboriginals, owners and labourers – share a common perspective and common purposes. And his assumption seemed to have been confirmed as he took Reform beyond Alberta into the other western provinces, the hinterland of Ontario, and the suburbs of Metropolitan Toronto such as Mississauga West. The only things that changed, he claimed, were local nuances and traditions. "We found that if we stuck to our core messages, they resonated everywhere."

Perhaps, but Manning also found that there was a limit to the resonance of fiscal and social conservatism beyond the membership and the caucus. He framed balancing the budget as the way to *preserve* medicare and welfare assistance, for example, and he chided the Royal Canadian Legion for not allowing Sikhs to wear their turbans in its halls. "The purists are content to end up as a right-wing NDP and influence other people's agendas," he said. "But we ought to aim to be a governing party, which means adding people who subscribe to our base but aren't perhaps driven by it. The free market is an economic democracy. Now we have to extend it to bring in people who want decentralized, localized, personalized social reforms and more democratic decision-making like freer votes and referenda. If the NDP had not narrowed down to a coalition of socialistic interest groups, if it had focused instead on the democratic part of its name, it would have had more of a future."

To many of Reform's western conservatives, that implied an abdication of political leadership. Worse, it smacked of the very sort of mainstream, Central Canadian pragmatism they felt had destroyed both the Progressive Conservative party and the country. That worry was the subtext beneath the internal dispute over Preston Manning's expense allowance. It was no coincidence that the sharpest attack came from Stephen Harper, MP for Calgary West, a one-time Tory who had emerged as Reform's most intelligent conservative, or that the Manning-controlled executive council rebuked Harper for criticizing their party leader in the press. The real feud between the two men was between ideological principle and consensual populism.

"We can't avoid pragmatism altogether," Harper explained, "but Reform has to find a way of broadening itself without shedding a significant element of its existing electorate. That's where the Tories erred. They made a decision to become a party of the centre – 'Liberal Party B' – and shed their right-wing element. Now they're the most endangered party because they're the party with the weakest core, even though they may be everybody's second choice. Populism can be seen as just a less elitist form of centrism, and it risks the same dangers in its lack of principles and its appeal to base majoritarianism."

It was the very lack of principles, Harper argued, that would condemn Reform to the NDP's fate. Lack of principles would allow it to be captured by extreme, egocentric interest groups such as the gun lobby and the religious moralists. "In the past," he said, "as long as populist parties were homogeneous or faced common-interest issues, they were okay. But they tended to explode when confronted with important issues that revealed the heterogeneity within them. Since we must become more heterogeneous if we're going to grow, we will either divide on those issues or adopt a philosophy and show traditional signs of party solidarity."

In the spring of 1995, as though to demonstrate the fatal weakness of Manning's populism, Harper announced his intention to break with the party platform and support the Liberals' gun-control legislation.

Not because it matched his own beliefs about law and order, he hastened to add, but because it reflected the wishes of his constituents as overwhelmingly confirmed in householders' surveys and scientific polls in Calgary West. As well as signalling tensions within the party and the caucus, Harper's little "experiment" in free votes tested Manning's own doubts about whether "a grassroots, bottom–up party [could] maintain the unity and self-discipline necessary to fight a successful election campaign and to act as a cohesive force in a divided Parliament." It also raised an embarrassing question: How had Preston Manning come to the opposite conclusion about the will of the people on gun control, when his riding was immediately south of Stephen Harper's? More confusing still, by the time the final legislation arrived in June, Harper voted against it, while three other Reform MPs, including the Whip from Calgary Centre, now said their constituents wanted them to vote for it!

"Preston hasn't got an authoritarian personality," said Tom Flanagan, who shared Harper's conservatism. "He doesn't like conflict and he's reluctant to give orders. If he feels he can't carry the party, he will veer, like he did with the Charlottetown referendum. But he has a clear conception of what he wants and he doesn't like being pushed off his own agenda. And because the link between the leader and the grassroots is so important and so direct in the Reform party, he is the ultimate interpreter of what the people really want. He selects the appropriate mechanism for determining their will – questionnaires, straw votes, task forces, trial balloons – and he has all kinds of procedural devices and rhetorical tricks to try and shape it. That's why he's been having so much trouble with his caucus: elected MPs aren't willing to accept that kind of leadership."

On the whole, however, Reform MPs rarely broke ranks on a parliamentary vote. Like Carolyn Parrish, they had experienced the pressure to defer to the leadership and behave as a team, not least because a divided caucus looks bad in the eyes of the very same voters and editorialists who regularly denounce the herd mentality of party discipline. And, unlike the Liberals, the Reformers were so similar in their backgrounds and interests that they did not have to contend with major regional, ethnic, or philosophical strains. Reform was more like the Bloc Québécois in this way. It saw almost every issue from the viewpoint of one region with one language and one agenda.

That had begun to change as Manning gradually manoeuvred his membership from western protest movement to national political party and his MPs adapted to the customs of the political class. Within months of arriving in Parliament, a number of them – including Manning – started taking French lessons, and some were soon seen strolling through the tunnels under the Hill swapping ideas and laughing with members of the Bloc. Then, within a year of the election, the party brass decided to hold Reform's 1994 assembly in the national capital, even though the vast majority of its seats and members were in Alberta and British Columbia. "Politically, some may view Ottawa as the centre for bureaucratic intrusion in their lives," the glossy souvenir program reassured the more nervous delegates, "but physically, you will find a city of quiet beauty, diverse nightlife, and friendly, hospitable people." All the documents and proceedings were available in French translation; tours of the Parliament Buildings came with a chance to "be treated to coffee in the infamous Commons cafeteria"; there was even a visit to see the controversial Barnett Newman painting the National Gallery had purchased in 1990 for $1.7 million of taxpayers' money.

At first, despite their undisguised pride and pleasure in the election results, the thirteen hundred delegates seemed determined to resist all the temptations of this rapacious Sodom and its French-speaking Gomorrah across the river. They even clung to their illusion that Reform was not really a political party, but instead, as the chairman of the executive council reminded them, "a movement of concerned Canadians fighting the status quo and the entrenched political elite." Though they reversed their resolution to send anyone convicted of three or more serious offences to jail for life after several Reform MPs alerted them to some legal and practical ramifications, they were determined not to be railroaded by the so-called pros. And though they backed away from a union-busting resolution so as not to offend their working-class vote in British Columbia and Ontario, they pressed ahead with a series of hard-line policies on immigration, crime, gay rights, and social spending.

Manning was not perturbed. He didn't think the grassroots resolutions had pushed Reform into the ideological cul-de-sac that had doomed Social Credit and the NDP. "We're sticking basically to the principles that got us here and we're doing well with those," he told the press. "I don't think we have to change a lot, but we have to communicate better in order to see some political increase."

He was also counting on something much more powerful than communications to sweep his party into office: a political or economic crisis that would smash the old order and unite the people behind a strong and single purpose. "When it becomes evident in the 1995 budget that the deficit is still out of control and higher taxes are in the offing, what then?" he asked the delegates. "And when Chrétien goes into a Quebec referendum campaign offering only status quo federalism, and it becomes evident that that isn't good enough for Canadians coast to coast, what then?"

What then, he implied, was a Reform victory – so long as Reform took care to position itself cleverly. "He believes that, because populist parties are too small to make waves, they have to paddle around in the trough and wait for the waves to hit," said Tom Flanagan, who titled his insightful history of the party *Waiting for the Wave*. "That accounts for his sudden shifts and the sense of opportunism." Thus, Manning rode the wave of western alienation, then the wave for lower deficits and lower taxes, then the wave against the Meech Lake and Charlottetown agreements, then the wave against immigration and crime. Now, it seemed, he was going to ride the wave of speculation about the future place of Quebec within Confederation to establish himself, not Jean Chrétien, as the legitimate spokesman for English Canada.

While the separation of Quebec would represent an obvious setback to Manning's faith in reconciliation and the common sense of the common people, he once thought it highly likely. "I think there's a bunch of Quebec politicians who are going to make a break for trying to get out in the 1990s," he was quoted as saying in Jeffrey Simpson's book, *Faultlines*, before the success of the Bloc Québécois in the 1993 national election and the victory of the Parti Québécois in Quebec in September 1994. "Some federal leader, some prime minister, is going to wind up sitting across the table discussing a secession agreement." But, within that dark prophecy, there was a golden chance for the Reform party. Given Quebec's seventy-five seats in the House of Commons and the odds against Reform's ever capturing any of them, Manning stood a considerably better chance of becoming prime minister of the "rest of Canada" than of Canada as a whole.

Until that fateful day, he had to deal with the possibility – later the probability – that Quebec would decide to stay. Hence his promise to organize a full slate of candidates in the province before the next election. Hence, too, his call for a "third option" between separation and the status quo. "We say exactly the same thing to Quebeckers that we say to discontented and disillusioned Canadians everywhere," he told the Reform assembly. "Provide equality for all provinces and citizens.

Decentralize federal powers. Make language and culture matters of personal and provincial responsibility. Make the streets safer for ordinary Canadians. Make elected officials more accountable to the people. And balance the federal budget, providing tax relief and more jobs. This is the third option."

Miraculously, instead of yawning and jeering at what surely sounded like the beginning of yet another round of consultations and negotiations leading to yet another constitutional initiative, the delegates leapt to their feet and gave Manning the loudest ovation of the evening. Some even waved small Quebec flags. Gone was the grumbling about his leadership. Gone, apparently, after just four days in Central Canada, was the old fury about all the time the political class wasted blathering about national unity instead of concentrating on economic growth. There did not even seem to be any suspicion that Manning's devolution of federal programs and language policy was nothing but the latest variation on the Tories' old game, as practised by Joe Clark and Brian Mulroney, of catering to the Quebec nationalists for medium-term partisan advantage.

Once again, in his own coy way, part evangelical rhetoric, part management technique, Manning had led the grassroots to accept his way as though it were their own. "If the people believe you will defer to them when they really want it," he once revealed to the *Star*'s Richard Gwyn, "they will let you get away with a lot." And so, by his deference – or seeming deference – to their workshop debates and policy resolutions, he won the greater battle. He got them to crave more than moral rectitude and mere influence. He got them to crave electoral victory and executive authority. "I think the hard core of our membership is determined to build a national party," he declared, "and their goal is to form a national government before the end of the century."

The Reform party had come a long way in seven years. Out of nothing, it captured fifty-two seats, attracted two and a half million voters, displaced the Conservatives in Western Canada, and pulled the political debate of the nation toward its own priorities and policies. Success was now transporting Reformers into a broader political world, where their simple solutions ran into complex trade-offs and their common assumptions clashed with diverse interests. There they began to learn the same lesson it had taken the Conservatives almost twenty years in opposition to appreciate: Unless you can win power, your best ideas and soundest principles will be like dogs barking at the caravan.

Thought-Control Centre

What should have been one of the happiest days of Paul Martin Jr.'s life, the day he finally became a minister in the government of Canada like his beloved father fifty years before him, was wrecked by the news that his eighty-year-old mother had just suffered a serious stroke. Martin had to dash directly from the ceremony at Rideau Hall, where he was sworn in as minister of finance on November 5, 1993, to get to her bedside in Windsor's Hotel-Dieu Hospital, where she lay in a coma.

Presently, she opened her eyes and saw him standing in the unfamiliar room. "Why?" she mumbled. Martin explained to her that she had fallen ill, that he was there to be with her. Five minutes later she again studied his face and asked why. He again explained what had happened. "No, no," she said. "Why do you want to be minister of finance?"

Why, indeed. Given that the job entailed responsibility for the nation's half-trillion-dollar debt and is considered a career-killer in politics – only four finance ministers in Canadian history, including Jean Chrétien, had succeeded in becoming prime minister – it was a question that Martin had often asked himself. He had even let it be known that he wanted to get his hands on Industry and become, like C. D. Howe in the 1950s, the czar of Canada's economic development. When Chrétien asked him to take Finance, however, he was ready to agree, thanks largely to the anxious appeals of his friends in the business community and a convincing argument from Ed Lumley, a former minister of industry under Pierre Trudeau.

"He'd been there," Martin explained, "and he told me I was crazy not to want Finance instead. Finance is where the action is, it's at the centre of the whole thing. Did I want to be forever trying to convince a reluctant minister of finance about something or did I want to be the minister of finance whom everyone else was trying to convince?"

Power proved the irresistible lure, in other words, for Paul Martin had left behind an extremely successful corporate career and comfortable private life in Montreal in order, as he put it, "to get things done" in Ottawa. That's why his five years on the opposition benches had been so frustrating for him – nothing but whining and snivelling, as

Preston Manning was learning, for the sake of whining and snivelling
– and that's why he did not really care if he sacrificed his chance to
become prime minister so long as he could realize his economic
vision.

Above all else, Martin dreamed of reconstructing the federal government into an effective instrument for economic growth, while
simultaneously dismantling the obstacles Ottawa had put in the way of
growth. In theory, that meant manipulating the levers of state to facilitate the creation of small businesses and help them blossom into
transnational companies that dominate "niche" markets all over the
world, just as the United States had been doing through its defence
contracts and Japan through its Ministry of International Trade and
Industry. "The biggest problem," he thought, "is that government has
tried to do a whole lot of things, instead of concentrating on doing
what it has to do really well. The role of the nation-state is not to be
protectionist or pour huge sums into megaprojects. Surely to God it's
to make sure, in terms of comparative advantage, that its people are
constantly increasing their productive capacity through education,
innovation, and entrepreneurship. If it focused on getting the crucial
things right, everything else would flow."

In practice, it meant promoting research and development; training the young and the unemployed for the knowledge economy;
gathering and disseminating information and ideas; building linkages
between businesses; helping small companies get access to venture
capital and the latest technologies; reducing payroll taxes; updating the
infrastructure; and opening the doors to new export markets. "Take
the need to provide loan capital to small business as an example," Martin explained. "The Tories would simply withdraw, saying that the
private sector should do it. Fine, I say, except that the banks themselves admit there's a limit to what they can do. The answer isn't for
government to do it directly, because I don't think government can
do it right. But Ottawa can make sure that it gets done."

More painfully, as the Liberals' Red Book admitted, "any strategy
to foster the growth of the small and medium-sized business sector
will fail if it does not recognize the negative impacts of excessive government debt, interprovincial trade barriers, and taxation policies."
Unlike the old activism, in other words, the new activism would not
be built on money, rules, and intimidation. It would be built on partnership, leverage, and salesmanship. And that required a breadth of
understanding and depth of conviction able to stand firm against the

onslaught of financial and political pressures – an understanding and conviction some of Martin's greatest admirers weren't sure he had.

"He understands the social reform side because of his dad," said one, "and he understands the fiscal conservative side because he's probably the richest guy in the House of Commons who's made it on his own. But he hasn't ingested or metabolized the innovative economy side to the same degree. He has to work at it. It isn't in his guts or his instincts."

In fact, though Martin's ideas owed much to the American economist Lester Thurow, the guru of national growth strategies who had been invited to give a keynote speech at the Liberal policy conference in 1991, the new finance minister was equally impressed by Paul Krugman's *Peddling Prosperity*, with its emphasis on improving domestic productivity, and David Osborne and Ted Gaebler's *Reinventing Government*, the best-selling manual on how to imbue the public sector with entrepreneurial zeal, which was (as he once said, pointing to the book) "what I want to do in spades."

Martin may have been more a doer than an intellectual – he himself credited his hands-on business experience as "the single most important influence" on his economic thinking – but he had the bright, curious mind of a policy wonk with an excitement about the latest idea and the big picture. He had grown up as a child of the political class with the table talk and huge library of a brilliant man who had three academic degrees and almost forty years of public life, after all, and he himself had studied philosophy and law at his father's urging. He might well have become just another right-wing stockbroker like Michael Wilson, he admitted, if not for being the son of Paul Martin Sr.

His father's legacy as the architect of Canada's postwar social programs, and John Fitzgerald Kennedy's rhetoric of the early 1960s, inspired young Paul with an altruism that first expressed itself in a desire to serve in the Third World. But Martin was persuaded by Maurice Strong, then president of Power Corporation in Montreal, later chairman of Petro-Canada and Ontario Hydro, that the developing nations had little need for either a philosophy graduate or a lawyer. So, in 1966, Martin went to work for Strong to learn something more useful, and he stayed on after Paul Desmarais bought control of Power two years later because he had discovered in himself an aptitude and a passion for business.

In 1981, with interest rates above 22 per cent and little money of his own to invest, he took an enormous gamble by acquiring his boss's stake in CSL Group, which included Voyageur buses and Kingsway trucks as well as the Great Lakes carriers of Canada Steamship Lines, after raising $197 million in equal partnership with shipping magnate Laurence Pathy (whom he bought out after seven years). "He saw a unique opportunity and had the courage to take it," said Maurice Strong, "and that's unusual because very few business people take both the company route and the entrepreneurial route. Though he was safe where he was, he put all his resources on the line to make a major acquisition that could have broken him."

On the contrary, it made him a fortune estimated at over $30 million, partly because interest rates quickly eased and partly because Martin had the vision to turn the stolid company into a high-tech, international conglomerate. "When he bought it," said David Herle, an Ottawa consultant who had worked for Martin both in business and in politics, "CSL had an aging fleet going up and down the St. Lawrence River and a shrinking market. Now it has ships all over the world, and its self-unloading cargo carriers are world-beaters in the industry. If he hadn't forced those changes, CSL might now be bankrupt."

Martin's private-sector training, tinged no doubt with the bitterness he had felt about his father's humiliating defeat at the 1968 Liberal leadership convention, made him an ardent critic of most of Pierre Trudeau's high-spending and interventionist policies. He thought that the made-in-Canada oil price of 1973 and the National Energy Program of 1980 were particularly bad decisions. "Trudeau tried to isolate us by claiming we could withdraw into ourselves and operate on oil prices lower than the rest of the world," he used to argue. "From then on we stopped evolving." Indeed, in his belief that the creation of wealth was as important as its distribution, Paul Martin Jr. often sounded closer to his old friend John Turner and his Westmount neighbour Brian Mulroney than to his left-wing father or his golfing buddy Jean Chrétien.

"The great advantage of the marketplace isn't that it's smarter than government," he said. "It's that it has a multiplicity of players, some making mistakes, some doing things right, so that in the end there's a positive evolution. But because government acts in such a big way, when it's wrong, an awful lot of people get hurt."

Martin was always a loyal Liberal, nevertheless. Despite his growing wealth and status, he never cultivated Turner's Bay Street style or Mulroney's addiction to the rich and powerful. Nor did he adopt the airs of a self-made tycoon. It was a trait he had inherited from his mother Nell, an "I'm from Missouri" kind of woman who delighted in pricking her husband's pretensions with a sharp "Poppa, subside!" Though Martin did indulge himself by gentrifying a three-hundred-acre farm in Quebec's Eastern Townships, he preferred spending weekends with his wife Sheila and their three sons, tending his herd of cattle or reading a serious book, to sipping martinis with the sailing-and-tennis set in nearby Knowlton. And, unlike most of the corporate elite among whom he moved, he was more interested in building a better society than in building a better widget.

"I *really* loved business," Martin said, "but I never felt that you could make the contribution in business that you could in public life. Maybe I chose politics because I subconsciously absorbed all those speeches in which my father said it was the highest vocation after the clergy."

Despite the qualms of his wife and parents, he ran in the 1988 federal election in the working-class Montreal riding of LaSalle-Emard hoping to do for Canada what he had done for CSL Group: put it on a sound financial footing, increase its productivity, and make it a leader in technological change and the global economy. "Very few business leaders have the courage or will to leave their comfortable, exciting positions to go into politics and do something about what they think has to be done," said Tom d'Aquino, president of the Business Council on National Issues. "Paul did, and that's a real sign that he cares enough. He wants to do good. He has a genuine desire to serve his country."

Barely established in Ottawa, Martin took on Jean Chrétien for the leadership of the Liberal party in 1990, not because he had much chance of winning or a prime-ministerial destiny to fulfil, but to gain a wider audience for his ideas. "What we are seeing in this leadership race is a confrontation of two visions of government and of the country," he told *Maclean's* at the time. "One says that it's not necessary to have a clear agenda, and that muddling through is the way to govern. The other says that muddling through has led the country to the pickle that it's now in."

"He doesn't love politics, he may not even like it," said Herle, who directed Martin's campaign. "What he likes is government and public policy. Though he's getting better, he used to be dreadful working a room or engaging in small talk. 'What'll I talk about?' he'd ask when we forced him to phone convention delegates. 'Talk about the weather, anything, it doesn't matter,' we'd say. So he'd call and say, 'How's your weather?' then hang up!"

Martin lost the fight for delegates, but he managed to win the fight for ideas. In 1991, at the party's policy conference in Aylmer, he was instrumental in reversing the left wing's protectionist and interventionist sway. Subsequently he got most of his agenda in the Red Book. With the Liberals' victory, the routing of the left, and Chrétien's self-confessed aversion to grand plans and fancy ideas, Martin had ample reason to imagine himself the thought-control centre of the new government.

Indeed, though the Department of Finance had always been a locus of power in Ottawa, it was soon to garner even more clout than in Ed Lumley's day. Trudeau had checked it by building a strong Privy Council Office and introducing a collegial system of cabinet decision making. Mulroney had controlled it by trumping its fiscal projections with his own political calculations and making his deputy prime minister its boss. But Chrétien reduced the strength of the PCO and abolished all but two cabinet committees, thus weakening the collective counterweight to Finance's authority. And, mindful of his own humiliation at Finance in 1978 when Trudeau had unilaterally announced huge spending cuts, Chrétien conceded Martin remarkable independence within the whole field of economic and fiscal policy.

Screw the Red Book

Shortly after taking over Finance, Paul Martin asked to have a look at Kim Campbell's deficit reduction plan. He discovered, to his surprise, that the department had never made one. When first presented with three huge briefing books, he threw them across the room because of their inadequacies. But what frustrated him most were those bureaucrats who insisted on treating the Red Book, which had been patched together with the scant resources available to an opposition party, the way fundamentalists treat the Bible. Time and again, in order to get them to think beyond it, Martin himself was heard to yell, "Screw the Red Book!"

It had never been intended, in fact, to carry the Liberal government through its entire first term in power. "It gave the political direction," said Chrétien's policy adviser Chaviva Hosek, with whom Martin wrote the Red Book, "but it didn't do the work for us. Its limitations were always apparent with the resources and information we had. For example, it touched gingerly on the need to remove disincentives to work built into the UI and social-assistance system, partly because it wasn't clear what the right answer was, partly because the right answer would have to emerge from federal-provincial debate. So there wasn't a consensus about what to do, only an understanding that this was a problem area."

Once in office, Prime Minister Chrétien's own bias was to look to the civil service for answers. His experience had taught him that the best policies emerge from strong ministers working in close partnership with strong deputies. "I never pretended to know everything," he wrote in his memoirs, "and many Ottawa bureaucrats are extremely well educated, well read, and nobody's fool. Knowledge is power, and in many cases these people got to power because of their knowledge. Of course, a minister must place the facts and opinions in a political perspective and not be overwhelmed by them, but on the whole the stronger and more intelligent the officials, the better the minister."

The bureaucracy he had inherited from Brian Mulroney, however, was neither as strong nor as intelligent as the one Chrétien had known under Pearson and Trudeau. Not only had it yet to fully absorb the massive departmental restructuring Kim Campbell had ordered in June 1993, it was still hurting from the neo-conservative contempt for federal public servants and the populist attack against the entire political class. The very word *bureaucracy* had become synonymous with fat, faceless apparatchiks, at best a stupid leviathan of top-down management, at worst an evil tyrant. After a decade of unrelenting cutbacks and reorganization, its ranks were battle weary, demoralized, and underpaid. "Particularly in the last couple of years," added Arthur Kroeger, "when the Tories became alarmed by the rise of Reform, they wanted to show they could be tough too. So they turned on their own people. Demeaning things were said, even though the public servants were no less competent or loyal than they had been before."

In addition to money and honour, the public service lost many of its best and brightest to early retirement or the cash-green fields of corporate lobbying. There were few rewards and little demand for thinking, and Mulroney's habit of yanking the sharper minds from policy development into crisis management – or, worse, into his own office – crippled the system's capacity to offer long-term, broad-ranging advice. Fixing yesterday's problems, especially those produced by the failure of the Meech Lake Accord, took precedence over developing tomorrow's solutions. "That's why it was a double tragedy for Mulroney to have destroyed the Economic Council of Canada and the Science Council," Martin observed. "To have destroyed the policy-making side of the bureaucracy *and* two important think tanks was just crazy."

Consequently, though the Liberals arrived with almost no mistrust of the civil service (despite the large number of Tories who had prudently insinuated themselves into its comfiest ranks before the election), they were faced with the formidable task of rebuilding its policy capacity at a time of no money. "We thought the bureaucracy would be ready to bounce back after the Mulroney years," said one of Chrétien's confidants, "but every major file was really exhausted and brain-dead. When we went looking for advice about what to do, we were told, 'You give *us* the answers and we'll do the analysis to show you're right.' That's how things had been done for a decade. They were actually afraid to think, in case it cost them their jobs or promotions." Even late into the Liberals' second year in office, a witness to a meeting involving many of the bureaucracy's senior policy officials described the scene as "really scary and depressing. With only two possible exceptions, none of them had a clue what to do or even what was expected of them."

Finance, which had not been as decimated and discouraged as most departments under the Tories, was an exception, but it too suffered from the general fatigue and empty-headedness that had contributed to Kim Campbell's defeat. Even the public had cause to wonder about its competence after budget upon budget of erroneous forecasts, the impolitic introduction of the GST, and the particularly severe effects of its anti-inflation policies in the wake of the Free Trade Agreement and the cyclical downturn.

"I don't blame the bureaucracy for not having the ideas or the sense of direction," Martin said. "It's the responsibility of the elected government to have a vision of where it wants to go. I would have blamed the bureaucrats if they had tried to stall on it, but I didn't run into that in Finance. Sometimes they fought me, but they didn't stall."

To the electorate, Paul Martin was an affable and unassuming guy. He was generally liked and well regarded, even by his adversaries in the Commons and the press gallery, and he had developed into a popular stump-speaker with ready humour and passionate conviction. Sometimes he slammed the table a little too hard in stating his case; sometimes he showed a flash of anger or raised his voice to an exasperated whine; but rarely did he appear arrogant or unapproachable. He often told the story of coming within inches of being hit by a car when absentmindedly jaywalking in Toronto one day. The driver rolled down his window and shouted, "Martin, you horse's ass, don't tempt me!"

"Sometimes I think he should look more worried," Preston Manning joked. "My father remembers old James Ilsley, who was finance minister during the war and the walking embodiment of worry. Everybody used to really think twice about adding to his burdens."

In the middle of many a night, in fact, Martin did lie awake worrying. "What am I going to do about the country?" he sometimes asked his wife – then promptly fell asleep, leaving her to do the worrying. Often he carried his nightmares into the office the next day. Contrary to his nice-guy image, he was a demanding taskmaster with relentless stamina and an explosive temper. Though his tantrums blew over with amazing speed and few lasting grudges, his officials often toiled in an atmosphere of high suspense, never certain what mood or idea would possess their minister next. David Dodge, his deputy minister, had to scold him from time to time for shouting at departmental juniors who felt understandably reluctant to shout back. "He's very high maintenance," admitted Terrie O'Leary, his key political adviser. "He's emotionally and physically exhausting. He believes in tension. He sees it in a positive light."

"When he gets interested in something," Chaviva Hosek added, "he bores his way through it by reading everything about it, asking everybody about it, and taking nothing for granted. But once he's made up his mind, it's a major struggle to get him to change it. You think you've convinced him, and then you have to convince him again. Sometimes he just returns to his original bent. Sometimes he's decided he's lost too many fights that month and doesn't want to lose another one."

"Government is concerned with umpteen thousand things and it's constantly getting diverted from its top priorities," Martin said in his own defence. "But I'm not psychologically capable of deviating from the goals I've put on the agenda. I'll tell my people, 'Christ Almighty! These are the things we've got to get done, so don't come to me with other things, we'll talk about them later. In the meantime, by God, you'd better do *this* and there's no excuse!'"

As a high-risk entrepreneur, Martin had little patience with Finance's reactive, stay-the-course mentality, and he found its abstract macroeconomic theories somewhat disconnected from the day-to-day realities he had known in business. "Don't give me the forty thousand reasons I can't do that!" he would shout. "Tell me the one thing that will make it happen." Rather than purging the department, he preferred to bring it around to his own power of positive thinking and to bolster its weak areas by reaching for advice from "every goddamn person I could talk to." Terrie O'Leary became, as one official called her, "Dodge's second master," and, in February 1994, Martin brought in his good friend and intellectual soul mate, Peter Nicholson, as "visiting economist."

Nicholson, a former Liberal member of the Nova Scotia legislature and an executive with Canada's largest fisheries company before he joined the Bank of Nova Scotia as a senior vice-president, was immediately commissioned to write the eighty-seven-page statement of objectives, *A New Framework for Economic Policy*, dubbed the Purple Book, that Martin released the following October. Despite its economic angle, the Purple Book was received as the revised version of the Red Book by all twenty-two departments of the federal government. (The public missed almost all of its proactivist import, however, because the media went as usual for the negative and confrontational, fixating on the document's one chapter about the deficit.)

"In a knowledge-based economy," it stated, "success depends less on a nation's natural endowment and more on its skills and innovative capacities – in other words, on 'comparative advantages' that can be shaped by government policy." As examples, in addition to high-quality education, health care, and infrastructure, the report cited the federal government's financial and regulatory role in developing the "information highway," its direct and indirect spending on science and technology, and its strategic emphasis on expanding trade with the rapidly developing markets in Asia, Latin America, and Eastern Europe.

Several press commentators cleverly noted that purple is what you get if you mix Liberal red with Tory blue. Yet the Purple Book's ideological base was neither neo-conservative politics nor neo-classical economics. It was, in its respect for the state and its reservations about the market, the latest expression of Canadian Liberalism. "It's hard for Liberals to give up the idea of an industrial strategy," Preston Manning noted, while his party's finance critic wondered if "the same people who brought us the post office are going to bring us more job training."

"That has worried me a great deal about Paul," said Tom d'Aquino, who otherwise greeted the Purple Book with a loud hallelujah. "Like the 'Atari Democrats' in the United States, he wrongly believes that government should have a stronger, proactive role, that it can be creative and inventive. The truth is, governments have been very damaging. Finance is the best place to realize the limitations of government, but Paul still has some travelling to do on the road to Damascus."

As it turned out, neither Manning nor d'Aquino had much reason to worry. Martin was made aware of the limitations of government, and the particular constraints of his portfolio, very quickly. "If our tax system were competitive, if our debt were low, if our regulations weren't a burden, I would be a bit of an Atari Democrat," he admitted after a year on the job. "But those things aren't right."

It was only a matter of months before critics – and not a few of his friends – started wondering if Paul Martin Jr. had not been brainwashed by the bureaucrats in Finance into becoming just another Michael Wilson after all. Not that he hadn't been warned. "Before Paul got into politics," said Wilson, happily back on Bay Street after fourteen punishing years in the political class, "he used to ask me, 'What's it like, Mike?' and I'd say that making a decision in the private sector is easy in comparison. In government you may make absolutely the right decision in a business sense, but the politics can come along and push it in a direction you can't control."

Up Against the Wall

Paul Martin had barely got comfortable in his office on the twenty-first floor of L'Esplanade Laurier before his officials confronted him with the awful truth. The fiscal situation, which he had assumed would be bad, was much, much worse. According to the Tories' last budget, the 1993-94 deficit was expected to be $32.6 billion and on its way down to $8 billion within four years. Instead, the new finance minister was told, the current deficit was now projected to be closer to $45 billion – more than a third higher! – with almost all of it being borrowed to pay the interest on the national debt. The interest itself would be more than the federal government would spend on the old and the unemployed combined, and the interest on the interest would be more than Ottawa's contribution to either agriculture or postsecondary education.

Both Martin and his prime minister remained committed, nevertheless, to the Liberals' election pledge to reduce the deficit to 3 per cent of Canada's Gross Domestic Product, about $25 billion, by 1996-97. Chrétien had chosen that target because it was the standard the European Union had set for its member nations. Martin – who, for what Hosek called "macho" reasons, had tried to get the party to commit to a balanced budget within a specific period in the Red Book – agreed, after roughly calculating that it was where the growth in the economy would finally exceed the growth in the debt under normal circumstances. It was a level Ottawa had not reached in two decades.

"I didn't know how difficult it was going to be to reach," he said, "but I understood the riveting effect of focusing on a short-term target and not deviating from it. A long-term, unrealistic target wouldn't have given me the 'anchor' to take the tough steps now and build up my credibility."

With little better than three months to put together his first budget, he only had time to contemplate cuts in the costliest areas. Lloyd Axworthy, the minister of human resources development, who had already had cabinet experience in the area of social policy, was ready to trim unemployment insurance benefits; David Collenette, in Defence, was prepared to close a large number of obsolete facilities; and Ottawa carved $1.2 billion out of federal-provincial transfers over two years. "They were sufficient to get us to our target," Martin said, "*if* my economic assumptions held."

It was a very big if, he realized, though he had set his growth projections on the safe side and squirrelled away considerable emergency reserves. "I *knew* something would bugger me up," as he put it, "I just didn't know what the hell it would be."

Whether his assumptions held or not, Martin was still not satisfied with stopping at the 3-per-cent interim or taking a slash-and-burn approach to deficit reduction. He understood why it was necessary to strive for a balanced budget before the next cyclical downturn. And he wanted to use the necessity of cuts to force every department to make *selective* decisions about the best role for the federal government, within its own areas and in relation to the provinces and the private sector.

"In the past," he explained, "government would chip away at its operating costs without looking at the programs themselves. In the few areas where real cuts were made, the problem was not necessarily the 10 or 15 per cent that was lopped off. The problem was that they did not pay any attention to doing better with the 85 or 90 per cent that was left. That led to a situation where, in some areas, there were too few people delivering programs that were priorities – and, in other areas, too many people delivering programs that didn't make sense."

While Lloyd Axworthy launched an extensive review of social-assistance payments and old-age pensions, which together accounted for about half of Ottawa's $120 billion in program spending, Martin set the "targets and parameters" for a complete re-examination of the other half under the aegis of the minister of intergovernmental affairs, Marcel Massé, himself a former federal mandarin. Every department was asked to re-evaluate each of its programs according to six guiding questions: Does it continue to serve a public interest? Is there a legitimate and necessary role for government in it? Is the current role of the federal government appropriate? What could or should be transferred, in whole or in part, to the private or voluntary sector? How could the efficiency of what remained be improved, and is it all affordable? If not, what would be abandoned?

Not only did Martin expect the answers to start helping his numbers in the second budget, he hoped to use the budget as "the shock troops" to advance his own ideas about the way government should work. Every major Liberal initiative, from Art Eggleton's $6-billion infrastructure program to Doug Young's commercialization of airports, from Brian Tobin's overhaul of the fisheries to Ralph Goodale's musings about farm-subsidy cuts, had a philosophical link to Martin's Red Book and a practical link to the Finance Department.

"There's no question that Paul's reputation in the cabinet exceeds his authority over the numbers," said John Manley, the industry minister, who consulted Martin several times in preparing his own proposals for building an innovative economy. "In my case, it's because I know that he's been through the issues that concern me."

By April 1994, however, Martin himself became preoccupied by the numbers. Just as he had predicted, something did bugger up his first budget's projections: interest rates unexpectedly jumped by 2 per cent in the wake of inflationary pressures in the United States and the threat of Quebec independence, with each percentage point translating into more than $1.5 billion of new spending – and new borrowing. The jump cancelled out the gains Finance was making with a better-than-expected recovery and the subsequent creation of

hundreds of thousands of jobs. If Martin wanted to meet his targets –
as he was publicly committed to doing "come hell or high water" –
growth and a few more taxes were not going to get him there: he
needed a lot more cuts.

"That wasn't a change of mind, it was a change of economic circumstances," he insisted. "A year ago there was no growth and lower
interest rates. Today there's lots of growth but an interest-rate problem, and failure to deal with the deficit will mean escalating interest
rates. That's what changed."

Facing both hell *and* high water, he went back to Marcel Massé and
said he now wanted to use program review, which had been intended
as a methodical five-year process, to help get him his second- and
third-year projections. He even requested savings as high as 50 per
cent of some departmental budgets. Deliberately or inadvertently,
Martin charged the entire apparatus of government with the bottom-
line discipline he had applied to Canada Steamship Lines and the creative tension he had brought to Finance.

With an upswing in both the nation's economy and the government's popularity, not a few of his colleagues started challenging the
accuracy of Finance's economic assumptions and the urgency of its
demands. "What planet is he coming from?" Deputy Prime Minister
Sheila Copps asked in dismay after Martin proposed tampering with
old-age pensions. Even a decentralist like Massé was heard to say that
he was reluctant to downsize the civil service, save by attrition, given
how many of his constituents in Hull-Aylmer were federal bureaucrats. "Finance came to us trying to wear the deficit problem like a
giant gorilla costume," one ministerial adviser grumbled. "It still
behaves like a superpower, but it's only a shadow of its former self
because its numbers have been so often wrong."

Turf wars erupted all over the capital. However much Martin's
colleagues in the cabinet and caucus still agreed with his basic thrust,
they proved a lot more helpful about where *others* should cut. Thus,
while Lloyd Axworthy accepted the realities of Martin's job and
shared his desire to rejig social programs to fit the new economy, he
grew increasingly unhappy about having to take the heat for the cuts
for which Martin was trying to reap the glory. At the same time,
though the two men maintained a cordial relationship – despite a
rivalry for intellectual supremacy which, as a mutual friend commented, "Lloyd wouldn't concede and Paul wouldn't notice" – their
officials became engaged in a classic competition between those trying

to maximize the benefits to their client groups and those in charge of slashing expenditures.

During a major speech in September, Prime Minister Chrétien strengthened Finance's hand by again reaffirming the 3-per-cent-of-GDP goal, but he refused to back Martin over any other minister or knock heads. Martin had to take "the crap," as he called it, all by himself. Eventually, as departments, regions, and particular interests snarled over the remaining morsels, a cabinet subcommittee was established, with Massé in the chair, to broker the trade-offs. "That's the only way to build cabinet consensus," Martin understood, "and when I sit down with the prime minister and tell him how I see the priorities, I want to have more than my own judgement. I want to be able to say that this is where people are. But, in the end, this budget will be made by two people: the prime minister and his minister of finance."

It remained uncertain, however, whether Martin had the focus and control to reinvent government according to his vision of what it should do well and what it should abandon. As he repeated time and again, "the devil is in the details," yet he had neither the authority nor the inclination to manage the fine details. His job was to manage the nation's finances, and his distaste for political schmoozing and backroom deals prevented him from exploiting the time-honoured ways by which ministers have got what they wanted. Some departments tried hard to meet their financial targets in ways that met the economic principles articulated in either the Red Book or the Purple Book. Many others did not try at all: they just slashed their programs across the board.

"The economics in the Purple Book is solid," Judith Maxwell, former chair of the Economic Council of Canada, observed, "but it's not at all clear how you transform that into a redefinition of the role of government or a microeconomic agenda. The ambiguities of getting out of business subsidies are horrendous, for example – is the CBC or the CMHC a business subsidy? – and we haven't seen how those ideas can be actually implemented in the present context."

As a result, Martin soon discovered, his power to get less government did not necessarily translate into a power to get better government. "Paul's view is to give people the parameters and let them go into their departments and do what they want," David Walker, his parliamentary secretary, said in the midst of the review process, "and that's put him in a sort of halfway house because it's been difficult to get the ideas going in the right shape. So right now we're just using the budget framework, rather than any overriding principles, to force departments to rethink what they're doing."

There wasn't really any choice. The Liberals had put themselves so far out on a limb that failure to meet the 3-per-cent goal would undoubtedly precipitate a political and financial crisis (assuming higher interest rates and the Quebec referendum did not trigger one first). There was also a profound skepticism in the bond markets that Martin would press on toward a balanced budget – or even, as some analysts now thought necessary, a surplus – with the economy heading for a downturn, so much blood already on the floor, and another election in sight. "He may have vague intentions," Preston Manning commented, "but I don't think he has any concrete plans to get there or that he'll be allowed to go as far as he wants by his colleagues and his prime minister."

In January 1995, while the cabinet was gathering to broker the results of the program review in final preparation for the second budget, currency traders ran the Canadian dollar down to a nine-year low, prompting yet another hike in interest rates and further speculation about an impending "lenders' strike." The *Wall Street Journal* dubbed Canada "an honorary member of the Third World." Then, two weeks before the budget, Moody's investors service announced it was going to review Ottawa's credit rating. Though the moves were probably reactions to the fall of the Mexican peso in December rather than calculated attempts to influence Ottawa's decisions (which had already been made anyway), they did serve to remind the cabinet, the caucus, and much of the country that the global money managers were watching very, very closely.

"Indeed," Thomas Friedman wrote in the *New York Times*, "Moody's message to both Canada and Mexico is that either you vote the economic pain on yourself – in the form of deep cuts in government spending and higher domestic interest rates to suppress inflation – or the bond market will force you to do it by withholding capital."

There was no longer any question, it seemed, in whose interest the political class of Canada was governing. It was governing to satisfy the bearers of its debt, 44 per cent of which was held by foreigners, all of whom were demanding a higher rate of return to compensate for their fears that Ottawa was going to let inflation climb and the dollar tumble at their expense. "The sovereignty of the country has been undermined," Martin himself confessed, in what sounded like a *cri de coeur*, "by the ability of the bond market to dictate policy." Which was reason enough to eliminate the deficit. "We owe an awful lot of money, and those kids in red suspenders are playing with that money, driving rates up and down. But we have the ability to regain power by getting our act together."

Bob White, the president of the Canadian Labour Congress, suspected a more complicated motive. "Paul talks a lot about learning social issues at his father's knee," he said, "but he himself became a wealthy businessperson, and I think his relationship with those pushing the business agenda has moved him toward taking more from people he used to argue you shouldn't take from. So, just because some international market says so, interest rates are transferring our tax dollars from the poor to the bondholders and the banks, who are wallowing in goddamn money."

A Private Government

On May 20, 1994, while Paul Martin was busy trying to turn the federal government upside-down and shake it for loose change, Jean Chrétien was at a prelunch ceremony in the Toronto suburb of Scarborough to officially open the Bank of Montreal's $40-million Institute for Learning. Designed by the renowned architect Raymond Moriyama and supervised by a former director of the University of Western Ontario's M.B.A. program, the institute was a corporate college of classrooms, residential quarters, conference areas, and recreation facilities where some fourteen thousand employees would gather each year to further their professional development in a comfortable and cloistered environment.

It was also the pride and joy of the tall, good-looking man who unveiled the plaque with the prime minister, the BMO's forty-nine-year-old chairman, Matthew Barrett. Never perhaps had something of such expense and originality passed through a bank's tight-fisted procedures with such rapidity. Never perhaps had a CEO devoted so much time and fussiness to the planting of trees and the access for wheelchairs. In fact, the institute was as much a fulfilment of the chairman's psychological needs as of the bank's corporate requirements, for, like many other self-made people who had never attended university, Matt Barrett had an obsession, a romance, and an insecurity about higher education. "When I have my heart attack," he gushed as he strode through the institute amid an entourage of deferential staff and a chorus of obsequious well-wishers, "I'm going to come here."

In many ways, the institute symbolized the ongoing shift of power from the public arena to the private sector. Education and training had long been considered state responsibilities, after all, until deficits and debt began compelling every level of government to downsize its bureaucracies and offload its services. And though the "Big Six" banks are not in fact major players in the games of the international bond-holders and currency speculators who manipulate the Bank of Canada's central lending rate, they are where most people encounter a hike in mortgage payments or the hurdles of getting a small-business loan. They are also, by dint of their dominant presence in the broker-age industry and trust companies, the undisputed titans of Canadian financial concentration. Indeed, watching Matt Barrett escort Jean Chrétien through the crowd of dignitaries as waiters in white jackets offered glasses of champagne and a string quartet played Mozart, an observer might well have wondered which man had the real power.

"If you speed in your car and have a very bad accident that breaks every bone in your body, you become dependent on the doctors," Barrett himself said of Ottawa's debt situation. "It's hardly a criticism of the hospital that you end up in the emergency ward."

The prime minister still had the prestige of public office, of course. He was the ultimate boss over more than a quarter-million civil ser-vants, he had access to heads of state around the world, and he will be remembered for good or evil in the history books when Matthew Bar-rett is as forgotten as his predecessor Sir Charles Blair Gordon. "I would not change my job to be president of a bank," Chrétien once com-mented. "It's an important job, you're not a bum if you're a bank pres-ident, but it's not a big complicated business to collect money and lend money. It's not as complex or as satisfying as running a government."

Much of the art of running a government had been reduced to get-ting people to pay more for less, however, and Chrétien seemed left with more power to do harm than to do good. As if to confirm that drop in esteem and authority, Canadians paid him less than the average doctor or hockey player, called him to account for each plane ride and household expense, subjected him to ruthless ridicule and condemna-tion in the press, and compelled him to defend every one of his gov-ernment's decisions on national television against a rude barrage of questions and accusations from his opponents.

"Why would any sane human being go into politics given today's journalism, TV, and the tabloids?" Barrett wondered. "You must either be a saint or a little bit deranged. I've often reflected that the psychic rewards of political leadership, power, and profile must be much greater than they look because, rationally, the rewards are so modest. They're even excoriated for their pensions."

Barrett, in comparison, earned $1.8 million in salary and bonuses in 1993 – more than ten times as much as the prime minister. He was under no pressure to swap his chauffeur-driven Lincoln for a Chevrolet, and if he ever chose to use a company jet to go fly-fishing on the Restigouche or vacationing in Mexico, not many people would know and fewer would care. He was accountable to a board of directors and his shareholders, of course, but his performance was essentially judged by the bottom-line numbers he presented to the bank's annual general meeting. And because those numbers had been steadily improving since Barrett became chairman in 1990, reaching record profits of $700 million in 1993, he was allowed to get on with the job as he saw fit – including the construction of the Institute for Learning.

"There's a point of view that politics is a higher calling," he said, as though in direct response to Paul Martin Jr. "But a business leader can serve his country very well by running a good business, by creating jobs, by training and educating its people, by improving its competitiveness."

Barrett even visualized the Bank of Montreal – with more than $100 billion in assets and some 35,000 employees, directly or indirectly responsible for the well-being of as many as 350,000 people, connected through its four million customers and its distinguished history since 1817 to the whole of Canadian society – as a city full of "saints, scholars, geniuses, and scoundrels." And in that city, slapping the branch managers on the back or pausing to grant an interview to a reporter, basking in all the perks and vanities of high rank, Barrett seemed every inch a politician – and, like Jean Chrétien, rather a populist one at that.

"I was struck all my life about how pompous bankers are," Barrett remarked. "They love being seen as imperial and aloof. But that is dangerous for banking and not good for business. So, while I was glad to have scratched and clawed my way to the top, I wasn't about to – as Shakespeare says in *Julius Caesar* – 'when he once attains the upmost round, he then unto the ladder turns his back, looks in the clouds, scorning the base degrees by which he did ascend.' It's the old humble-beginning thing, I guess. There's no point trying to fake it as David Niven."

He could, with his military posture and dark moustache, fake it as David Niven, but he had neither the stiff manner nor superior tone of a British expatriate. He moved lithely and spoke with the soft melodiousness of his native Ireland, where he had grown up in a town an hour from Dublin, the son of a well-known bandleader. His irrepressible sense of humour kept breaking through the tedious meetings and formal occasions to which his position condemned him. Sometimes, it was true, at a podium or after a couple of drinks, holding court or laughing too loudly, he could seem rather too pleased with his own wit and intelligence. But more often, by a sudden look of worry or a quick drag on one of his constant Craven A's, he betrayed the unease of the young "Mick" who had been tossed upon this foreign shore without money, connections, or decent education.

Though obviously bright – he developed an early passion for literature, for example, and could recite the *Rubaiyat* from memory at the age of twelve – Barrett had dedicated himself to good times rather than good grades and barely finished high school before embarking, at eighteen, for London with the dream of becoming a great novelist. There, to support himself, he clerked in the Bank of Montreal on Waterloo Place, but neither his bohemian ambition nor his boisterous behaviour suggested the makings of a career banker. In 1964, however, his father died of a heart attack at age forty-five, leaving Matthew as the sole provider for his mother and sister. Uncertain of his literary talent, he began to apply himself to his job, which he had come to enjoy, and when the bank offered to send him to Canada in 1967, he thought it would be a two-year lark with the chance to do some excellent fishing. Instead, on his first day as a $3,800-a-year clerk on St. James Street in Montreal, he met Irene Korsak, a beautiful Polish immigrant working in the foreign exchange department, and they soon settled down to a middle-class life with children and a mortgage.

Even though he had arrived with nothing and knew no one, Barrett marvelled at the "whole world of opportunity here and no restraints, *none.*" Despite his devil-may-care veneer – and now ashamed of having made so little effort at school – he became determined to demonstrate, especially to himself, that he could achieve the impossible. It did not take him long to be appreciated as a hard-working troubleshooter with a mania for thorough preparation, an aptitude for rigorous analysis, and a talent for rallying others to his cause. After twenty years of skilfully climbing the greasy pole, he was named president, and in 1990, still only forty-six years old, he succeeded William Mulholland as chairman – with no expensive campaign, no media scrutiny, no words of French, no statements of policy, and no televised convention.

Mulholland, an American toughened by the Second World War and trained on Wall Street, had been hired to knock an anachronistic institution into shape – and, as he himself noted, "charm wasn't going to do it." He rode roughshod over the Westmount old boys who still treated the Bank of Montreal as a kind of Edwardian gentleman's club. He re-engineered the management structures, advanced the computer revolution, and overhauled the credit process. He moved aggressively into corporate financing and Third World loans. He bought Harris Bankcorp in Chicago and the brokerage firm Nesbitt Thomson. But, by the end of his reign, he also left a head office weakened by his rude and autocratic style and numerous branch managers disoriented and demoralized by the effect of his changes. "It was easy for Barrett to look good after Bill Mulholland," one insider said. "All Matt had to do was look normal."

"He was a godsend for me professionally," added Dick O'Hagan, who had been a newspaper reporter, advertising executive, and media adviser to two Liberal prime ministers, Pearson and Trudeau, before joining the bank in 1979 as vice-president, public affairs. "Matt was obviously a man of great potential as a public-communications resource."

A generation older than Barrett, but with an Irish charm and irrepressible laugh of his own, O'Hagan knew that image is as crucial in banking as in politics, because the differences tend to be subtle and the allegiances hard to sunder. "How can we demonstrate that we're different?" O'Hagan asked while the new chairman and his senior executives were developing a comprehensive strategy for the Bank of Montreal. "How are we going to put a patina of newness on ourselves?"

The simplest way was to showcase the youth and personality of Barrett himself. So, assuming the role of wise uncle, O'Hagan started introducing him around town and into the public consciousness. "Before Matt became president," said one old friend, "he had almost no contacts outside the bank and knew zero beyond banking and books. Dick had the pieces Matt didn't have – who was who in the clubs, what was what in politics, when to serve the cigars. He and his wife brought Matt and Irene into a different class."

In May 1990, *Canadian Business* featured a flattering profile of Barrett and his efforts "to recapture the bank's forgotten asset: ordinary Canadians." Two months later, with a rakish grin on his face and a bag of money in his hand, he appeared on the cover of *Maclean's*, captioned "The Banks' New Weapon: Being Nice." And for six weeks that fall, he was sent from coast to coast in a tour of the bank's operations that had, in O'Hagan's words, "the aroma of a political campaign." He visited thirty-four towns and cities, was seen by some fifteen thousand employees, and played to the cameras of the CBC-TV crew that followed in his wake. The highlight, as in many an election, was a huge rally in Toronto, where Metro-area staff filled Roy Thomson Hall to hear him. That meeting had an impact beyond what could have been predicted by Barrett's experience in staff communications, his perfunctory media training, or even the show-biz environment of his childhood. "That's where Matt's mettle as a speaker and a leader came through," O'Hagan observed. "He himself was surprised by his ability to reach people, and maybe slightly sobered by the responsibility that attaches to it."

But the biggest break had already occurred, thanks to a bold public-relations gamble based on polling results produced by Allan Gregg. On August 14, at a meeting in his elegant office on the sixty-eighth floor of Toronto's First Canadian Place, Barrett listened to his officials agreeing that the Bank of Canada would reduce its lending rate the following Thursday, then asked them a simple question with profound consequences: Why wait? The Bank of Montreal kept anticipating the downward trajectory week after week over the next couple of years, and, to its utter amazement and delight, its competitors were remarkably slow to follow.

"We did an environmental scan," Barrett said of Gregg's surveys, "and wrote down all the things that people say about banks. Remote, insensitive, mean-spirited, black-hearted. Then we developed a strategy built on the assumption that the public is right and we are wrong. The prime-rate strategy was a direct result of that. At the time interest rates were the public villain. If we could be seen making a contribution to drive those rates down, then people would feel good about it."

People did feel good about it. Business immediately poured in, even in areas such as mortgages and small-business lending that were not connected to the prime rate, and BMO soon regained its fair share of the Canadian retail market that Mulholland's concentration on corporate financing had lost. And the spin-off success of the prime strategy gave Barrett's young management team the confidence to push forward in other areas of social concern. Not only did BMO significantly increase its percentage of female executives and appoint an aboriginal vice-president, not only did it start a pilot project for financing knowledge-based innovations and participate in the Ontario Venture Capital Fund, it guarded against failure and backsliding by putting its goals and results on the public record.

That wasn't business do-goodism: it was doing good business. It made customers loyal and employees productive. It generated positive publicity and substantial revenues. It strengthened the intellectual muscle and global perspective of the bank's officers. And it indulged Matt Barrett, perhaps the best-read and most intellectually directed executive in Canada (despite, or because of, his lack of a university degree), in his love for "connecting the dots" by tying sociology, anthropology, economics, and politics to his basic business. The spacious office and corporate jet were, he claimed, just "someone else's stage props that have nothing to do with me, except that they make the performance better." The exorbitant salary and society parties were far less rewarding to him than the access to renowned thinkers and weekends at home with half a dozen books on the go. Indeed, his own greatest "psychic satisfaction" came from the belief that he would be able to influence the national debate.

"If you were a fly on the wall at our two-and-a-half-hour breakfast meetings on Monday mornings," he said, "you would hear the preoccupation of our executive team with what the customers want, what is happening with the employees, how we can be relevant, how we can catch the wave ahead of the others. You would rarely find a team as externally focused as ours."

Though the others in the Big Six countered that they had been doing the same things – some longer, some better – the Bank of Montreal appeared part think tank, part experimental laboratory, part social activist. "Ultimately public relations has to be founded on substance," a senior executive at a rival bank observed, "but BMO has shown the rest of us the importance of communications."

By 1992, as a result, Matthew Barrett was high on the short list of people a survey of 433 business leaders would like to see as prime minister. A year later his name was also put forward by a group of economists and businessmen as their candidate to replace John Crow as governor of the Bank of Canada. "When we were looking for a model of the kind of banker we wanted to see," their spokesman explained, "we all agreed on Barrett. He's proven himself financially, he's socially sensitive, and he struck us as the most enlightened of the bankers."

"All it means," Barrett responded, "is that they're seeing some-body acting differently than the stereotypical image they have of a bank chairman or CEO. It actually all stems, believe it or not, from a corporate strategy, a sophisticated form of marketing strategy."

It was, more accurately, a political strategy, with the shareholder, the customer, the employee, and the community as four distinct "constituencies" whose interests the bank had to satisfy in order to prosper. Barrett even carried in his head a merit score – 6.8 in 1993, despite the record profits – in which the Bank of Montreal's financial performance accounted for only 40 per cent. The rest was based on customer satisfaction (30 per cent), employee competence (20 per cent), and public image (10 per cent). To boost the score, BMO conducted telephone surveys of approximately 500 people a day – some 175,000 a year – and in 1994 it launched a $15-million adver-tising campaign with the slogan "It *is* possible," designed to sell the same general sense of hope the Liberals had successfully sold in the election.

If the political class had learned about mass advertising and market research from the private sector, in other words, the private "city-states" were now learning about the cult of personality, media spin-ning, and public accountability from the political class. And those slow to learn began encountering grassroots uprisings – as Rogers Cablesys-tems did with its "negative billing option" and MacMillan Bloedel its logging in Clayoquot Sound – that echoed the popular revolt against the Charlottetown Accord.

Enlightened Self-Interest

Better and earlier than most of his fellow CEOs, Matthew Barrett understood the hidden price of political power. As government became increasingly unable to perform its traditional tasks, business would be pushed into a new activism – not by "a regime of regula-tion," he believed, but by "a regime of expectation." People would look to it to assume more of the responsibility for creating jobs, improving productivity, capturing markets, training the work force, developing research, advancing technology, and even caring for the disadvantaged. Business executives would no longer be allowed to occupy themselves exclusively with the making and selling of their widgets or rest content with their simplistic cant about socialist politicians and welfare bums.

"The person who is really greedy will be a social activist," said Barrett, "because order, stability, and all those other flaky things are in his self-interest. I am still confused by a dialogue that thinks we don't have to worry about one and a half million unemployed."

In 1992, in fact, he had suffered the wrath of the Mulroney government and its friends at the *Globe and Mail* by publicly suggesting that instead of treating "the unemployed as the cannon fodder in our economic battles," Ottawa should spend money on a major job-creation and training initiative. And though he understood why companies had to downsize, Barrett saw massive layoffs as an admission by management that it had not been able to adjust to the new economy in a way that did not inflict pain and uncertainty on its staff and the public. For its part, the Bank of Montreal undertook to spend up to two years to retrain or relocate its employees, with the result that it was able to eliminate thousands of positions without any large-scale firings.

"When a company downsizes," Barrett explained, "it's shifting its burden to the society. So we need a more sophisticated view of our collective obligation to make adjustments when adjustments are required. I have a problem personally with proposing that people are Kleenex, people who want to work but are thrown out on the street because the company didn't invest any capital in them or train them earlier. And the notion that there should be no safety net to help them is *obscene*." Even when he condemned the existing safety net for "creating a moral hazard where there is a prize in being unfortunate" or criticized politicians for their outdated and discredited approaches, he shared their concerns. "We have not found the new ways of coping with the loss of the nation-state, with globalization, with the inability to control capital markets and technology," he said.

In the meantime, unlike Jean Chrétien or Paul Martin, he was not required to make the brutal trade-offs between fiscal stability and social justice or justify his decisions to a disillusioned Canadian population. While it was evident, as Bill Mulholland once put it, that "bankers can't afford to piss away public support by seeming haughty and unresponsive," if only to minimize the likelihood of government interference through taxation and the Bank Act, no one ever claimed that the Bank of Montreal was a democratic institution or its chairman a public servant. On the contrary, however much pride Barrett took in having decentralized decision-making authority out among his executives and down toward 236 community-oriented clusters of BMO's 1,214 branches, he had no illusions about where the buck stopped. Some of his closest friends even worried that a couple of years of high power, high profile, and high profits had already corrupted his cockiness into conceit, his acumen into arrogance. One called him as "a well-socialized autocrat," akin to a prime minister at the cabinet table.

"Collegiality doesn't mean that everyone agrees," Barrett said. "It means that everyone has an opportunity to express their views fully and without fear, then you as the boss have to make choices amongst competing points of view. You've got to consult, but then you've got to go into the back room. That's why I think it's nonsense about how wonderful it is that we're getting all these men in suits out of the back rooms. We've got to get people back *into* the back rooms. It's the only way you'll get decisions made."

Ultimately, no matter how enlightened, every corporation faces a perennial conflict between long-term payoffs to its society and short-term payouts to its shareholders. Banks have a duty not to gamble with their depositors' money, for example, which has made them notoriously cautious about financing the knowledge industries and new technologies that Canada needs for sustained growth. Nor, for all his gifts as a communicator, did Barrett feel effective in convincing Canadians why BMO's decision to invest at least $1 billion to expand its American subsidiary would produce Canadian jobs, boost Ottawa's revenues, and increase Canada's standard of living. He wasn't even certain how many of his own employees understood why he deserved his seven-figure income or knew that he faced a seven-figure tax bill every April.

Indeed, as bank profits and interest rates soared in tandem during 1994, so did public criticism of the Big Six – and, for all its good efforts and positive press, the Bank of Montreal was not spared. There was widespread outrage at the news that the banks had claimed $300 million in tax credits for routine improvements under a federal initiative intended to promote computer research and development. A report of the parliamentary Industry committee, of which Carolyn Parrish was a member, called attention to the number of small businesses who "have experienced increasing difficulty in obtaining finance for start-up, normal operations, and expansion, while banks have been quick to close lines of credit, call in loans, or withdraw financing." A spokesperson for the Canadian Organization of Small Business urged the government not to fear becoming "more assertive" with the banks, since they could hardly move their branches to Mexico or Taiwan. Paul Martin himself was heard to make threatening noises about reviewing the conditions of the Bank Act while he swore at bank executives for starving the credit needs of business and thus undermining the economy.

"I can live with bank-bashing being good politics," Barrett countered, "but what scares me is if politicians really believe we're big and bad. You find some of that in Ottawa, and you find it in all three parties, which is quite disturbing. We have not done a very good job in raising the consciousness of the politicians, the media, and the people about what we do for a living and why it's an honest buck or that we're paying 18 per cent of the country's taxes while representing only 6 per cent of its GDP."

As a result, on the eve of the government's second budget, in February 1995, Matt Barrett's sources warned him that the banks were going to be hit hard. Nothing personal, they said, just politics. If the Liberals were going to be able to sell a tough budget, it had to look fair, and what could look fairer than taxing the banks' record profits of $4.3 billion (up 47 per cent in a single year)? Image politics cuts many ways, Barrett was discovering to his anger and dismay, and public popularity has neither a memory nor a conscience.

Nor, he fumed, did his friend Paul Martin.

The Courage to Act

In the event, the banks were not hit all that hard: a special surtax of $60 million in year one (less than 1.5 per cent of their 1994 profits) and another $40 million in year two, as well as the possible loss of the R and D tax credits. There was also an ominous announcement that Ottawa would begin "working with the banks to hammer out meaningful performance benchmarks for small-business financing." Matthew Barrett thought the money grab unjust and unjustified; he particularly hated seeing the Liberal benches greeting it with a standing ovation. His only consolation was that Martin himself had not compounded the injury by implying that "these guys have been ripping us off and now we've got them."

Canadians, meanwhile, were going to pay an extra $500 million a year at the gas pumps. The unemployed were going to suffer another $500-million drop in benefits. Western grain farmers were going to lose their $560-million transportation subsidy and eastern dairy producers were going to get 30 per cent less within two years. Immigrants and refugees were going to be slapped with an entry tax of $975 per adult. The regional development agencies were going to be downsized by more than half. The CBC and the other cultural industries were going to be squeezed once again. Federal funds to the provinces for health, education, and welfare were going to plunge by $7 billion in three years. And forty-five thousand federal jobs were going to be axed as total departmental expenditures fell by 20 per cent.

"This is by far the largest set of actions in any Canadian budget since demobilization after the Second World War," Martin boasted. "Relative to the size of our economy, program spending will be lower in 1996-97 than *at any time* since 1951." The result, amounting to more than $25 billion by 1997-98, was projected to get him easily to his 3-per-cent interim. Indeed, given his cautious forecasts and contingency reserves, most analysts calculated that Ottawa was on the way to zero.

The message behind the cuts contradicted almost everything the Liberal Party of Canada had represented during the past thirty years – if not the past century. Mackenzie King's unemployment insurance, Louis St. Laurent's old-age security, and Lester Pearson's Canada Pension Plan were to be revamped with an eye to savings. Wilfrid Laurier's Canadian National Railways and Pierre Trudeau's Petro-Canada were to be privatized. Much of the work of at least two generations of Canadians in building national institutions, national policies, national programs, and national standards was about to be undone – including the work of Paul Martin's own father.

That seemed to have appeased the domestic and foreign financiers for the instant, though interest rates and the dollar continued to bob up and down for weeks afterwards. Prime Minister Chrétien, on the other hand, was hardly leaping for joy. "It's no pleasure at all," he admitted to Peter Gzowski on CBC-Radio. "I'm not a doctrinaire, a right-winger. I'm a Liberal and I feel like a Liberal and it's painful. But it's needed."

The question that gripped the political class was whether the people of Canada were any more ready to accept such a dramatic reduction in federal services and social programs from him than they had been from Brian Mulroney or Kim Campbell. The previous autumn, according to the Liberals' own polls, no more than a quarter of Canadians considered the deficit as the nation's number-one problem or could even define what a deficit is. And though Paul Martin had become convinced that announcing new cutbacks was now more popular than announcing new projects, Terrie O'Leary admitted a couple of months before the budget that most people had not "bought into" the debt problem. They tended to think it was still just a matter of eliminating bureaucratic inefficiencies and closing some tax loopholes for the rich.

Preston Manning, for one, blamed the Liberals for not having sought a specific mandate from the electorate to slash the deficit. "They accepted the old line that you can't get elected in this country without promising to spend public money," he said. "That makes their position so much weaker now."

To which Martin curtly replied that his party had indeed sought and obtained a mandate: to hit the 3-per-cent target, as promised in the Red Book. And since the economic recovery had reduced the immediate pressure to deal with the Liberals' first priority, by creating 433,000 full-time jobs in 1994, he expected to get away with concentrating on the fiscal problem. "But you could have the strongest mandate possible for deficit reduction and you'd still get a reaction from those who are hit," he understood. "Because government is no longer about arbitrating between a right and a wrong. It's about arbitrating between two rights."

For that reason, he had set up four public forums and a televised meeting with forty economists before his first budget; he had laid out an economic framework for general discussion in his Purple Book, and accompanied it with another book of detailed information about the government's expenses and revenues; and he had opened up the budget-making process to an unprecedented degree through the cross-country consultations of the Finance committee in the late fall of 1994. More than simply gathering input, Martin wanted to implicate as many people as possible in the arduous task of negotiating the trade-offs and finding the common ground.

"It is important to ask the people who appear before you to make hard choices," he instructed the committee members. "If they are asking to be shielded from cuts, ask them who they believe should pick up the difference. If they are saying we should cut even more, ask them to say precisely what they would cut to meet the targets they prefer. If people say that taxation should be off the table, ask them if they believe that every tax now in place is fair – and every tax expenditure the most efficient way to achieve our policy goals. And if people come before you and say that now is not the time to cut, ask them to describe the morality and justice of letting the debt continue to run wild."

The committee had some success in luring people to its hearings and getting them to confront each other's needs. But, given the arcane technicalities involved, most of the participants were the very same "elites" who had shown up at the five advisory conferences preceding the Charlottetown constitutional debacle: the same think-tank gurus, the same interest-group chieftains, the same lawyers and lobbyists. And though no one denied the necessity of spending cuts, they all seemed to have a self-serving case as to why they were worthy of exemption.

"My biggest frustration with most of the so-called experts in this country," Martin remarked, "is that they fail to understand that setting a target without dealing with the details is bullshit. Look at the business community. It tells me that I've got to get to a balanced budget. But apart from an important contribution by the C. D. Howe Institute – and even it didn't get into the details – what were its first two significant interventions? The auto companies said I've got to change unemployment insurance in a way that affects the fishermen in Newfoundland, but not in a way that affects them. And the investment guys told me not to touch RRSPs, supposedly because they want to protect people's retirement income, but I suspect because that's what they sell. It shows you the extent to which the debate has got to evolve."

Most business leaders and many media pundits were of the view that the debate had evolved far enough. They agreed on what had to be done – less spending, less taxation, less centralization, and less regulation in order to produce more jobs, more investment, more entrepreneurs, and more growth – and they wanted the government to get off its butt and demonstrate what the C. D. Howe Institute called "the courage to act," regardless of what the people thought or wanted.

Instead, as Peter Cook argued from his soapbox in the business section of the *Globe and Mail*, "Federal ministers and MPs now sally forth into the ballrooms and basements of the nation, and into the middle of rallies on Parliament Hill, to hear out the resistees. Most of what they hear is rubbish. Some of it is farce." His worry, he said, citing the constitutional debates as an example, was that consulting "often does the opposite of what is intended and erodes consensus."

That was surely a twisted reading of both the constitutional debates and the democratic process. In 1992, stalwarts of the political class had got together and constructed a very neat accommodation, which they smugly assumed could be sold to the Canadian people as the national interest. They were wrong. Most Canadians liked neither its inherent vision nor the elitist isolation in which it had been contrived. So, too, in 1994, there wasn't the type of broad-based consensus that had united Canadians around economic reconstruction in the 1950s and social justice in the 1960s – nor was there the loose cash to buy it or the public deference to impose it. People seemed deeply confused and divided about the role of the state, the division of powers, the viability of the safety net, or even the values upon which choices could be made and a consensus built.

Though the Purple Book and the Finance committee hearings may not have achieved the level of public engagement and in-depth understanding for which Martin had hoped, he thought they had played a more vital role in coalescing popular opinion than the peso crisis or the threat from Moody's. "The mere fact of going out to build up a consensus had a lot to do with the building up of support," he said, equating his no-surprises strategy of budget making to how the Liberals had pieced together the Red Book, "and it enabled us to develop or discard a lot of ideas. By the time everything was done, we had really tried and tested all the ideas, mechanisms, and how to put them together."

Eventually, of course, time ran out. The "debt clock" was ticking at $85,000 a minute, the bankers were at the door, and Parliament was awaiting the annual budget. "In the end," Paul Martin said, "governments have to decide among the conflicting choices, and some people will not be happy. There's no alternative. So if I'm going to be unpopular anyway, I might as well be unpopular for doing the right thing." And, with that mantra of the political class on his lips, he marched stoically toward his fate.

The 3-Per-Cent Solution

In the wake of the February 1995 budget, there was shouting and confusion, shots were fired from left and right, the odd skirmish broke out, and a few foot-soldiers bolted from the ranks. But the Liberals advanced in tight formation and were astonished to discover, when the smoke had cleared, that their popularity was up five points to 63 per cent and more than two-thirds of Canadians deemed Martin's budget "on the right track."

Why, considering the protest demonstrations and plunging polls with which tough budgets were traditionally greeted, hadn't this one been cited as further evidence that the political class always ends up pursuing its own agenda regardless of the party in power and its election promises?

The answer lay in a confluence of skilful management, clever communications, and good luck. The absence of any whack on personal income or RRSPs, which had been strongly rumoured, was not only a relief but a sign that Ottawa had heeded the complaints of many middle-class taxpayers during the consultation process. The severity of the government's cuts to its own operations and employees not only satisfied those who assumed that the source of the problem was there, but disarmed those provinces and interest groups who felt especially hit. Martin's commitment to meet the Liberals' 3-per-cent target had served as a loud warning of the terrible things to come, and since 3 was a much simpler number to comprehend than 25,000,000,000, it established a mark of relative progress in the minds of people who may not have known what a GDP was or why it mattered. Nor, considering all the judicious leaks and trial balloons preceding this budget, could the media register the same shock as they had on previous budget nights, when the bad news used to drop like a secret weapon upon an unsuspecting population. The instant reaction was tempered, too, by the coyness with which the most controversial measures were buried in technical complexities, mitigated by the transitional payouts to farmers and fishermen, or timed to detonate later.

Most important of all, like a Chinese water torture, the drip, drip, drip of the deficit numbers had finally affected the public's brain. In the weeks preceding the budget, government polls started showing for the first time that concern about deficit reduction had surpassed concern about job creation, in part because the boom had brought unemployment down under 10 per cent, in part because the media had been in full cry about the peso crisis in Mexico and the fiscal revolution in Alberta, in part because the Liberal establishment had adopted Kim Campbell and Preston Manning's Mother of All Issues. Almost as soon as Canadians switched priority, moreover, they seemed ready and eager for Ottawa to stop talking and do something. In this twist of circumstance the Martin budget looked highly activist even while it set out to make Ottawa less activist. Its deep cuts to business and the provinces looked like a courageous refusal to accommodate the elites even though the underlying effect was to empower them.

The Liberals were given the benefit of the doubt, for a while at least, in large measure as a reward for the trust and stability Jean Chrétien had instilled since the election. It wasn't just that he had none of the extravagances and pretensions of Brian Mulroney, though that alone would have given him a hallowed place in people's hearts. His populist image and flexible approach let Canadians believe that if he cut national institutions and programs, it must have been because he really had to – not because he was a corporate flunky like Mulroney or a mean-spirited policy wonk like Campbell or an Albertan yahoo like Manning. As Chaviva Hosek explained it, "Only Richard Nixon could have gone to China." And if brutal choices had to be made, went the corollary, better they were made by warm guys like Chrétien and Martin whose values were in the right place and whose heads were not in some ideological cuckoo-land.

"Canadians' instincts were deeply troubled by something in Brian Mulroney's style, which eroded the logical case for his policies," the *Globe*'s Bill Thorsell came to realize in a belated and somewhat understated assessment of his old friend's failure as a leader. "Mr. Chrétien satisfies public instincts much more easily, both because he is an apparent 'straight-shooter,' and because he gives so much priority to the 'soft' side of politics. Mr. Chrétien is demonstrably much more effective in sustaining and even expanding the constituency for change."

That was not just a matter of leadership style, Chrétien himself pointed out. Canadians, as moderate and pragmatic people, simply felt more comfortable with the moderation and pragmatism of the Liberal party. Because of Canada's size and diversity, he once explained, "no doctrinaire party of the left or right beholden to specific groups can ever succeed at the national level. What may be valid in one part of the country or one period of time won't necessarily work in another. And if you're in the centre, the centre moves."

In 1995 it moved so far to the right that it swallowed most of the Conservatives' agenda and nibbled into Reform's. There were no credible forces on the left to tug it back. Bob Rae launched an angry assault against the budget, declaring that "the Canada we have known is no more," but he himself was at 17 per cent in the Ontario polls and widely assumed to be posturing for the June election everyone knew he would lose. Nor did Rae, or his NDP colleagues in British Columbia and Saskatchewan, carry much intellectual weight and moral suasion after their own bloody battles with provincial deficit reduction. In Ottawa, meanwhile, the New Democrats were scarcely visible, with virtually no leader, no status, and no alternatives. That left only the Bloc Québécois to twist itself into knots trying to denounce the budget as both a centralist attack on Quebec's jurisdiction and a callous abandonment of federal help to the province. "The real opposition lay with each and every cabinet minister," Martin said. "They all felt that their department was a special case."

Left-of-centre Liberals had no attractive refuge for their vote, and there was no compelling voice to incite Canadians to rise up against the political class as many of them had done after hearing Pierre Trudeau denounce the Meech Lake and Charlottetown accords. The budget was condemned, of course, by a familiar chorus of extraparliamentary voices. The National Action Committee on the Status of Women called it "a bankers' budget, a businessman's budget." The National Anti-Poverty Organization called it "a total disaster." The Action Canada Network called it "not a budget made in Canada." But their thirty-second clips were quickly superseded by thirty-second clips from Preston Manning, Bay Street brokers, conservative think tanks, and Wall Street analysts, all denouncing Martin for not going further faster. Even the media pundits, who probably would have denounced the Conservatives and Reformers for doing half as much, either applauded the budget for its bravery or criticized it for its caution.

"What's satisfying is that our more balanced judgement has been accepted," said Chrétien. "We convinced the people that if we had gone to zero right away, we would have created a recession. Manning and all those guys on Bay Street did not worry about that, they just wanted to get to zero. On the other hand, when our currency is being pushed down and our real interest rate is at a record level of 7 per cent, you can be a bleeding heart all you want, but you have to face reality.

It's as if you wanted to buy your son a car but have no money. If you don't buy it, it's not because you're tough. It's because you can't afford it."

With this middle course, the Liberals accomplished a deft political manoeuvre. By co-opting many of the arguments and policies of their strongest and most vocal adversaries, they sapped the strength of the right without evident risk to their own support. And, by means of his experience and salesmanship, Chrétien seemed to have done what Brian Mulroney and Kim Campbell had found impossible to do – bring the ungovernable to accept the unpalatable. He seemed, indeed, to have bridged the huge divide between the political class and the Canadian people.

"The government has a lot of credibility and people feel comfortable with us," he said. "When I was leader of the Opposition, I noticed that the government of the day had a tendency to tell Canadians that if it didn't get its way, it would be the end of the world. I've been around long enough to know that it's never the end of the world. So I have my agenda, I was elected on it, and I'm following it closely. And when I move, I want to feel I have a mandate to do what I'm doing." That said, he later added, "If you asked me if I ever thought that, after eighteen months in office, I'd be fifteen points or more higher in the polls, I would have answered, 'Never!'"

Here Lies Paul Martin Jr.

In the sunny spring of 1995, with tulips and tourists lending colour to Parliament Hill, scores of Liberals skulked in dark corners and musty offices, wondering how much longer their honeymoon could last. They knew that the budget's cuts had yet to register as painful losses to community organizations or welfare services. They knew that the radical overhaul of old-age pensions and unemployment insurance was still to come. They knew that global forces would likely conspire to keep interest rates, income disparities, and unemployment levels high, whatever efforts Canada took to lower them. They knew that the present cyclical boom – which hadn't been much of a boom in consumer confidence or in many sectors – was already stalling and would eventually turn into a bust. And, having survived their first two budgets by

the seat of their pants, they knew that Paul Martin was already screaming at his officials over in Finance to prepare the third, which was
expected to be his last almighty attempt to crack the back of government spending.

"I perceive next year as still being tough," said Winnipeg MP David
Walker. "After that, I'm too much of a politician not to think about
what I want to do in the months leading up to the election. People,
sooner than later, have to be given some reward or some sign that
there is a reward. No government can survive without some social
project of some order. People are economically insecure, they're worried about their health and social programs, and the national government will have to begin to address that, even though we are very, very
limited in cash."

Martin himself was more confident that the people would hold
with him until the fiscal crisis was over, however long it took. Com-
paring his duty to that of the minister of national defence in the Second World War, he didn't think he had any option to retreat anyway.
"I've been lucky," he said. "My desire to do this was done against the
backdrop of a Canadian people who more and more wanted to convince the government of the same thing." He nevertheless shared
Walker's point that deficit reduction could not be an end in itself.
"When the public decides that the problem is solved, it will immediately ask for a better vision, a broader vision, of what this country is
about and how to get there. We have to start talking about the bigger
picture now, as well as about the deficit, or when public opinion
shifts, it's going to look elsewhere."

Apart from his own wish to reconstruct a federal government that
was kinder and smarter, as well as smaller, he remembered that most
Canadians had rejected Kim Campbell's deterministic message that
nothing could be done but slash and wait. Even when people believed
that the provincial governments better reflected their interests or were
more efficient administrators, they still looked to Ottawa for leadership in job creation, education, social justice, the environment, and
cultural identity. It was the very absence of such leadership that had
caused so many of them to react so negatively to the Conservatives'
economic and constitutional agendas. And while a majority may have
come to accept "rethinking government" in order to make it less
costly and intrusive, as advertised in the Liberals' Red and Purple
books, only a minority went toward the right-wing extreme of wishing it to vanish altogether.

"If written on my tombstone is 'Here Lies Paul Martin Jr. – He Got the Deficit Down,'" he said, "I'll be really disappointed."

He was already disappointed, in fact, that the activist side of the Purple Book and his first two budgets had not penetrated the sensationalism and bellowing about spending cuts. Some of that was his own fault. In his speeches and answers as finance minister, the government's nation-*building* role usually sounded soft and fuzzy compared to the hard fact of being, as he once put it, "in hock up to our eyeballs." A few political operatives around the PMO even advised him to moderate his apocalyptic rhetoric, though in hindsight they conceded its short-term benefit in selling the budget.

Whatever Martin's intention, the overwhelming message of the budget itself was of downsizing, devolution, and deregulation, rather than a coherent indication of what would be left afterwards. Trade and technological research were flagged as crucial pillars of a national industrial policy, but that only meant they were to be cut *less* than most other areas. Social security reform was another national priority, but that only meant giving fewer people less money in order to make the programs financially sustainable. And the public's desire for national standards in health, education, and welfare was going to be achieved, it seemed, by distributing federal grants to the provincial governments in a single chunk – the Canada Health and Social Transfer (CHST) – with few strings attached and a lot fewer dollars.

Since 1977, under the terms of the Canada Assistance Plan and the Established Programs Financing, the federal cash for those social areas had been running down and was eventually expected to run out, leaving Ottawa with less and less ability to insist upon its minimal and often outdated conditions. Pooling the two into one block fund would reinforce its clout – particularly in the prime area of Liberal concern, health – and liberate the provinces from what Martin called the "blanket chloroform" of antiquated regulations. "If they're good governments, and most of them are," he argued, "let them do their own thing, or else give the money directly to people. And the great advantage of 'competitive federalism' is one province may do things that the others can learn from," in the way that Saskatchewan had introduced socialized medicine in the 1940s.

The CHST had other unstated, but no less practical, advantages. It would obscure the fact that Ottawa was in effect announcing huge cuts to welfare and education. It would offload the increasingly heavy financial and political burden on to the backs of the provinces. It would undermine the decentralist demands of the Reform party and the Bloc Québécois. It would demonstrate to Quebeckers that Canadian federalism could be supple and responsive without having to tamper with the Constitution. And, apropos of the British North America Act, weren't health, education, and welfare provincial responsibilities, before Ottawa had started intruding through its spending power?

They were indeed, but Ottawa had only started intruding because most of the provinces were doing such a mediocre job in meeting their responsibilities – some because they could not afford to do better, some because they did not want to do better, some because they did not know better. Nor had the provinces been able collectively to impose or arrange sufficient uniformity to establish comparable benefits in every part of the country. Canadians, therefore, had turned to their national government – more often than not, a Liberal government – which responded with old-age pensions and unemployment insurance, universal medicare and postsecondary education grants, welfare standards and provincial equalization transfers. And those programs did more than intended: they became closely identified with Canada's national pride and sense of unity.

Not that Canadians weren't willing to see them administered more effectively and cheaply. On the contrary, everyone had a horror story about the abuse of unemployment insurance, and few believed that either medicare or the Canada Pension Plan was financially viable in its present form. But if a major restructuring was both desirable and unavoidable, as the Liberals themselves had declared in their campaign Red Book, best to take "an integrated and coherent approach" that would mesh social policy with fiscal policy and industrial policy.

"The next generation of social programs must not just share the wealth, and protect those who are disadvantaged among us," Lloyd Axworthy, the human resources minister, elaborated in the government's discussion paper on social security reform in October 1994, "they must actively create opportunity for Canadians and, in so doing, help drive economic growth. By helping to equip Canadians with the skills to excel in today's – and tomorrow's – Information Age, our social security system can play a vital role in turning Canada's shrinking middle class into an expanding one again."

That discussion paper was supposed to be the first step. Itself the result of the advice of an outside task force of fourteen social-policy experts, the findings from a week of public hearings by a parliamentary committee, and a mountain of bureaucratic studies begun under the Tories, the Green Book sought to link employment, education, and the alleviation of poverty into one reform package – though health reform, pension reform, tax reform, and constitutional reform were not included. As tentative, limited, and old hat as most of the Green Book proved to be, the debate was barely under way before it too hit the debt wall.

Critics from the right pounced on the fact that Axworthy had not put a price tag on his various options. Critics from the left held up a confidential memo leaked in the *Toronto Star* to prove that his true agenda was to cut social spending by another $7.5 billion within five years (which was higher than the working number Axworthy had in mind, but lower than the eventual figure in Martin's budget). Martin himself was soon on the rubber-chicken circuit declaring that "if a country is to continue to care for its citizens, it must be a country that can pay its bills." Behind the scenes, meanwhile, Finance continued to demand more and more savings from Human Resources. Axworthy had to take his unhappiness public, in a carefully staged bit of political theatrics for the media in January, to signal to Martin and the prime minister that he couldn't be squeezed further.

Any pretence of a comprehensive national strategy on social reform was exposed by the Canada Health and Social Transfer. The CHST lifted all but one of the conditions on how federal money for welfare programs should be spent, gave up on the idea of a more direct federal role in financing university education, and merely prayed that the provinces would eventually agree to a set of shared principles and objectives (over the dead body of Quebec's separatist government, no doubt). "I think they are losing the moral authority to set national standards for these programs," Ontario's NDP Finance Minister Floyd Laughren immediately reacted in a Global TV interview. "They can say they want to maintain national standards, but I know what I say to them, representing Ontario. I say, 'Take a hike. You're not going to reduce your transfers that dramatically and then still set all the rules.'"

The result, many feared, would be an inexorable decline toward gross disparities and the lowest standards, a "rush to the bottom" that had already begun in Alberta and New Brunswick. Even the Liberal chairman of the Finance committee, Jim Peterson, after hearing those fears expressed by scores of people who did not trust their provinces to be the sole guardian of the social programs, declared (to the fury of Martin's officials), "We cannot abandon the field. We have to keep a presence. Cash means clout. No cash, no clout. And, therefore, the bill should be amended because it does not confirm that there will always be a cash component in our transfers to the provinces."

Prime Minister Chrétien, for his part, vowed that "there will always be some cash," but he didn't believe Ottawa had any option other than to shift almost all the responsibility back to the provinces. "A lot of people in the caucus might get up and say, gee, the city of Toronto is not good at collecting the garbage so we should do it. No!" he said. "If the municipal government isn't collecting the garbage properly, kick it out. It's not our job. We don't have a British-style government that runs everything. We have different levels of government, there is some conflict, but that's better. Eventually, you know, things sort themselves out." And because Ottawa retained its spending power, he added, it could always intervene if the inequities became extreme.

That may have been some comfort to Canadians – assuming Ottawa ever again had money to spend on the young and the poor – but the Canada Health and Social Transfer was hardly a clarion call to national purpose with the aim of mobilizing the population to compete in the Information Age against the savage world of the twenty-first century. Axworthy himself conceded, given the fiscal constraints imposed by Finance, that the best his department could do was to concentrate on UI and pension reform and put a "framework in place, pointing in the right direction, that can be built on as times get better, as resources are made available."

Nor was it obvious how the budget's cuts to the research-and-development agencies and the cultural industries would help meet the Red Book's resolve "to create a national system of innovation," not least by promising to increase spending on R and D and culture over four years. Instead, among the long list of casualties in the budget's fine print, the Technology Outreach Program and the Canada Scholarships Program were eliminated, the Industrial Research Assistance Program and the Natural Sciences and Engineering Research Council were eviscerated, and the Canadian Broadcasting Corporation and the Book Publishing Industry Development Program were emasculated. The CBC's president, Anthony Manera, immediately announced his resignation, claiming he had been betrayed. Pratt & Whitney Canada soon threatened to move the R and D of a new aircraft engine out of the country if federal subsidies disappeared. The University of Toronto's normally affable president issued a sharp public rebuke.

"The reductions run contrary to all the advice given to the government by its own advisory bodies over the past decade," Robert

Prichard declared. "Coupled with funding decreases to research infrastructure as a consequence of the new Canada Social Transfer (block-grant) program, it is inconceivable that these actions are in the best interest of the country." (Which caused Paul Martin to wonder how Rob Prichard was managing to fight the deficits at the University of Toronto.)

"If the best of those programs had any chance of surviving the fiscal imperatives," said one Liberal backbencher, "they needed ministers with a very strong alternative story about why they should be spared. Unfortunately, [Heritage Minister Michel] Dupuy was weak and totally obsessed with the Quebec referendum, and [Industry Minister John] Manley was no C. D. Howe. He wasn't even up to the Red Book intellectually. So that left Martin and Peter Nicholson to defend the vision. But they fell victim to the Stockholm Syndrome: they had been cooped up in so many late-night meetings over so many months with David Dodge that their minds and hearts were captured by that gang at Finance."

What had captured them, of course, was the pure arithmetic of compound interest. "The patient was in the emergency room," Nicholson said of Canada's economic situation, "and the first priority was to stop the fiscal haemorrhaging or else the patient would die. The reconstructive surgery, the physiotherapy, the life-style changes can come later. Unlike the constitutional amendments proposed in the Meech Lake and Charlottetown accords, there's nothing we've done now that's irreversible."

But the lack of money was exacerbated by lack of policy. "The truth is, *we really don't know what to do!*" said a senior official, whose bewilderment was felt throughout the capital in the spring of 1995 as Eddie Goldenberg and Chaviva Hosek sallied forth from the PMO to visit every minister and try to piece together a positive agenda before the next election. "Take all the hopeful talk about training. According to the evaluations so far, we're just not getting the bang for the buck. We don't know what jobs will be needed in the future, we don't know how to create jobs, so why not let the provinces or the private sector try? At least we're not throwing any more good money after bad. In the old days we'd get a call from on high that the minister needed to showcase a big announcement the day after tomorrow, so we'd throw $200 million at some problem. That's all gone, because the money's all gone. We have no damned choice!"

The Last Period

"End of the second period," Jacques Parizeau declared from the stage of La Capitole, a renovated music hall in Quebec City, on the night of September 12, 1994. "The third starts tomorrow morning."

In Parizeau's version of one of the Canadian political class's favourite metaphors, politics-as-hockey, the first period had been the 1993 federal election. Lucien Bouchard's Bloc Québécois captured over two-thirds of the seats in Quebec and half the popular vote: Separatists 1, federalists 0. Now Parizeau and his Parti Québécois had just won a majority government in the provincial election: Separatists 2, federalists 0. And sometime before the end of 1995, as Quebec's new premier stated again and again, the PQ would hold a referendum in order "to become a normal people in a country that belongs to us." The result, he was convinced to the point of arrogance, would be a 3-0 shutout, the final defeat of Canada.

Parizeau's smile looked as false as his hair colouring that night, and his bloated self-assurance was perceptibly deflated. In truth, his victory had not been a great triumph. The Parti Québécois had carried only 44.7 per cent of the vote, less than half a point better than the provincial Liberals, whom everyone expected to be trounced after almost nine years in power, two failed constitutional negotiations with the rest of Canada, a long and severe recession, and the retirement of their very sly fox Robert Bourassa. Nor had the Liberals' new leader, Daniel Johnson Jr., been expected to have much appeal, given his physical ungainliness, his businessman's perspective, and his support of Canadian federalism. His campaign was noteworthy, in fact, for how little he catered to the usual rhetoric of bashing Ottawa and demanding more powers – or else! – despite his being a son and brother to two highly nationalistic Quebec premiers. Parizeau himself had had to change direction, from the promise of independence to the promise of good government, as it became clear that most Quebeckers wanted jobs and economic growth above all else. "This election is first of all a choice of a government," he said in mid-campaign, "and after that we'll decide on sovereignty in the framework of a referendum."

That was not to be Parizeau's last change of direction. Through late 1994 and early 1995 the polls consistently reported that the Parti

Québécois would lose the referendum, even if separation were disguised under the ambiguous "sovereignty." Gone were the passions that had followed the collapse of the Meech Lake Accord, when Mulroney, Bourassa, the separatists, and most of the province's political class perpetuated the falsehood for their own self-interested reasons that Quebec had been left out of Trudeau's constitutional reforms in 1982, knifed in the back by English Canada. Even if Quebeckers fancied being recognized as a "distinct society" or given more autonomy over culture and manpower training, a startling CBC-CROP poll revealed in February 1995, 51 per cent still preferred the much-maligned status quo to sovereignty.

It came as something of a shock to Quebec's nationalist elites, including those in the media and universities, to discover themselves as alienated from majority opinion as their English-Canadian counterparts had been during the Charlottetown referendum. They had often bragged about being on the same side as the people – "No" to the accord in 1992, "Yes" to the Bloc Québécois in 1993. It confirmed their fantasy that Quebec was of one heart, one will, one great common purpose. But, however true it was that Quebeckers did not share the same degree of fury and cynicism that other Canadians had been venting against their politicians and governments, it did not necessarily follow that they shared the same agenda as their political class. The success of the Bloc Québécois may have been just "a safe way to express one's visceral nationalism while venting a deep-seated anger against the political class and the economic quagmire," as *La Presse* columnist Lysiane Gagnon put it, not unlike the Reform phenomenon in Western Canada or the Créditiste movement in the 1960s. The success of the Parti Québécois certainly did not represent a popular consensus for what the separatists had in mind.

This was all the more remarkable considering how weak the federalist voice had been in the province during the previous decade. Mulroney's Conservatives had snuggled up to the nationalists in order to get their votes and electoral machines. The intelligentsia had created Uncle Toms out of Pierre Trudeau and Jean Chrétien – who were used, as Parizeau put it, "to achieve things that anglophones would not dare try to achieve on their own" – and the media had turned dissenters such as the Jewish novelist Mordecai Richler and native chief Matthew Coon Come into enemies of the people. Despite the social intimidation and selective reporting, however, despite the rhetoric of humiliation and constitutional impasses, support for sovereignty was about what it had been in the 1980 referendum: 40 per cent.

As a result, Parizeau was forced to move more cautiously in the third period than his game plan had called for. He postponed any "solemn declaration" of Quebec's wish for independence to the National Assembly, and took until December to come up with a draft proposal for separation that would not be passed until it had been discussed in hundreds of televised public hearings by seventeen regional committees and polished in a final report of their findings. The resulting legislation was then supposed to be put to a people presumably aroused to a pitch of flag-waving enthusiasm by this month of orchestrated, multimillion-dollar momentum.

The actual effect was a massive yawn. The committees either preached to the converted or bullied anyone who dared to question the party line – one federalist participant compared the experience to being dragged in front of the Spanish Inquisition – and if they caused any shift at all, it seemed to be away from the separatist option.

In early April Lucien Bouchard, after his narrow escape from the "flesh-eating" disease that cost him his left leg but added a heroic dimension to his popularity, called for another "sharp turn" in the PQ's strategy to avoid the dire fate of losing the referendum. If the people weren't ready for full independence, he argued, perhaps they might be persuaded to accept an independent Quebec that maintained formal economic and political associations with the rest of Canada, such as a customs and monetary union, a joint council of ministers, and a parliamentary assembly, along the lines of the European Union. According to the polls, a majority of Quebeckers were prepared to vote "Yes" if they were guaranteed the Canadian market, the Canadian currency, the Canadian passport, and some sort of representation in Ottawa.

"The whole thing is about giving the people of Quebec bargaining power," Bouchard explained, "a real change in dynamics where any proposal coming from a sovereign Quebec would have to be considered very favourably and quite seriously by the rest of Canada." The fatal flaw, of course, was that a sovereign Quebec could not guarantee any sort of association without Canada's consent. However sincerely Bouchard believed that good sense and mutual self-interest would deliver that consent, he obviously failed to grasp either the irritation most Canadians were feeling after thirty years of threats by Quebec's political class or the emotional backlash that a "Yes" vote would trigger in English Canada.

Parizeau, on the other hand, thoroughly understood the dilemma, which was why he had opposed René Lévesque's soft option of sovereignty association in 1980, resigned from the PQ cabinet in 1984, and returned as leader four years later on a platform of outright independence. "We gave so many powerful handles to English Canada and English Canadians on the issue of sovereignty," he lamented in hindsight, "that as a wave of protest took hold across English Canada at the time, it became quite obvious to a majority of Quebeckers that we could not pull it off."

Now Bouchard's public challenge and the stagnant polls compelled him to overrule his own logic. And, wonder of wonders, he was handed a suspiciously convenient excuse to change his mind when the committees' report came out in April with an unexpected recommendation for new economic and political ties with Canada "when circumstances so permit." "All right, I'm game, I'll try," Parizeau conceded, though he had to admit he was not "the most credible of individuals" to sell the idea. Delaying the referendum until fall, with the hope that something dramatic might yet boost the numbers, the "Vibrant Weasel" (as he was called in the Boy Scouts) went off to prepare whatever question would assure the answer "Yes."

"They are not changing the substance of the problem," Prime Minister Chrétien retaliated. "They still want to separate but they don't have the guts to say so."

And West Is West

Ottawa remained surprisingly equanimous throughout this third-period farce. Jean Chrétien belied his reputation as a scrappy street fighter, only occasionally getting caught in a feisty exchange with Lucien Bouchard in the House or gloating about his climb in the Quebec polls in the press. His low-key approach was simply to provide good government in order to show Quebeckers that Canada works and they have a strong place in it. "That's the best strategy," he said. "And not trying to sell them dreams about changing the Constitution. The problems in Canada are not constitutional. They are social and economic problems."

There was little to be gained from promising constitutional reform anyway. Nothing would ever satisfy the hard-line separatists, who had opposed both of Mulroney's accords after all, while anything that smacked of appeasing them with extra powers or special status would ignite the wrath of English Canada in general and the Reform opposition in particular. "If you never talk about the Constitution," Chrétien often recalled a man telling him in the Gaspé during the election, "you'll be prime minister forever."

He didn't, and he helped convince Daniel Johnson and other weak-hearted leaders of the "No" campaign in Quebec not to bother trying to come up with futile offers and counter-offers of a new deal. Every Friday since the beginning of 1995 his two most important advisers in the PMO, Jean Pelletier and Eddie Goldenberg, travelled to Montreal for secret meetings to make sure that everyone kept singing that same song. Meanwhile, in February, the federal government launched a series of high-profile events designed to divert attention away from the PQ's committee hearings: the swearing in of Canada's first Acadian governor general, the capture of Brome-Missisquoi from the Bloc in one of three byelections, the appointment of Lucienne Robillard to the cabinet the day Lucien Bouchard returned to the Commons, the first visit of President Bill Clinton to Ottawa, and the release of Paul Martin's second budget. "So who was in the news during that crucial month?" Chrétien asked rhetorically. "Not bad for people who had no strategy!"

It was Preston Manning, strangely enough, who seemed to panic. Despite the country's obvious preoccupation with economic issues, he chose to hop on the wavelet of anxiety that had seized the political class and the Ottawa media on the eve of the Quebec election. "Prime Minister," Manning wrote in an open letter to Jean Chrétien in June 1994, "we cannot stand by passively and allow Quebec voters to make a decision – separation or Canada – without offering them a vigorous defence of Canada, including a positive federalist alternative to the status quo. And we cannot let them make their decision without disputing the separatist contention that separation will be a relatively uncomplicated and painless process."

Whether through ignorance or guile, he himself was not offering Quebeckers a very attractive alternative to what he liked to caricature as the "Pearson-Trudeau-Mulroney approach." In reality, of course, Trudeau's vision of Canada as a national community of individuals founded upon the sovereignty and will of the people was closer to Manning's than either Lester Pearson's or Brian Mulroney's accommodations with Quebec's nationalist elites – which was precisely why Trudeau and Manning had found themselves allied during the referendum on the Charlottetown Accord. Just as Manning wanted constitutional and political guarantees to protect the interests of western Canadians from the numerical superiority of Central Canada, so Trudeau had wanted constitutional and political guarantees to protect the interests of French Canadians from the numerical superiority of English Canada. Those were not "collective rights" so much as an extension of the rights by which every citizen could participate fully in Canadian society. They certainly did not recognize any special status for Quebec.

"French and English are equal in Canada," Trudeau once noted, not because they were founding nations superior to the immigrants from Italy or China but "because each of these linguistic groups has the power to break the country."

Manning, however, was not content with disputing collective rights and special status for almost all the same reasons as Trudeau. He also denied that Canada had been created out of a historic compromise between two powerful European peoples. "A Canada built on the union of the English and the French is a country built on the union of Quebec and Ontario," he argued. "And in this union the other provinces are, in a fundamental sense, little more than extensions of Ontario." Like the separatists, he essentially twisted the underlying unity of Canada into a conflict between Quebec and the rest of Canada.

In truth, Reform represented the very sort of English-Canadian narrow-mindedness that Trudeau used to fear would shove Quebec out of the federation. Despite Manning's protestations that his party was not anti-French, its core support consisted of Anglo-Saxons who refused to accept the history of 1867 and only saw bilingualism as a barrier to their own careers in national politics and the federal public service. And without any prominent Quebec francophones to sell its economic and populist messages, Reform was stuck with the same alien image that had prevented the New Democrats and the pre-Mulroney Tories from finding acceptance in the province.

Thus, while Reform was willing to support official bilingualism "where need is sufficient to warrant provision of minority services on a cost-effective basis" and in key federal institutions – Manning even welcomed Lucien Bouchard back to the Commons after the Opposition leader's illness with a speech totally in French! – it called for the repeal of the Official Languages Act, vowed to slash hundreds of millions of dollars from Ottawa's bilingualism programs, and proposed handing over to the government of Quebec the primary responsibility for preserving and developing the French language and culture. Though its sincere intention may well have been the practical "recognition of French in Quebec and English elsewhere as the predominant language of work and society," as party policy put it, the consequence (as foreshadowed by Reform's own efforts to become the voice of English Canada) was likely to be the further evolution of two distinct societies centred in two distinct territories, what Manning once described optimistically as "a better but more separate relationship between them, on equitable and mutually acceptable terms."

Like many westerners, Preston Manning did not seem to have much emotional stake in whether Quebeckers stayed or left. "Sooner or later," wrote David Bercuson, a University of Calgary historian, on the front page of the *Globe and Mail* the day after the PQ's victory, "a majority of English-speaking Canadians will come to the conclusion that the secession of Quebec has become unavoidable." Instead of resisting such a conclusion as sad, short-sighted, and probably wrong, Bercuson embraced it. "Canadians can never be a constitutionally defined people," he declared, adopting an argument that Bouchard and Parizeau often used, "as long as Quebec is part of Canada."

Western Canadian politicians and thinkers were caught in a conundrum. To define Canada, even without Quebec, as a single, unhyphenated nationality with a national will and culture led logically, as it had with Diefenbaker and Trudeau, to defining Ottawa as the ultimate guardian of the national interest. But that contradicted the western provinces' claim to being distinct cultures with distinct interests that had been victimized by Central Canada's imperial grip on the national identity. Without Quebec, in fact, Ontario would have an even stronger grip, with half the population, half the seats in the Commons, and half the Supreme Court. Hence arose the persistent denial, contrary to Manning's own notion of a majority will, that English Canadians were a "monolithic" people. They formed, instead, a community of diverse communities, an entente of disparate regions, a pact of equal provinces. Hence, too, arose the constant demand for decentralization – usually a code word for the provincialization of power – which neatly suited Reform's conservative ideologues and the West's failure to strengthen its position in Ottawa through the Triple-E Senate. On health and welfare, for example, Manning not only objected to the intrusion of national programs into provincial jurisdiction but to the imposition of national standards as well. The best interests of the Canadian people were to be defined by the sum of the interests of the provinces, apparently, and the best interests of the provinces were to be defined by each province's political class.

The crazy spectacle going on in Quebec cast serious doubt on both those tenets. More English Canadians had voted for the Liberal vision of Canada than for Reform's, after all, and the public support behind Preston Manning and Ralph Klein in the West was as contradictory and nuanced in the polls and focus groups as the success of Lucien Bouchard and Jacques Parizeau in Quebec. Even Reform, in an ambiguous and understated defence of federalism, argued for a strengthening of Ottawa's commerce power in order to knock down internal trade barriers, and for a non-coercive role for the national government in financing education.

Yet the federal Liberals themselves ended up negotiating a weak settlement to the problem of those costly trade barriers, which they had promised to eliminate altogether in the Red Book, and they handed over postsecondary funding without asking for anything in return. Why, instead, hadn't they mobilized Jean Chrétien's national authority and personal popularity to go over the heads of the self-serving elites to the people of Canada, as Pierre Trudeau had done so effectively in the early 1980s? Partly because they had no money to mount new initiatives or buy off the opposition, partly because they had no strategic agenda worth putting all that stress on the federal system, and partly because they had no Trudeau. ("Thank God for that," a Liberal cabinet minister sighed with relief.)

Path of Least Resistance

At heart, Jean Chrétien was a middle-of-the-road pragmatist with a sharp eye to the politics of the moment and a deep skepticism about mega-strategies for the future. However much he understood the threat of provincialism to national unity, he tacitly went along with the Meech Lake Accord in 1990 lest he lose his Quebec delegates at the Liberal leadership convention; he openly campaigned for the Charlottetown Accord in 1992 lest he be tarred with its defeat; he categorically rejected Pierre Trudeau's suggestion to force an endgame to

the political and economic uncertainty in Quebec by holding a federally sponsored referendum on a clear question of Canada or independence. And however much he defended the notion of a proactive
central government during the 1993 election, he knew the limitations
and pitfalls all too well.

"People say, 'Oh, Chrétien, you're too practical. You don't like
long-term planning,'" he explained in his memoirs. "That's not true.
Canada needs long-term planning, and I've done a lot of it. I'm willing to discuss and work with those who think they know precisely
how many microchips and dentists the society will need in five
years. Their forecasts are useful and if they are accurate, so much the
better; but my experience doesn't allow me to be fooled about the
chances of success. There are simply too many decisions to be made
by too many people in Canada and around the world that can affect
any strategy."

As prime minister, his ambition was more to provide good, realistic, decisive management of whatever crossed his desk each day than
to go off on great crusades against the entrenched interests. He wanted
to cool things down, not heat things up; he wanted to simplify things,
not make them complex; he wanted to do what made sense, not what
fit some abstract theory; and he believed that the less people heard of
their government, the happier they were. If Trudeau had "gone
Cadillac" as Franklin Roosevelt, Chrétien was content to "go Chevrolet" as Harry Truman. "I am not reaching for the spectacular," he
told *Maclean's* at the end of his first year in office. "I don't spend a lot
of time dreaming about my place in history. I would like to be a competent prime minister."

Chrétien's bias toward departmental autonomy also meant that
energetic ministers such as Lloyd Axworthy or Ralph Goodale could
try to do as much as they wanted – within the bounds of cabinet solidarity and fiscal restraint, of course – but there would be minimal
interference and coordination by either the Privy Council Office or
the PMO. The PMO did keep a close watch on what everyone was
doing, particularly in hot areas such as social reform and budget cuts,
but more to make sure they avoided bad decisions than to push them
in a particular direction. "Go there and ask the bureaucrats and the
minister what they think," Chrétien barked at some PCO officials who
wanted him to intervene in a particular department's problems on his
very first day in power. "Let them do their job. If they're no good,
we'll let them go."

The upside of Chrétien's approach was a welcome decrease in the sort of central intrusions that had plagued the Trudeau and Mulroney regimes; the downside was a frustrating inability to accomplish national objectives by rational methods across department lines. Marcel Massé's program review was shot full of philosophical inconsistencies and practical anomalies largely because each department was allowed to reassess its priorities by itself. John Manley's science and technology review proved next to useless not least because Industry could not mastermind a report that ranged very far beyond the department's boundaries. And though Chrétien joked that he worked harder on Paul Martin's second budget than he ever did on one of his own, fretting over the politics of the CHST and forcing a delay in pension reform, there was no "policy shop" mighty enough to stand up to Finance's will.

On the contrary, while the Liberals were anxious that Martin's agenda not be seen by English Canadians as a sop to Quebec on the eve of the referendum, they were grateful that it would provide ammunition to the federalist cause among moderate Quebeckers who wanted greater autonomy within Canada. Giving the provinces the CHST was a hell of a lot safer than trying to impose some centralizing authority over welfare or education for a long-term strategy that Ottawa could not afford anyway. Chrétien expected that would remain the case, for solid political and financial reasons, even after a "No" to the separatist option. "There's a notion that tomorrow I'll have billions of dollars to move and take over the provincial governments," he said. "I have no interest in that at all. I want them to do their job well. The better they do it, the happier I am. I have enough on my plate in Ottawa, and I'm not an empire builder. So I'm not looking for problems. I'd like to relax."

There was, at the same time, a powerful body of decentralists in the cabinet, the bureaucracy, and the rest of the political class who believed – politics and the deficit aside – that the concept of building elaborate national policies in order to preserve an artificial northern market from sea to shining sea had been rendered obsolete by free trade, global capital, and sensible economics. "Canada should no longer be viewed as a single east-west economy, but as a series of north-south cross-border economies," Queen's University professor Tom Courchene stated bluntly in his study *Social Canada in the Millennium*, and in person to Paul Martin and David Dodge, "and, relatedly, comparative advantage is more and more appropriately viewed as a regional, or in some cases a provincial, rather than a national phenomenon." Different regions with different industrial and trading systems required different economic and social policies.

"The decentralists made common cause with the deficit-reduction boys in arguing that we shouldn't be doing much of anything," a government insider explained, "and even if we were doing something, we shouldn't trumpet it or else it would just become another target for the separatists."

With the centre drained of resources and policies, there was growing concern about whether Canada was about to win a thirty-year battle and lose the hundred-year war. While money was not the glue that bound most Canadians to their country, it was the grease by which the machinery of government had been made to run smoothly. Robert Bourassa was not the only player in Canada's political or business class whose patriotism seemed contingent on "profitable federalism." Indeed, in its efforts to appease Quebec's elites without granting special status, Ottawa had conceded to all the provinces over 50 per cent of total government spending and 60 per cent of national tax revenues. Pierre Trudeau, in a rare moment of regret, thought he had been "naive" to have gone along with block funding in 1977. He simply never believed that the people would let their provincial leaders slash their own contributions to health and education.

"It is the nature of provincial governments to demand more money and more powers, but rarely if ever do they offer Ottawa money or powers in return," no less experienced a player than Jean Chrétien had observed in 1985. "Many times they take federal funds to build useful projects or provide beneficial services without even acknowledging the national contribution, yet it was usually torture for me to get them to hand over some territory for national parks that would benefit primarily their own citizens and economies. The problem was that the rich provinces were getting richer and the poor provinces were getting poorer. Provincial power for the sake of provincial power was diminishing the federal government's ability to transfer funds to where they were needed."

Ten years later, the national government still seemed to be acknowledging that it was more incompetent and remote than the provinces, as though provincial politicians were paragons of incorruptible intelligence or their schools and hospitals models of public administration. But that belief originated with the very elites – in the provincial capitals, among the Quebec nationalists, on Bay Street, in the West – whose own fortunes and empires would grow the more Ottawa's diminished. They had been shocked by Trudeau's success in bypassing them by appealing directly to the people in his last term. As Jeffrey Simpson remarked, citing Maréchal Bosquet's observation about the attack of the Light Brigade, *"C'est magnifique, mais ce n'est pas la guerre."* Many in the political class were determined to make sure Ottawa could never conduct such a magnificent attack again. That was clear in the rhetoric and psychology behind the elites' intellectual arguments in favour of the Free Trade Agreement, the Meech Lake and Charlottetown accords, and deficit reduction.

If the basic problem of American government was the gridlock between the White House and the Congress, the basic problem of Canadian government was the gridlock between Ottawa and the provinces – even without the bunch of ornery separatists in Quebec City throwing bricks in the road. Paul Martin found that out trying to replace the GST and the myriad of provincial sales taxes with a single, lower, and much more efficient national sales tax. Lloyd Axworthy found it out trying to get the provinces' cooperation for his paltry social-policy reforms, which Lucien Bouchard characterized as "an all-out offensive against provincial jurisdiction." Diane Marleau found it out trying to organize a federal-provincial summit on health care. With few exceptions, such as the Team Canada trade mission (in which every premier but Parizeau accompanied Prime Minister Chrétien to China), the provinces were inclined to resist every national initiative as a matter of principle. It would be a scorching day in January before they voluntarily recognized a national interest in securities regulation or high school curricula.

But it was far from certain whether the majority of Canadians were in greater harmony with their provincial leaders than the majority of Quebeckers. According to a mammoth survey by Ekos Research in 1994, most people felt more of a personal sense of belonging to their country than to their province. Most people thought the federal government's top priority should be in the provincial fiefdom of education. And most people were fed up with all the territorial disputes. *"Canadians are clearly not seeking a minimalist model of government,"* its report emphasized with italics, *"or even a massive withdrawal of government. They are undoubtedly interested in a leaner, smarter government which works more closely in partnership with other key stakeholders and institutions. . . . Canadians are seeking a moral community from government as much as an economic association."*

In a separate survey of one thousand political and economic decision makers, the Ekos researchers stumbled upon the "chasm" that had developed between the political class and the Canadian people. "Competitiveness, minimal government, and prosperity appear near or at the top of the elite values for government – the opposite of their positioning for the general public," they discovered. "Compared to broader public perceptions, it is rather like the elites look at government through the other end of the public's telescope. Everything is attenuated. Not only is everything related to government reduced, it is also purged of its moral content."

If anybody once harboured fantasies of a strong and independent country, apparently, it was the people of Canada more than the people of Quebec – which helped explained the grassroots jingoism that flared in March 1995 when Ottawa went to war against a Spanish trawler in defence of a fish few had even heard of. The Turbot War was the closest Canadians had felt to a clear victory in a common purpose for a long, long time. More often, in this age of government debt and global capitalism, their political class seemed as unable to indulge that dream of a nation as Quebec's was to foist its own, more parochial version upon an unwilling majority.

Who Shall Speak for Canada?

A Ridiculous Task

T HE SEEDS of Canada were planted by public enterprise. In 1663, the government of France took over the administrative and economic management of its North American colony from a corrupt and dysfunctional group of private investors who had led New France to the edge of ruin. "The King is now master of this country," a colonist wrote to her son from the tiny outpost at Quebec, and her gratitude only increased when His Majesty sent a governor to rule in his name, an army to subdue the Iroquois enemy, an intendant to oversee the development of agriculture and industry (which included, as one historian said, "the doling out of monopolies, subsidies, contracts, and jobs"), even a contingent of young women to marry the soldiers and breed a new people known as *les Canadiens*.

There were, to be sure, many occasions in the following one hundred years when their feudal allegiance to God and king was sorely tried by mad officials, odious prelates, debauched commanders, and stupid judges. Nor did the abuses and regulations inherent in the mercantile system encourage commercial growth and individual initiative. But without the central state's political and economic support, there would have been as little likelihood of French settlers living along the icy banks of the St. Lawrence River as American astronauts walking on the moon. Indeed, as soon as the powers in the French court decided that Canada's "few acres of snow" represented an unaffordable drain on the king's purse, they cut back their military commitment to New France and allowed its sixty-five thousand inhabitants, vast lands, and limitless resources to pass in 1763 to the king of England.

As a consequence, *les Canadiens* missed both the life, liberty, and pursuit of happiness of the American Revolution and the liberty, fraternity, and equality of the French Revolution. Their new British masters were themselves refugees from the liberal democratic rebellion in what became the United States of America. The English-speaking Protestant governors and some forty thousand Loyalist settlers found common cause with the French-speaking Catholic seigneurs and habitants in their wish to build a traditional, hierarchical, agrarian, and devout garrison in the northeast corner of the continent. The political culture of Canada was constructed, in other words, by two preindustrial European societies that valued social order above personal freedom, the rule of law above the rights of man, religious obedience above secular materialism, and executive privilege above the will of the people.

Like all primal stories, this one carried psychological import long after it had become the stuff of history books. The determination of French Canadians to survive in the modern world flows from the adversities they had to overcome: disease, winter, Indian raids, and English invasions. The persistence of Quebec nationalism stems from the humiliation many Québécois still harbour about having been defeated in a battle and bartered away in a treaty more than two hundred years ago. Yet their conquerors had not arrived as a triumphant host. They too were a defeated remnant who bequeathed to their own descendants a love for the imperial monarchy, a suspicion of mob rule, and an odd mixture of moral superiority and practical insecurity regarding all things American. From the very start, given the wealth and population of the United States, given its markets and manifest destiny, English Canadians looked to the Crown for military expenditures and protective tariffs, business subsidies and state monopolies, patronage jobs and endowments to the arts.

"We were grounded in the wisdom of Sir John A. Macdonald, who saw plainly more than a hundred years ago that the only threat to nationalism was from the South, not from across the sea," the Tory philosopher George Grant observed. "To be a Canadian was to build, along with the French, a more ordered and stable society than the liberal experiment in the United States."

For that purpose (as well as to line the pockets of the elites in the Family Compact or the Bank of Montreal), Canadian conservatism underwrote the capital costs of canals, railways, and land development. It protected central manufacturers from American competition and gave them artificial advantages down East and out West. It modelled the Senate on the House of Lords so that appointed members of the elites could provide "sober second thought" to the enthusiasms of the elected MPs. It commissioned the CBC to create, like the BBC, commercial-free quality programming. But, also from the start, that tradition-bound and class-conscious ethos was challenged in both its French and English expressions by a radical and egalitarian strain that eventually came to predominate.

In the fresh air of New France, an ocean away from the medieval despotism of the Old Regime, there was an almost tangible attraction to equality and freedom. The local nobles were hardly better off than their tenants, after all, and when the laws and mores of the colony proved too suffocating, the wilderness offered a ready escape. Within every French-Canadian family, there were always some who broke from the piety and conformity of the St. Lawrence valley, went out as fur traders or explorers all the way west to the Rocky Mountains and south to Louisiana. Instead of barricading themselves against hostile intruders, they adapted the ways of the native peoples and opened trade links with the English colonists. Instead of shunning danger and enterprise, they established an empire that once covered most of North America.

Even after the English Conquest, while most of their kin huddled on farms within sight of a church steeple in order to keep their language and their faith, the heirs of Radisson and La Vérendrye learned about international commerce, gained parliamentary concessions from the English majority, and moved west to better land or south to better jobs. In time they produced great political and corporate leaders who advanced the wealth and culture of their people within Canada – and across Canada – in defiance of their compatriots who argued that the only safe course was to withdraw into social isolation or political independence.

Those liberal-minded French Canadians found sympathetic allies in English Canada, largely among the tens of thousands of immigrants who had fled the poverty of the British Isles a couple of generations after the Loyalist influx. Most of them were not true-blue conservatives anxious to reconstruct in North America a Little England based upon God, king, and empire. Instead, they were English Methodists, Scottish Presbyterians, and Irish Roman Catholics who had been influenced by the liberation movements and social consciences of the early Industrial Revolution. Some were barely off the boat in the 1830s, in fact, before they launched one of the few rebellions in Canadian history – in defence of liberal ideals and democratic institutions, and in tandem with French-speaking "reds."

In Canada, there arose a unique ideology in which conservative values such as community, oligarchy, and stability sought constant balance with liberal values such as individualism, majority government, and the free market. When the various British colonies of North America decided to join together in 1867, their conservative bias inclined them toward a strong unitary state like the motherland had, but their liberal bias led them to duplicate the decentralized checks-and-balances of the American system. The compromise was Canadian federalism. So, too, the conservative bias toward national authority and state intervention was increasingly joined to the liberal bias toward economic progress and social justice. Throughout the twentieth century, Keynesian macroeconomics, Roosevelt's New Deal, the Second World War, immigration, industrialization, urbanization, unionization, Yankee capital, mass communications, technological innovation, the decline of religion, and the collapse of the British Empire all converged to make Canada one of the most progressive and democratic societies in the world.

The liberal bias also killed off the Loyalist dream of making Canada a distinct and independent country, according to George Grant. "The impossibility of conservatism in our era is the impossibility of Canada," he argued in his bitter polemic, *Lament for a Nation*, which appeared in 1965. "As Canadians we attempted a ridiculous task in trying to build a conservative nation in the age of progress, on a continent we share with the most dynamic nation on earth. The current of modern history was against us."

State of Disrepair

George Grant had barely finished proclaiming the death of the old national myth when Pierre Trudeau showed up to herald the birth of a new one. Instead of associating the Canadian identity with the Union Jack and the imperial pound, Trudeau associated it with the Maple Leaf and the metric ton. Instead of defining the Canadian government by the English language and the British Constitution, he defined it by official bilingualism and the Charter of Rights. Propelled by the wave of English-Canadian patriotism unleashed during Canada's centennial celebrations and the wave of French-Canadian nationalism let loose by Quebec's Quiet Revolution, he overthrew a litany of archaic assumptions that had in effect excluded francophones, immigrants, and the young. Simultaneously he articulated – and personified – a more accurate and attractive vision of Canada as a bilingual, multicultural, and just society symbolized by regional equality and medicare.

Trudeau's liberal substitute was implanted with remarkable speed, and became the core of what distinguished Canadians from Americans and bound them as a community. Without it, one could argue, the nation would not have survived Quebec's 1980 referendum on independence. But it alienated a lot of people, too, including many of the same elites who had killed George Grant's dream. White Anglo-Saxon Tories – Kim Campbell's father George, for one – were upset by the displacement of their own mythology. Quebec separatists and unilingual westerners were aggrieved that bilingualism gave a boost to the power of French Canadians in Parliament and the federal civil service. Corporate executives and branch-plant managers were alarmed by the inherent emphasis on social justice, equal opportunity, and national sovereignty. Provincial premiers and suburban taxpayers were distressed by the activist thrust of the national government and the size of the national debt. They all eventually found their political champions among those who had their own motives for breaking the Trudeau legacy: Progressive Conservatives, Reformers, the Bloc Québécois, and right-wing Liberals.

Whether in power or opposition, each was bent on discrediting and dismantling the model Pierre Trudeau had constructed. Some, notably the separatists in Quebec and the West, had nothing to gain by constructing yet another myth to sustain the unity of Canada. Some, especially war veterans and small-town Loyalists, fantasized in vain about going back to the peace, order, and good government of their youth, when the sun had never set on the British Empire. A few, such as Joe Clark and Preston Manning, struggled to give resonance to their rhetoric about a "community of communities" or a new Canada in ways that added up to Ottawa's being more than "a headwaiter to the provinces" or in cahoots with the Quebec separatists. But most never bothered trying to conceive an alternate national vision. Like Brian Mulroney after the Free Trade Agreement and the Charlottetown Accord, they merely threw up their hands in the midst of the economic, social, and political turbulence through which the country was passing. It was like being up the creek not only without a paddle, but without a map, a knapsack, or a canoe.

The more governments slashed sacred programs and historic services, the less citizens came to see their state as a useful or necessary tool, and the faster the conventional wisdoms began to unravel. If people could no longer depend on the state for fair treatment, they would have to depend on themselves, and everyone else could go to rot. Parties that had once presumed generation after generation of support from a majority of families and constituencies now saw the electorate swing wildly from election to election, indeed from week to week. Ideas and policies that had been unthinkable a few years ago became commonplace. Some members of the political class started doing very well by pushing the hot buttons of conflict rather than compromise, faction rather than nation, self-interest rather than common good, ideology rather than consensus.

"There's no longer the political climate or the economic resources for politicians to fulfil the expectations of a wide range of people," Reform MP Stephen Harper suggested. "Now they have to make choices, which means saying no to ethnics or bankers or whomever. They can't be all things to all people any more. And many of them are having trouble adjusting to that different role because it's new and because consensus politicians aren't well suited to conflict management or conflict exploitation."

Thus, in the spring of 1995, the voters of Ontario clearly decided they had had enough of the fiscal incompetence, ministerial ineptitude, and social engineering of the NDP government they had elected in 1990. According to the polls, about half of them turned to the provincial Liberals, whose federal cousins had actually grown in popularity since winning ninety-eight of Ontario's ninety-nine seats less than two years earlier. Their leader Lyn McLeod didn't just take a page from Jean Chrétien's book: she took the whole Red Book, offering a pragmatic balance of deficit reduction and social programs in eighty-two pages of helter-skelter promises. In the opinion of the pundits and historians, her victory was all the more assured considering that the once-great

Conservative party of John Robarts and William Davis, the bastion of "Red" Toryism and national statesmanship, had fallen into the hands of a right-wing golf pro from the hinterland named "Chainsaw Mike" Harris.

Harris had deliberately abandoned the party's traditional formula of bland moderation and paternalistic government to appeal to over-taxed, underappreciated, middle-class and working-class voters whose liberal principles had been shaken up by the savage recession in Ontario, Ralph Klein in Alberta, Preston Manning in Ottawa, and Newt Gingrich in Washington. Harris talked about putting welfare recipients to work; he talked about sending young offenders to boot camp; he talked about a 15-per-cent cut in the civil service and tax cuts of 30 per cent; he talked about ending the NDP's employment-equity and JobsOntario programs. Not surprisingly, or so the pollsters and pundits thought going into the campaign, he was doing only slightly better than the Reform party had done in the 1993 federal election. Just a few weeks later, on June 8, he emerged with a majority government and 45 per cent of the popular vote. His Common Sense Revolution was launched among a people to whom "revolution" had been a dirty word for more than two hundred years.

"If there were any errors made by analysts in all parties," Harris said, "it was in not realizing the extent to which old voting patterns had gone and the public was really looking for a change." And since Lyn McLeod's 142 promises had not added up to a coherent statement of what the Liberals stood for and why they were worth supporting, the Conservatives were able to get away with singling out welfare families, minority groups, and labour unions as scapegoats for what was wrong with Ontario. Conversely, they took care not to threaten the health services, classroom facilities, and crime-fighting programs that were of such below-cost benefit and psychological comfort to their suburban, small-business supporters in ridings such as Mississauga West, where a Tory defeated the Liberal incumbent – to the conster-nation of the federal MP, Carolyn Parrish.

In the absence of any grander purpose, neo-conservatism was able to sell the idea that individual prosperity was all that mattered. "The best way to keep the country together," the BCNI's Tom d'Aquino argued, "is to make sure it's wealthy." And that was best achieved, went the corollary, by letting private companies go about their private business with almost no interference from the state. As a reaction to the entrenched political class, it was helpful in knocking down a host of outdated shibboleths and some bad social habits. But, whether or not it would bring balanced budgets and renewed prosperity, it was certain to widen the gap between the haves and have-nots. The highest incomes would gain the most from the tax cuts; the lowest incomes would lose the most from the welfare cuts; some in the middle would do better in a dog-eat-dog world; more would slip down into harder times. And that outcome seemed inevitable whatever Mike Harris did at Queen's Park or Jean Chrétien did on Parliament Hill, because it was being driven by the economic and technological transformations happening around the world.

"If the Industrial Revolution gave us mass production, mass consumption, mass media, mass education," said Alvin Toffler, the American prophet of what he termed the "Third Wave" of human history (and a guru to Newt Gingrich), "the Third Wave reverses the direction: customized production, micro markets, infinite channels of communications, heterogeneous family styles, and instead of mass political movements, we see thousands of single-issue grouplets."

Those who could compete on a world scale in the knowledge industries and niche markets were going to enjoy extraordinary growth and profits. Those blessed with university educations and innovative minds were already experiencing a boom in their opportunities and salaries. Those stuck in declining sectors with little training were finding fewer jobs, lower wages, and less help getting through the epic transformation, which happened to coincide in Canada with the collapse of East Coast fisheries, the chaos in prairie agriculture, the restructuring of the transportation industry, and the adjustment to free trade. Thus, between 1990 and 1993, those with a high school education or less suffered a net job *loss* of 640,000, while those with more than a high school education had a net job *gain* of 450,000.

After analysing the previous transitions from farming to factories and steam to electricity, many economists concluded that the world was only halfway through a forty-year lag between the old order and the new prosperity – except that this one was liable to eliminate a lot more full-time jobs than it would create. At the same time, governments everywhere were encountering the tremendous resistance from the transnational corporations and money managers to any schemes to redistribute wealth through progressive taxes, minimum wages, and social spending. Even when the deficit gets under control, Martin's deputy minister David Dodge already warned, Canada will have to face the fact that its high level of taxes on corporations and professionals has put the country at a competitive disadvantage, particularly vis-à-vis the United States, and Ottawa will still have to spend about a third of its tax revenues on interest payments in the foreseeable future just to stay even.

"Whether you're talking about Canada, the United States, Europe, anywhere," Matthew Barrett said, "you see governments struggling with a transitional period. Nobody knows how to manage the transition. I'm an optimist in the long run, but what I don't know – and what I don't think the politicians know – is how do we make it through the night, when you're going to have an unemployable underclass, when the rich are getting richer and the poor are getting poorer. I mean, with all the retraining in the world, you're not going to retrain most fifty-year-olds with a Grade 8 education into becoming black belts in Microsoft. It's just not going to happen."

Such was the range and rate of this global revolution that even the haves were feeling insecure and besieged – if not for themselves, then for their children. To survive, they had to move faster, farther, and lighter, which meant lower taxes, fewer regulations, bigger markets, and a lot less obligation to carry the have-nots on their backs. Debt-heavy government was not just of little use to them any more; it was now seen as an obstacle. And the political class was no longer able to buy back the favour of upper-income earners through generous write-offs, subsidies, procurements, and universal social programs. As the economic elites assumed almost total responsibility for their retirement and old age, as they sent their kids to private schools and their parents to American clinics, as they protected themselves behind security systems in insulated enclaves, as they roamed the Earth for the best place to put their factories and invest their capital, they begrudged having to pay for public services they considered wasteful, incompetent, counterproductive, and unaffordable.

"I think what's happening is the two nations are no longer French-English," the pollster Michael Adams commented. "There are those who can get along on their own and those who can't. This is a society of winners and losers. There are those who feel they have the resources – psychological, financial, educational – to survive in a social Darwinistic world and there are those who don't."

Nor was the withdrawal from public life confined to the rich and powerful. According to the Ekos study, it had spread throughout the well-educated, upwardly mobile social class – which American economist Robert Reich now called "the anxious class" – that used to pride itself on liberal values of tolerance, generosity, and social justice. They felt that Ottawa hadn't downsized its own operations and expenses enough during the recession; they had friends in middle and upper-middle management who had been laid off; they heard about people on welfare who wouldn't look for work; and they saw their tax bills going up and up. If taxes had once been the price willingly paid for the privilege of living in a peaceable kingdom, they were now only a rung above cancer treatments in everybody's list of things to avoid. The Ekos researchers found "Canadians themselves acknowledging that economic stress is reducing their sense of compassion. In areas such as immigration and foreign aid we see an inexorable decline in a more tolerant-compassionate posture to public policy. Somewhat disturbingly, this increasing mean-spiritedness has continued unabated despite the end of the recession and a mild easing of economic insecurities."

Downtown streets, in a state of disrepair, became ever more rife with drunks, panhandlers, the homeless, and the mentally ill. Structural unemployment, child poverty, single-parent families, suicides among young men, and the demand for food banks all increased. Living standards declined, especially among those under thirty-five. Media stories detailed the growing incidents of racist attacks in suburban neighbourhoods, teenaged gangs in shopping malls, brutal beatings in domestic disputes, and drug deaths in city parks. Private school enrolment doubled in twenty years; many public school students were crowded into poorly equipped classrooms in makeshift extensions. Toll booths went up on public highways and in national parks. In the midst of all this, there was a minority whose paycheques had never been higher, whose life-styles had never been richer, and whose futures had never been brighter.

Hardly a national institution was left with its dignity intact. The appointment of a new governor general was marred by charges of sleazy patronage. The new prime minister was reluctant to entertain guests at his residence in case the new puritans on the Hill queried the size of his food bills. The minister of foreign affairs announced that human rights would not be allowed to stand in the way of any trade deal. A distinguished military regiment was exposed as a viper's nest of racists and thugs. Not a single Canadian was judged capable of being the publisher of the *Globe and Mail*. The Quebec Nordiques were sold to Denver. Commercial operators such as Garth Drabinsky and Moses Znaimer replaced the Stratford Festival and the CBC as icons of cultural excellence. And, in the face of government cutbacks and layoffs, the brightest, most ambitious graduates headed toward the big bucks and expansive horizons of the banks, the law firms, the multinationals, and the United States, leaving politics and the civil service vulnerable to the special interests and mediocre careerists, thereby threatening to further erode public confidence in the political class.

There wasn't anything particularly wicked or illogical in all of this. It is human nature, in periods of unsettling change and diminishing income, for people to look out for themselves and their families first; and it is in the nature of corporations, bureaucracies, interest groups, and the media to clash for their own benefit. But the absence of a greater vision and the weakness of the federal government did pose the question of what values, institutions, and declarations of national community would counterbalance all the pressures and interests that were tearing the Dominion of Canada into ten little Canadas, or no Canada at all. What would motivate Albertans, who had suffered hospital closures for the cause of a balanced budget, to continue sending transfer dollars to support unemployed fishermen in Newfoundland? Why should Ontario put up any longer, as Bob Rae once complained (and Mike Harris would no doubt repeat), with being "seen as the big guy at the end of the bar who would pick up the tab at the end of the night"? Indeed, what motives beyond sloth and fear would drive Quebeckers to choose federalism over the passionate arguments of their own political class and the apparent indifference of the rest of the country?

To paraphrase George Grant, is the impossibility of liberalism in our era the impossibility of Canada? Michael Adams, for one, suggested that the roller-coaster of emotions that Canadians had been feeling in recent years – denial, anger, bargaining, depression, resignation – were just classic stages in the dying of a nation.

Bugs in the System

There is a theory, mostly borrowed from the Americans, that freedom and avarice are all any society needs to survive. As long as the state does not intrude unduly in the lives of its citizens, as long as people really believe that anyone can become a millionaire through hard work and a decent chance, social harmony and national unity will follow as day does night. Conveniently ignoring that the United States itself has had to bolster its patriotic brag as the Land of the Free with a civil war, an anti-Communist crusade, a space program, and civil-rights legislation, Canadian neo-conservativism postulates that Canada will get along just fine without a strong central government or an integral national vision. Indeed, it claims, Canada will get along better than ever if Ottawa stops shoving industrial policies, social standards, and bilingualism programs upon an unwilling people.

Neo-conservatism was most enthusiastically received among two groups that have little else in common: the corporate elite who had a vested interest in disarming their only serious rival for power – the federal government – and disaffected WASPs in the suburbs and hinterlands who, despite their middle-class status, felt left out of the political class's liberal consensus and sliding down the economic ladder. Strangely enough, the latter did not seem to care whether they were merely being used as the votes by which remote and irresponsible politicians would be displaced by even more remote and irresponsible CEOs. Certainly the CEOs never lost much sleep worrying whether the devolution to the provinces or the recall of MPs would hurt them. On the contrary, the more political authority is divided, the more corporate concentration will conquer. And the people will only ever get what the global investors are willing and able to give them anyway.

"I used to think that if there was reincarnation, I wanted to come back as the president or the pope," the Washington political strategist James Carville joked in the *New York Times*. "But now I would like to come back as the bond market. You can intimidate everybody."

Populism is much like anarchism in its fantasy that societies can function without some sort of executive decision making. Like Marxism, populism is also more likely to lead to an authoritarian leader determining the will of the people below from his position on a high balcony than to the withering away of the state. Indeed, even if it becomes technologically possible to amass everyone in an electronic town hall as the Greeks once did in the agora, it may not be socially desirable to let a majority of votes overwhelm the interests of significant minorities on many complex issues or crucial trade-offs. That isn't to suggest that the people are incapable of reaching an appropriate decision. It's merely to suggest that, in a country as diverse as Canada, and in a time of dwindling funds, most conflicts need a subtler resolution than majoritarianism can provide with its "Yes" or "No." The major exception, of course, happens when the people are called upon to judge proposed changes to their fundamental social contract, the Constitution, as they were in Quebec in 1980 and across the country in 1992.

There are all kinds of populist reforms capable of checking the authority of a parliamentary government – citizen-initiated referenda, free votes, an elected Senate, proportional representation – but they share a single attribute. All grow out of the opposition mentality that people develop when they feel themselves out of power and don't trust their elected politicians to do the right thing. As soon as these "outs" get into power, however, they want their own leaders to be able to act decisively and swiftly. They turn out not to want governments to do nothing, but to do a lot of *other* things, closer to the new insiders' interests. Right-wing parties, in particular, discover that pushing through deficit cuts, social reforms, and cultural revolutions in a pluralistic nation requires much more executive will and party discipline than spending money and maintaining the status quo. Thus, the basic issue is not really about institutional and constitutional reforms. It's about exclusion and trust.

"There's too much focus on what I call the system hardware – Parliament, the committees, the courts, the federal-provincial conferences," said Donald Johnston, the former Trudeau cabinet minister who later served as president of the Liberal Party of Canada under Jean Chrétien. "The weakest element is really the 'software,' which are the political parties."

In this analogy, the hardware is a neutral machine that, despite its operating modes and built-in proclivities, processes information well enough. The people, after all, got the political class to nix the Meech Lake and Charlottetown accords. The people elevated Kim Campbell and punished the Conservative professionals under what were considered fair electoral rules. The people gave Quebec separatists and western Reformers the power to check the potential abuse of cabinet government through the House of Commons and the media. Indeed, considering the Byzantine battles between the White House and Capitol Hill over health care and budget cuts, the tens of millions of dollars every American candidate must raise to seek public office and the consequent grip of corporate influence on the legislators, and the abject nature of media discourse and declining level of voter turnout in the United States, Canadians might well conclude that their hardware is not so bad after all – which is reason enough to protect its integrity with stringent rules about election spending, polling, lobbyists, and ethics.

"People talk as though our political system had been taken over by alien beings," one American study concluded about the apathy and rage in United States politics, which has produced Ross Perot populism, evangelical Republicanism, and the militiamen who blew up a federal building in Oklahoma City. "They point their fingers at politicians, at powerful lobbyists, and – this came as a surprise – at people in the media. They see these three groups as a political class, the rulers of an oligarchy that has replaced democracy."

Ultimately, the hardware is only as good as the facts, biases, policies, and principles that are fed into it and the quality of the human beings involved. Even if Brian Mulroney and Jean Chrétien were both driven to the same conclusions about deficit reduction and free trade, one would be hard pressed to suggest that it did not matter to Canadian government or Canadian society which man was prime minister. It mattered enormously to the management and mood of the country, just as it mattered enormously that the Bloc Québécois became the Loyal Opposition and the Reform party replaced the New Democrats as the third party. And what mattered most were their ideas. Lowering the deficit to 3 per cent of GDP obviously had a different political, social, and economic effect than bringing it to zero within three years. Refusing to engage in any more constitutional negotiations was hardly the same as inviting the premiers to revisit Meech Lake.

Given the brain-dead condition of the federal bureaucracy and the media's commercial obsession with sensational crime stories, the political parties were, even more than usual, the main vehicles for ideas. The Liberals came into office with the Aylmer Conference and the Red Book, both highly effective devices for involving the membership and the public in policy debates; the Reformers revered their Blue Sheet only a mite less than the New Testament; the Bloc Québécois had its separatist agenda. In practice, however, the parties proved a lot better at organizing campaigns, raising money, and fighting elections than at generating policies, encouraging participation, and explaining decisions. The government, especially, appeared to lose interest in what its own grassroots members thought, as ministers and MPs got bound up in the realities of the Hill and the cacophonous advice of civil servants, client groups, newspaper editorials, think tanks, and opinion polls. Indeed, the lowest support for Martin's second budget was among Liberal supporters.

"One of the problems of successful political parties is that they become governments and cease to be parties," Dalton Camp observed from his own experience in the Tory back rooms. "Instead, the governing party becomes a firmament of elites, the result being that more and more people in the party feel themselves left out. As well, the agenda of government is not party business but that of a faceless bureaucracy. Perhaps worst of all, what governments and their elites find they need most to sustain themselves is not followers or supporters but contributors with money."

By the time some two thousand Liberals gathered in mid-May 1994 for their first postvictory convention, senior campaign officials were already complaining that they had been frozen out by the Prime Minister's Office. Experienced veterans from the Pearson and Trudeau eras either did not know who to phone any more or were kept at a distance because of Chrétien's determination to avoid the taint of lobbyists, patronage, and cronyism. And, in what was billed as a policy convention to update the Red Book in the midst of the fiscal crisis and the social-security reviews, there was astonishingly little serious discussion about the 146 resolutions or the future of Canadian Liberalism. Except for a few young hotheads, nobody seemed prepared to quarrel with political success. "I'm not all that interested in the government-bureaucratic thing," said one Ontario organizer above the happy din of a cocktail party in the Centre Block. "I just like the game of getting them elected."

Almost all the delegates seemed content to pay $575 each to give their leader a standing ovation for his steady climb in the polls, slip Paul Martin a business card or approach David Anderson with a tax problem, network the corridors of the Congress Centre for a job or a contract, and celebrate from office to office on Parliament Hill like the ferrets that overran Toad Hall. At one breakfast meeting with the Ontario caucus, there were more MPs and cabinet ministers in the room than delegates to grill them, and the angriest charge heard in four days was that some Tory law firms were still getting work from the Department of Justice. Only a few riding associations had been able to get their active members to meet and prepare a policy resolution. As soon as the election was over, a Liberal backbencher observed, everyone's political participation reverted to staying home like other Canadians and yelling obscenities at the TV news.

The typical pattern is for an MP who really cares about ideas and issues to twist arms to get a couple of hundred people to one weekend session. Fifty of them show up for the second; no one shows up for the third. Most have prior responsibilities to their work or their families; many prefer to go to a movie or play tennis; few get any material reward for their efforts or even much psychological gratification in watching their labours vanish into the black hole of the PMO or the Ottawa bureaucracy. In Carolyn Parrish's riding of Mississauga West, party membership tumbled from over 15,000 to a mere 150 stalwarts, and she had trouble attracting more than thirty people to a couple of public meetings about the hot local issue of expanding Pearson Airport. Reform's own keeners had decreased by more than half. The truth is, the vast majority of citizens choose to become engaged in party politics only on E-day or when their personal interests are adversely affected in a visible way.

"Even university professors and business leaders with great ideas aren't prepared to work through the parties," Donald Johnston said. "They all whine about having no input, they all want special access to the prime minister and the cabinet, but they never try using the party apparatus because they aren't willing to get up in front of a microphone and convince other people to buy their ideas. The leader isn't obliged to adopt the positions of a convention, of course, but he does have to appear at an accountability session and explain why not."

However arduous, frustrating, tiresome, and even humiliating the party system can be, it remains the fundamental instrument by which leaders are chosen, governments are elected, policies are decided, and changes are made. All kinds of realities may limit the ability of politicians to meet the expectations of the people, of course, and governing parties always betray their membership to a degree in their duty to govern on behalf of the whole country. But democratic politics is the *only* vehicle by which ordinary citizens have any hope of achieving their desires among the various centres of power in society, particularly given the oligarchical tendencies of money. However effective some interest groups, however influential some editorial opinions, however gratifying some protest marches, they are nothing in the end but supplicants to those who hold public office. "Some people confuse consultation with decision," said Prime Minister Chrétien. "If you want to decide, you have to get elected." Success is difficult and far from certain, but participation is the way to achieve it, as "French Power" showed in the 1970s and the Reform party more recently.

All Right Now

The New Right came late to party politics in Canada, but it came with a vengeance, mobilizing a lot of marginalized citizens like Charles Conn to sign up and take charge for the first time. It treated their opinions with respect, it trained them in the games of election-eering, and it invested them with evangelical conviction and hope. The Old Left, by contrast, wallowed in confusion and despondency, its own evangelical fires having been doused by globalization and debt. The centre muddled through the contradictions, conundrums, and complacencies of postmodern liberalism. Indeed, the right was doing well throughout the Western world because it had become bet-ter organized and more fervent than either the left or the centre. Like its soul mate, fundamentalist religion, it found its strength in *believing* a few simple things in a time and place where most people could no longer believe in anything, then communicating its simple messages through the perfect medium of television.

Postwar prosperity had corrupted both the left and the centre. It made their victories too easy, their ideas too expensive, because there was enough money for every problem and everybody. Young leftists, never having had to fight for freedom, disdained parliamentary democ-racy. When they grew up, they carried that disdain into the uncom-promising righteousness of extraparliamentary groups, the irrelevant blather about constituent assemblies, or the uncaring cynicism of the eighties. By the time an issue arose that ignited their passions – the Free Trade Agreement with the United States – they lost to those who had been playing the party game longer and with more skill. If they had really wanted to defeat Brian Mulroney and his deal, they should have ousted John Turner from the Liberal leadership, forced a coali-tion between the Liberals and the NDP under Jean Chrétien, and pre-sented a credible alternative to continental protectionism – all of which presumed an ongoing and sophisticated involvement in elec-toral politics. Afterwards, instead of learning a lesson, many of them retreated into dispiritedness and disengagement, which merely relin-quished to Preston Manning, Ralph Klein, and Mike Harris the polit-ical and intellectual ground to put public institutions and social programs under the gun.

The centre, as represented by the Liberal party, may have had a more pragmatic and realistic view of politics, but it too ended up conceding more of the right's ideas than holding to its own. "It's not hard to find ideas to spend money," Chrétien explained. "The problem is finding money." Once the more straightforward promises of the Red Book were exhausted, once the fiscal crunch thwarted any ambitious rethinking of social policy and the innovative economy, the Liberals became fuzzier about their constructive vision for Canada. Being in office rather than in opposition, they knew that there weren't any cheap or clear solutions to counter the insecurities of the public, the demands of the media, and the delusions of the ideologues. Nor were the government's platitudes about helping the working poor or protecting national values able to stir the public and the media when, in apparent contradiction, it proceeded to slash UI benefits and regional development, social transfers and cultural agencies, immigration levels and old-age pensions. Despite their high standing in the polls, many federal Liberals grew worried about what the same sort of fuzziness had done to their colleagues in Ontario and to the Mulroney Conservatives.

"Apparently," Mulroney himself commented, in a dig at Jean Chrétien, "he's endorsed NAFTA, approved the cruise-missile testing, announced a freeze for public servants, cut back on unemployment-insurance payments, and he's appointed friends and relatives to high positions in government. Gee, for a minute I thought I was right back in office."

The political centre is called the silent majority because it is not accustomed to speaking up and usually does not have much to say. Some of that is leftover deference to authority. Some of it is due to the fact that neither the mass media nor the education system have done a decent job of teaching Canadians how decision making happens through the cabinet, the caucus, the committees, and the political parties. Much of it is because public life requires more time and interest than most people have to give. They want to feel that they can participate if and when they choose to; they want to know that someone cares about what they think; but generally they want the political class to come up with a plan and some ideas on how to implement it, which they can either study, ignore, accept, or reject.

"People are saying, if you listen to me, you'll make better decisions. They're not saying, let *me* decide," was Allan Gregg's interpretation. "The irony of empowerment is that the public doesn't have a fucking clue about what it wants. Sure, it wants lower taxes, more services, a more equitable country, and nothing for Quebec. But what it really wants is a leadership capable of listening and deciding." Indeed, a good deal of the apathy and frustration with politics is rooted in the feeling that governments can no longer do very much very well.

"After the defeat of the Charlottetown referendum in 1992, many observers suggested that Canadians would insist on constant consultation about the political issues of the day," the *Globe and Mail* noted in its attempt to explain the general boredom and right-wing drift of the Ontario election. "That's what 'populism' meant. Maybe they got that backward. Maybe populism means 'cool it.' Get back to your knitting, focus on serving us more effectively with less *Sturm und Drang*, get your hands out of our pockets, put your sermons back into your own pockets and, well, leave us alone unless something really important comes up."

That may have reflected the self-satisfied ennui around the *Globe*'s editorial offices and the evident decline of public life in Canada, but it was a rewriting of the history of the Charlottetown referendum, the federal election, and even the Harris victory. In each case, the losers lost more than the winners won, and they lost primarily because they were found wanting in leadership and vision. The architects of the Charlottetown Accord failed to design an idealistic model of Canada; Kim Campbell could not rise above the "do nothing" paralysis of her party; Lyn McLeod offered considerably less *Sturm und Drang* than Mike Harris and a lot fewer sermons than Preston Manning. Indeed, as the manager of the Ontario Tories' campaign explained it in the *Globe*'s own pages, the clearest message they heard in their town halls and bus tours was that people "wanted to believe so badly that things could be changed but they weren't sure if anybody was listening to them."

Take Me to Your Leader

Since the advent of mass communications, especially satellite television, most Canadians have looked ultimately to their national government for that kind of leadership. True, they have usually looked through different-coloured lenses – coloured by the region they inhabit and the language they speak, by the income they earn and the assistance they need – and more of their day-to-day contact is with the schools, hospitals, highways, parks, welfare bureaus, hydro offices, and liquor stores for which their provinces or municipalities are responsible. But, if the talk-show calls and voter turnouts are any indication, Ottawa remains the most significant political theatre in the country, its politicians the best-known actors, its debates the most engrossing dramas. Even French Quebeckers, who receive next to no information about the rest of Canada from their myopic media, pay close attention to the soap-opera feuds between Jean Chrétien and Lucien Bouchard on the Hill.

Part of that attention is attributable to the concentrated power of the national press gallery, which bypasses the local elites and brings the prime minister and the federal cabinet directly into people's homes. The Ottawa bureaus automatically generate a disproportionate number of prominent stories, which attracts a high number of the brightest and most ambitious reporters, who soon grow enamoured of basking in their proximity to history and their own quasi-celebrity status. One effect, as Peter Lougheed observed from his time as premier of Alberta, is that "the Ottawa media really had a very strong self-interest in a dominant central government. The more dominant the government, the more important their position as journalists." Though today's decentralists and deficit slayers at the bar of the National Press Club would undoubtedly disagree, Lougheed's point was reiterated from another angle by the *Toronto Star*'s Richard Gwyn. "National media like the CBC and *Maclean's* magazine rarely examine the national dimensions of provincially administered programs, such as higher education or worker's compensation," Gwyn noted, "because viewers/readers in Saskatchewan, say, don't give a damn about the state of these programs in Manitoba, let alone in Nova Scotia."

But the national focus of the mass media only tightened what history, climate, and mythology had already created: a strong sense among ordinary Canadians of a national community. According to Gregg's polling for *Maclean's* in July 1995, 74 per cent felt that Canada had a distinct character, based primarily on nonviolence, tolerance, and the quality of its social programs. The provincial premiers and special-interest spokespersons seldom want to admit that collective consciousness, because it undermines their ability to wrest authority and money from the system. Meanwhile, the federal elites and cultural nationalists have difficulty proclaiming the Canadian identity because it is so pluralistic and fluid. Its ideology isn't European or American, its language isn't French or English, its religion isn't Protestant or Catholic, its race isn't Caucasoid or Mongoloid, its culture isn't Western or aboriginal, its mentality isn't frontier or suburban, its occupation isn't manufacturing or mining, its distinction isn't health care or hockey. Canada is none and all of those things. Its people are often unable to find the words to express who they are, but they know in their hearts who they are.

As a result, Canadians – including most French-speaking Quebeckers – constantly seek an affirmation and elucidation of their commonality from their national government. Just as constantly, their elites bicker and brawl over constitutional powers, tax points, charter rights, spending cuts, parliamentary procedures, and political manoeuvres. The smaller and more crowded the water hole became, the louder and more ferocious the wild beasts became. The air was full of apocalyptic cries that Canada was about to break in two, that Canada was on the verge of fracturing into five pieces, that Canada would soon be sucked into the United States. For it was the nation's curse that so many of its social and economic cleavages were centred in different regions – whether Celts and fishermen in the Maritimes, dairy farmers and francophones in Quebec, Italians and automobile manufacturers in Ontario, wheat producers and oilmen across the Prairies, or natives and East Asians on the West Coast – rather than spread more evenly by ethnicity, religion, or class across the country.

Certainly the centrifugal forces were great. International capital pulled clout away from the national government, reducing it to the unhappy agent of higher taxes and fewer services. Provincial and local authorities pulled money away from the national programs. Regional economies, regional cultures, and regional entitlements weakened the bonds of national unity. Her Majesty's Loyal Opposition and the Parti Québécois were poised to launch their referendum on Quebec independence in the fall of 1995. Western Reformers used their podiums in the House of Commons, business-financed think tanks and lobbying organizations, and such national institutions as the *Globe and Mail* and *Saturday Night* magazine to undermine the very notion of national institutions. American populism and American entertainment overwhelmed the historic tenets of Canadian politics and Canadian identity from without, while mass immigration, Generation X, and the segmentation of media audiences challenged them from within. Indeed, between global economics and information technology, nation-states around the world were in imminent danger of fragmentation and impotence.

Arguably, however, many of the same forces of global economics and information technology were making Canada's national government even more necessary and possible. As the gap between the haves and have-nots widens, class divisions and ideological debates could well increase along national lines, not regional ones; the federal-provincial pendulum would have to swing back toward national programs and national standards as an eventual result. As the United States faces its own political turmoil, social tensions, cultural decay, and regional pressures, its decentralist and free-market ideology would likely become an example to fear (as happened in 1867) rather than a model to emulate. As the institutions of world governance such as the United Nations, the G7, the GATT, the IMF, and the World Bank strive to contain the power of international capitalism, Ottawa would become the "local" government that represents the "regional" interests of its citizens. It already does that to an extent, protecting Newfoundland fishermen in the councils of the European Union or giving Quebeckers a voice at the Asia Pacific Economic Co-operation meetings, and it does so with more political and economic clout than any single province or community could ever muster. On the world stage, therefore, Canada may perhaps have to speak with a stronger, more centralized weight to advance the interests of Canadians.

Computer communications, too, are dramatically reducing the distances and solitudes that have kept Canadians apart and frustrated their wish to speak to one another. High tech has already plugged the impoverished backwaters of New Brunswick into the Central Canadian economy; a lack of money has already pushed British Columbia into joining federal bureaucrats in a "one-stop shopping" information service for businesses; CBC's "Newsworld" and the CPAC channel already bring unfiltered national discussions into every home. Electronic technology, instead of being a tool for plebiscitary democracy the way Reform sees using it, could become an adjunct to representative democracy, much as telephone surveys and personalized letters have become adjuncts to election campaigning. Ideas, opinions, and grassroots knowledge could be fed directly into open debates, giving experts and laypeople an equal say while forcing them to take some responsibility for the trade-offs. Compromises, negotiations, and background material could be transmitted to every voter, giving ministers and MPs the final judgement but compelling them to provide a defence of their decisions. And if the national parties themselves brokered the input and output, through policy branches or affiliated foundations, they could supplement and weigh the self-serving positions of the provinces, the bureaucracy, the media, the party barons, the corporations, the think tanks, and all the other intermediary elites who now manipulate their superiority in data gathering to their own advantage.

Such an innovation would create, at the national level, the equivalent of perpetual policy conventions to which everyone is invited to address the issues, followed by perpetual accountability sessions at which everyone is free to ask a question. It would open a line of communication between the national leadership and individual Canadians that has been missing since television, opinion research, and technocratic government overthrew the old network of patronage, riding captains, and regional barons that used to connect the bottom to the top. A great deal of the dissonance in recent politics stems from the fact that the middlemen remained in place, cadging jobs and benefits for themselves, without retaining their ties and obligations to the grassroots. While these local bigwigs and special interests squabbled among each other for their own advantage, the people were stuck in an intimate but one-way relationship with Trudeau, Mulroney, and the rest of the guys giving thirty-second sound bites on TV live from Ottawa. And since party affiliation no longer meant a job in the post office or even a belief in common principles, why would any sensible person waste five dollars on a membership card?

In the meantime, if there were real prospects of instant prosperity and equal opportunity, perhaps the neo-conservatives would be right to suggest that Canadians do not need anything else to get beyond the cynicism and mean-spiritedness that hard times and lower incomes produced. But those are not real prospects. On the contrary, if Canada is to be pulled together by the forces of epochal change, rather than pulled apart, it needs a national purpose. And that purpose will have to be related to wealth creation as well as to wealth distribution. Certainly the United States, the Asian nations, and Europe do not act as if deficit reduction and deregulation are enough to create new growth. Often in working partnerships with their business communities, they are investing billions of dollars in science and technology, in continual training and long-term research, in software and consortia. The result is not socialism or *laissez-faire* economics: it's what Fraser Mustard of the Canadian Institute for Advanced Research calls "capitalism in a societal context," in which "the market is the final test of success in a free-trade environment, but substantial government guidance through policies, rules, and regulations is given to the forces of innovation and technological change." Without some such activism, which does not have to be costly, centralist, or protectionist, Canada is unlikely to drift on the Third Wave toward some utopia without any sense of urgency or foresight, while simultaneously discarding vital national programs and undermining crucial national values.

"The riskiest thing is risk aversion," Matt Barrett explained about his own expensive strategies in taking the Bank of Montreal into the United States and China. "You've got to do something unless you want to end up characterized as a competent steward who just kept order in the organization. But keeping order is easy – you don't become the CEO unless you know how to run the place – and it's worth about $65,000 a year. What you really get paid for is the transformation of the organization, the repositioning of it, the catching of the big emerging trends. Because the global environment isn't stable, nothing is stable, and there have been a lot of very large companies with household names that got into very serious trouble because their CEOs missed the waves."

Some very large countries, too.

Public Life

When Brian Mulroney arrived in the Prime Minister's Office in 1984, he liked to tell his staff that all his predecessors, with the possible exception of Sir John A. Macdonald, had run into problems as soon as they thought they could make a difference with some great sense of mission. The best prime ministers, he claimed, just tried to solve day-to-day problems as they arose. As if to prove his point, he himself developed a hubris about what he could achieve for the Canadian economy and national unity and consequently destroyed both his party and his reputation.

Mulroney's fate seemed to harden Jean Chrétien's resolve not to get swept into overenthusiastic crusades and polarized confrontations. "Is it caution to want to do something well?" he asked. "Rushing is not always a good thing. Being a flash in the pan is easy. But it's the result that's important." In the first half of his first term, aided by a buoyant economy and ineffective opposition, Chrétien showed himself a master at keeping order in the organization. The question around the PMO was whether that was enough, given the mammoth challenges of transforming and repositioning Canada for what Barrett called "the big emerging trends."

Letting individual ministers and departments establish priorities and axe programs may have a salutary effect on the general economy and some rather bloated public institutions, but the wrong priorities and programs could irreparably rip the economic and social fabric of the nation. At what point would forcing the CBC and the other cultural organizations to rethink their role by slashing their budgets destroy the ability of Canadians to communicate with each other and identify themselves through television, radio, books, magazines, and films in a limited market one-tenth the size of the American? What policies, if any, would take the place of the regulatory barriers and business subsidies that once helped create global giants such as Canadian Pacific, Northern Telecom, and Bombardier? Most importantly, perhaps, what values would young Canadians share when they no longer expect their national state to help them in sickness, poverty, and old age, and tune out from public affairs altogether?

The answers cannot be dictated from on high. They will have to evolve from the wisdom and wishes of the Canadian people through debate and argument. More and more citizens will have to become active in the political parties, instead of abandoning them to the single-issue fanatics and back-room opportunists, and party executives will have to develop new ways of involving the membership in policy formation by phone, E-mail, annual councils, and riding meetings. Business executives, labour leaders, and interest groups will have to work in closer alliance with politicians and bureaucrats to negotiate the social trade-offs and develop a Team Canada approach to taking on the world. The provinces will have to admit the important areas in which only Ottawa can do what has to be done for the benefit of everyone. The media will have to recognize that they have the power and obligation to broadcast constructive options as well as negative criticisms. Since none of those things is likely to happen quickly or easily, the national government will have to undertake the brunt of the task of soliciting, studying, and articulating an agenda, as the Liberals did with their Red Book and second budget.

"In both cases," Paul Martin said, "we started with a pretty good idea of where we wanted to go and went through a very extensive consultation process. We weren't saying to people, 'Here's the problem, we haven't a clue what to do about it.' We were saying, 'Here's the problem, this is what we're thinking about doing, let's talk about the trade-offs.'"

That was obviously a more effective style of executive leadership than either Brian Mulroney's this-is-what-we-have-decided-is-good-for-you or Preston Manning's please-tell-me-what-to-think-and-say. It presumed that the political class had done some homework, considered the possibilities, come up with a few options, and yet remained attentive and flexible to how Canadians responded. That is probably the kind of inclusive, accountable, and pragmatic style needed to forge a proactive consensus on how Ottawa should spend the tens of billions of dollars still available to it each year and how Canada will prosper as a united country in the next century. It cannot be ideological in the sense of uncompromising or preordained, but it must be ideological in its emphasis on ideas, rather than personalities and politics, and in its conviction that governments can serve as agents for the public good. "Governments are going to have to justify themselves like every other institution," Martin added. "If they can't deliver the goods – not necessarily by being the deliverer of services, but by making sure those services get done – then they will fall away."

In the end, if the consensus is to be something more than the cobbling together of yet another elite accommodation, the drive will have to come from the prime minister himself. He is the only one who, in conjunction with his staff and a strengthened Privy Council Office, could launch a coordinated effort by every minister, department, and party official to define and achieve some all-important goals. He is also the best one, through the prestige of his position and the focus of the media, to communicate those goals to the people. "Only with maximum prime ministerial involvement could the host of obstacles that stand in the way of reform be overcome," Tom Axworthy concluded from his time as Trudeau's principal secretary. "The crucial question in a strategic approach, then, is which big items?"

To date, it seemed, the big items on Chrétien's agenda were the Quebec referendum, the deficit, and international relations. None could be ignored in the short term; all were crucial to the country's growth in the long term; but they were hardly the major preoccupations in the daily lives of most Canadians. Jobs, education, and health were their concerns. Those also happened to be the interconnected bases for the future economic and social well-being of Canada. As such, any or all of them could be the subject of a national project that would reflect the values of the Canadian community – as could several other areas of national importance such as science and technology, communications and culture, or the environment. Since people seem to accept that jobs are best created by the private sector and schooling is best left to the provinces, medical care is probably the area in which Ottawa could have the greatest legitimacy as a player – not as an administrator of hospitals, but as a coordinator of programs, a facilitator of research, and a guarantor of services.

How would a National Health Program differ from what Ottawa does today under the Canada Health Act and the Canada Health and Social Transfer? It would have a competent minister such as Anne McLellan in charge of the portfolio instead of a second-rate novice like Diane Marleau. It would, through the PMO and PCO, make sure that every cabinet decision and as many federal programs as possible were linked to its coherent objectives. It would monitor and evaluate the health system in every province through the annual report of a federal commissioner, as Ottawa already does with human rights, and federal politicians would not hesitate to advise or lambast their provincial colleagues about any shortcomings. It would recognize that even a non-doctrinaire government has to be doctrinaire sometimes, as Chrétien's has already been, on key issues such as user fees and private clinics. Finally, during a period of tight money and hard choices, it would establish a collective purpose around which most Canadians may be persuaded to forgo other benefits and services, much like Martin did with his 3-per-cent target.

Within government, Finance could use its tax credits to help foster healthy children and medical research; Industry could direct its R and D budgets and export programs toward medical technology and pharmaceutical innovation; Environment and Agriculture could reassess their own priorities in light of health problems such as air pollution and poor nutrition; Human Resources could contribute a significant portion of its social spending toward improving the diet of infants and students; Justice could integrate the legal aspects of euthanasia and rehabilitation with the ethical debates and scientific advances of modern medicine. Beyond government, business groups such as the BCNI and the Public Policy Forum could be asked how to save – not simply dismantle – the public-health system through cost efficiencies and administrative reforms. Doctors, patients, and academics could be involved in grassroots feedback through the information highway or a permanent agency. In short order, Canada could conceivably establish itself as a world leader in health services, health technologies, and health issues – at a price perhaps lower than what it now pays in duplicated effort, malnourished children, mental illness, lost productivity, and bureaucratic waste.

It is politically correct these days to denigrate what Canadians have accomplished by acting together through national policies, social programs, and tax dollars, whether lifting the elderly from terrible poverty or closing the income gap for French-speaking Canadians, whether creating a public broadcasting system or facilitating the growth of the Big Six banks. Canada has become a country that dares not speak its name, lest it offend an array of powerful elites in Quebec, the West, the United States, or the world money markets. Ontarians are encouraged to regard themselves as regionalists, not Canadians. Federalist Liberals in Quebec are advised to go no further than a "quiet affirmation" of their country. The federal government is pushed by the C. D. Howe Institute to consider a policy of "radical disentanglement" with the provinces, a phrase that undoubtedly had that old minister of everything, C. D. Howe, spinning in his grave. And Matthew Barrett, talking about the investments his bank will be making in the United States, stares across Lake Ontario from his window high in First Canadian Place and says bluntly, "I don't see borders. At my desk there are no borders."

Restoring the integrity of government is not only about avoiding scandals and getting out of the way: it is also about proving that government can work in ways that are just and intelligent, inclusive and accountable. That doesn't mean grabbing revenues from the provinces or putting down Quebec, nor does it mean running up deficits and throwing away tax dollars. It means making Canadians of every background in every region feel a sense of ownership of their federal government, feel it is truly *theirs*. It means reminding them of their better instincts to serve the unfortunate and each other when so much of commerce and the media are appealing to their baser selves. It means convincing people that the biases of central power are not necessarily more impractical or less idealistic than the biases of local power, but may be rooted in a long history of thought and experience, of compassion and service, of blood. If the political class and the nation cannot do that, they will deserve whatever grim fate awaits them.

Every effort to check the abuse of power and money by any state is an effort worth taking. Still, there comes a point at which the national government may be rendered too hapless and broke to do what it must to help keep its citizens free, comfortable, and united. "You could have a zero deficit tomorrow," Chrétien used to warn during the 1993 election, "but you could also have, as a consequence, 25-percent unemployment. Then you won't be worried for a minute about the deficit, because you'll have a revolution on your hands." Yet there are already parts of the country where unemployment is higher than that. And there is already evidence that a revolution is possible, not as workers rioting in the streets, but as demagogues degrading Parliament and offering to impose law and order.

Canadians hardly need reminding that there has always been a cost in individual liberty and personal prosperity to making their country stable for democracy or their streets safe for children. When the people and the elites are no longer willing to assume that cost, they may well discover – too late – that they have not only lost their democracy or their streets: they have lost their liberty and prosperity too. That's why, as Václav Havel observed after his own nation was broken in two because the people did not stop the senseless games of their elite powermongers, "it is largely up to the politicians which social forces they choose to liberate and which they choose to suppress, whether they rely on the good in each citizen or on the bad."

Sometimes, seized by insecurity or a sense of inferiority, Canadians forget how fortunate they are compared to most human beings: fortunate in their abundant resources and advanced technologies, in their disciplined work force and standard of education, in their social peace and stable government. They have food, water, and a treasure house of minerals. They have oil, gas, and an eternity of hydroelectricity. They have competitive advantages in automobile products, forestry, telecommunications, banking, and knowledge-based services. They have hundreds of thousands of new citizens from around the world, empowered by ambition, work, and confidence to succeed in this land of space and opportunity. They have their good reputation as international peacemakers and honest traders, arduously earned by their participation in two world wars, the United Nations, the British Commonwealth of Nations, the French-speaking commonwealth, the G7, the GATT, NATO, the Organization of American States, and the OECD. Most importantly, Canadians have the spirit of their pioneer ancestors who left all that was dear and familiar to come and build a new nation in this harsh environment. Nothing Canada faces now is likely to match the hardships and adversities its people have faced in the past.

But those ancestors had an omnipotent ally in their struggles. They had a vision that they were building something together. More than money, more than policies, more than institutions, that ally is what is missing today. Unless it is rediscovered, and quickly, this mythic place called Canada may indeed fragment, or dissolve into the United States. Or it may continue to exist on maps for decades and even centuries to come, and no one will be able to remember why.

Acknowledgements

Portions of this book have appeared, in different form, in the *Globe and Mail*'s *Report on Business Magazine* and *Toronto Life* magazine. I am indebted to David Olive and Charles Macli, at the one, and John Macfarlane, at the other, for their support and advice. At MWR I would like to thank Bernice Eisenstein for her thorough editorial assistance, Jan Walter for her encouragement and professionalism, and Gary Ross for his constant guidance and friendship. And, as always, I owe more than my poor words can say to my darling wife Gillian.

Index